SCHAUM'S OUTLINE OF

THEORY AND PROBLEMS

of

ACCOUNTING II

•

by

JAMES A. CASHIN
Professor of Accounting
Hofstra University

and

JOEL J. LERNER
Chairman, Faculty of Business
Sullivan County Community College

SCHAUM'S OUTLINE SERIES

McGRAW-HILL BOOK COMPANY

New York, St. Louis, San Francisco, Düsseldorf, Johannesburg, Kuala Lumpur, London, Mexico,
Montreal, New Delhi, Panama, São Paulo, Singapore, Sydney, and Toronto

07-010212-0

2 3 4 5 6 7 8 9 10 11 12 13 14 15 16 17 18 19 20   SH SH   7 9 8 7 6

Library of Congress Cataloging in Publication Data

Cashin, James A
    Schaum's outline of theory and problems of accounting
II.

    (Schaum's outline series)
    Continuation of the authors' Accounting I.
    1. Accounting. 2. Accounting — Problems, exercises,
etc.   I. Lerner, Joel J., joint author.   II. Title.
III. Title: Theory and problems of accounting II.
IV. Title.: Accounting II.
[HF5635.C334]   657'.044   74-2350
ISBN 0-07-010212-0

Preface

This volume, the second in the Schaum's Outline Series in Accounting, covers the second part of the introductory accounting course. As in *Accounting I* the *solved-problems* approach is used and emphasis is on *practical application* of basic accounting concepts. The student is provided with:

1. concise definitions and explanations, in easily understood terms

2. fully worked-out solutions to a large range of problems (against which the student can check his own solutions)

3. review questions

4. sample examinations typical of those used by two-year and four-year colleges

The two books help him to develop the all-important know-how for solving problems — on the CPA examination and in his everyday work.

The subject matter has been carefully coordinated with the leading textbooks so that any topic can easily be found from the Table of Contents or the Index.

Accounting II differs from Accounting I in that specialized areas (Manufacturing Costs, Budgets, Standard Costs, Financial Ratios, etc.) are discussed rather than general practices of a business. This book will greatly assist those students who may have been able to complete Accounting I but are having difficulty with the specialized topics. Careful study of the solved problems will help such students, including those in special programs, to keep abreast of classwork, thereby reducing the number of drop-outs from Accounting II.

The wide range of areas covered will also benefit Liberal Arts majors and those Business Administration students not majoring in Accounting. In addition, this volume can serve as an accompanying text for various Management Accounting texts which need a tie-in to basic accounting.

The authors wish to thank the members of a faculty and student panel who offered suggestions and helped in designing the problems. They are: Cheri Adler, Joseph Bass, Barbara Catanese, Kenneth Cotty, Harold Eccleston, Louis Harmin, Sandy Kornheiser, Philip Malafsky, Elaine Morton, Vincent Newman, Robert Rolston, and Martin Siminerio.

JAMES A. CASHIN
JOEL J. LERNER

Hofstra University
Sullivan County Community College
April 1974

CONTENTS

Unit 1   Page

Chapter **1** **PARTNERSHIPS** 1

1.1   Characteristics of the Partnership 1
1.2   Formation of the Partnership 1
1.3   Admission of a New Partner 2
1.4   Division of Net Income and Loss 4
1.5   Liquidation of a Partnership 6

Chapter **2** **THE CORPORATION: ORGANIZATION** 23

2.1   Characteristics of the Corporation 23
2.2   Advantages of the Corporate Form 23
2.3   Disadvantages of the Corporate Form 23
2.4   Corporate Terminology 24
2.5   Equity Accounting for the Corporation 25
2.6   Common Stock 26
2.7   Preferred Stock 26
2.8   Issue of Stock 28
2.9   Book Value 29

Chapter **3** **THE CORPORATION: SUBSCRIPTIONS, TREASURY STOCK, AND RETAINED EARNINGS** 47

3.1   Stock Subscriptions 47
3.2   Default on Subscription 48
3.3   Treasury Stock 48
3.4   Retained Earnings 51
3.5   Dividends 52

Chapter **4** **THE CORPORATION: BONDS** 71

4.1   Bond Characteristics 71
4.2   Security 71
4.3   Payment of Interest. Options 71
4.4   Funding by Stock versus Funding by Bonds 72
4.5   Recording Authorized Bond Transactions 73
4.6   Premium and Discount on Bonds 73
4.7   Accrued Interest 75
4.8   Redemption of Bonds 77
4.9   Bond Sinking Funds. Restriction of Dividends 78
4.10 Review of Equity and Debt Financing 79

Examination 1 93

CONTENTS

Unit II   **Page**

Chapter *5*   MANUFACTURING ACCOUNTING 99

    5.1   Manufacturing Accounts 99

    5.2   Analysis of Manufacturing Cost 99

    5.3   Inventories 100

    5.4   Worksheet 101

    5.5   Cost of Goods Manufactured 101

    5.6   Income Statement 103

    5.7   Joint Products and By-Products 103

Chapter *6*   COST SYSTEMS 120

    6.1   Introduction 120

    6.2   Job Order Cost System 120

    6.3   Process Cost System 124

    6.4   Supplementary Costing Practices 124

    6.5   Flow of Goods. Equivalent Units 125

    6.6   Flow of Costs 126

    6.7   Comprehensive Illustration of Process Costs 127

Chapter *7*   BUDGETS AND STANDARD COSTS 153

    7.1   Nature of Budgeting 153

    7.2   The Master Budget 153

    7.3   Budgeted Income Statement 153

    7.4   Budgeted Balance Sheet 158

    7.5   Flexible Budgets 160

    7.6   Performance Reports 161

    7.7   Standard Costs 161

    7.8   Analysis of Variances 161

Examination II 185

Unit III

Chapter *8*   FINANCIAL STATEMENT ANALYSIS 189

    8.1   Introduction 189

    8.2   Amount and Percentage Changes (Horizontal Analysis) 189

    8.3   Component Percentages (Vertical Analysis) 190

    8.4   Analysis by Ratios 192

Chapter *9*   CHANGES IN FINANCIAL POSITION 210

    9.1   Introduction 210

    9.2   Changes in Working Capital 210

    9.3   Statement of Change in Financial Position 212

CONTENTS

Page

Chapter *10*   INCOME TAXES 230

   10.1   Introduction 230

   10.2   Taxation of Businesses 230

   10.3   Income Tax Formula for Individuals 232

   10.4   Gross Income 232

   10.5   Deductions from Gross Income 233

   10.6   Deductions from Adjusted Gross Income 233

   10.7   Exemptions 234

   10.8   Tax Credits 235

   10.9   Other Tax Considerations for Individuals 235

Examination III 250

INDEX 255

Chapter 1

Partnerships

1.1 CHARACTERISTICS OF THE PARTNERSHIP

According to the Uniform Partnership Act, a *partnership* is "an association of two or more persons to carry on as co-owners a business for profit." Generally speaking, partnership accounting is like that for the sole proprietorship, except in regard to owners' equity. The partnership uses a capital account and a drawing account for each partner.

The partnership has the following characteristics:

Articles of partnership. Good business practice calls for a written agreement among the partners which contains provisions on the formation of the partnership, capital contribution of each partner, profit and loss distribution, admission and withdrawal of partners, withdrawal of funds, and dissolution of the business.

Unlimited liability. All partners have unlimited liability and are individually responsible to creditors for debts incurred by the partnership. The debts of the business can be satisfied not only by the assets of the partnership but also by the personal assets of the partners.

Co-ownership of property. All property invested in the business by the partners, as well as that purchased with the partnership's funds, becomes the property of *all* partners jointly. Therefore, each partner has an interest in the partnership in proportion to his capital balance, rather than a claim against specific assets.

Participation in profits and losses. Profits and losses are distributed among the partners according to the partnership agreement. If no agreement exists, profits and losses must be shared equally.

Limited life. A partnership may be dissolved by bankruptcy, death of a partner, mutual agreement, or court order.

1.2 FORMATION OF THE PARTNERSHIP

When a partnership is formed, each partner's capital account is credited for his initial investment and the appropriate asset account is debited. If noncash assets are invested, these should be recorded at an *agreed* amount.

If liabilities are to be assumed by the partnership, they are credited to the respective liability accounts.

EXAMPLE 1.

William Morrison has agreed to go into partnership with Robert Caine.

1

Morrison's Accounts	Morrison's Ledger Balances	Agreed Valuations
Cash	$10,000	$10,000
Accounts Receivable	5,400	5,400
Merchandise Inventory	21,000	19,000
Equipment	16,000	14,000
Accumulated Depreciation, Equipment	4,000	
Allowance for Doubtful Accounts	400	400
Notes Payable	8,000	8,000

The entry to record the initial investment of Morrison in the firm of Morrison and Caine would be:

Cash	10,000	
Accounts Receivable	5,400	
Merchandise Inventory	19,000	
Equipment	14,000	
Allowance for Doubtful Accounts		400
Notes Payable		8,000
Morrison, Capital		40,000

1.3   ADMISSION OF A NEW PARTNER

The Uniform Partnership Act states that a partner may dispose of part or all of his interest in the firm without the consent of the remaining partners.

The individual who purchases the interest receives the selling partner's rights to share in income and expense. However, he is not a full partner, since he will have no vote or right to participate in partnership activities unless he is admitted to the firm.

ADMISSION BY PURCHASE OF INTEREST

When the incoming partner purchases an interest from another partner, he pays the purchase price directly to the old partner. The only change required in the partnership's books is an entry transferring capital from the old partner's account to the account established for the new partner. Assets and liabilities of the business are not affected.

EXAMPLE 2.

Ness and Owen have capital balances of $30,000 and $20,000 respectively. William Prey is admitted to the partnership by purchasing half of Ness's interest for $18,000. The only entry required is the changing of the capital balances of the affected partners.

Ness, Capital		Owen, Capital		Prey, Capital	
15,000	Bal. 30,000		Bal. 20,000		15,000

Prey's admission results in the transfer of half of Ness's capital to Prey, regardless of the amount paid by Prey for his share of the partnership.

ADMISSION BY CONTRIBUTION OF ASSETS

The new partner may contribute assets to the partnership, thus increasing both the assets and the capital of the firm.

EXAMPLE 3.

Assume that Prey is to be admitted to the partnership of Ness and Owen, whose total capital is $50,000

($30,000 and $20,000 respectively). Prey is to contribute $25,000 for a 1/3 interest in the new partnership. The entry to record his admission is:

Cash	25,000	
Prey, Capital		25,000

In Examples 2 and 3, it was assumed that the assets of Ness and Owen were stated in terms of the current market prices when Prey was admitted. Because of this, no adjustments were necessary in any of the assets prior to his admission. In some cases, when a new partner is admitted, assets may first have to be revalued or goodwill recognized in order to bring the capital accounts into line with current values.

(1) *Revaluation of assets.* The book values of certain assets of the partnership must be adjusted before they agree with current prices. The net amount of the revaluation is then transferred to the capital accounts of the old partners according to their income division agreement. If it appears that a number of assets need revaluation, whether to higher or lower figures, the adjustments may be made in a temporary account, Asset Revaluation, which will subsequently be closed to the partners' capital accounts.

EXAMPLE 4.

Ness and Owen share profits and losses equally. It was discovered that the merchandise inventory account is understated: the inventory, carried on the books at $21,000, has a current replacement cost of $25,000. The following entry would be recorded *prior* to the admission of Prey into the partnership:

Merchandise Inventory	4,000	
Ness, Capital		2,000
Owen, Capital		2,000

EXAMPLE 5.

Before admitting Prey to partnership, Ness and Owen decide that: (a) $600 is to be written off the Accounts Receivable balance; (b) Merchandise Inventory, carried at $19,000, is to be revalued at $21,000.

The entry to record the above revaluations is:

Merchandise Inventory	2,000	
Accounts Receivable		600
Asset Revaluation		1,400

After all adjustments have been made, Asset Revaluation is closed as follows:

Asset Revaluation	1,400	
Ness, Capital		700
Owen, Capital		700

(2) *Recognition of goodwill.* If a firm has the ability to earn more than the normal rate on its investment (because of a favorable location, established reputation, management skills, or better products or services), goodwill may be indicated, and an incoming partner may be charged for it. If so, the goodwill account is debited, while the old partners' accounts are credited in the ratios set up by the articles of partnership. On the other hand, if goodwill is created by the incoming partner, the goodwill account is debited and the new partner's capital account credited.

EXAMPLE 6.   Goodwill to the Old Partners.

The capital balances of Ness and Owen are $30,000 and $20,000 respectively. The partnership agrees to admit Prey to their firm, who is to contribute cash of $20,000 and is to receive a 1/4 interest in the firm.

Though the total capital of the firm before the admission is $50,000, the parties agree that the firm was worth $60,000. This excess of $10,000 indicates the existence of goodwill; it will be allocated to the old partners in their profit and loss ratio, which is 1 : 1 in this case. The entries to record goodwill and the admission of the new partner are:

Goodwill	*10,000*	
Ness, Capital		*5,000*
Owen, Capital		*5,000*
Cash	*20,000*	
Prey, Capital		*20,000**

$$*\frac{1}{4}(\underbrace{\$30,000}_{Ness} + \underbrace{\$20,000}_{Owen} + \underbrace{\$20,000}_{Prey} + \underbrace{\$10,000}_{goodwill})$$

EXAMPLE 7.   Goodwill to the New Partner.

Ness and Owen, with capital balances of $30,000 and $20,000 respectively, agree to admit Prey into the firm for a $15,000 investment, giving him a 1/3 share in profits and losses and granting him goodwill recognition of $10,000. The entry to record the above information would be:

Cash	*15,000*	
Goodwill	*10,000*	
Prey, Capital		*25,000**

$$*\frac{1}{3}(\underbrace{\$30,000}_{Ness} + \underbrace{\$20,000}_{Owen} + \underbrace{\$25,000}_{Prey})$$

1.4   DIVISION OF NET INCOME AND LOSS

Partnership profits and losses may be divided in any manner that the partners may agree upon. In general, a partner may be expected to share in proportion to the amount of capital and/or services he contributes. In the absence of a clear agreement the law provides that all partners share equally, regardless of the differences in time devoted or capital contributed.

Below are outlined the principal methods for profit and loss distribution. For simplicity the examples are limited to two partners.

FIXED OR CAPITAL BASIS

Profits and losses are generally divided equally, in a fixed ratio, or in a ratio based upon the amounts of capital contributed by the partners.

EXAMPLE 8.

Ness and Owen have capital balances of $30,000 and $20,000 respectively. The net income for the first year of operations was $15,000. If the partners have decided to share on an equal basis, the journal entry for the allocation of the net income will be:

Expense and Income Summary	*15,000*	
Ness, Capital		*7,500*
Owen, Capital		*7,500*

If, however, capital investment is to be the determining factor, the entry will run as follows:

Expense and Income Summary   15,000
    Ness, Capital   9,000*
    Owen, Capital   6,000**

$$* \quad \frac{30,000}{30,000 + 20,000} \, (15,000)$$

$$** \quad \frac{20,000}{30,000 + 20,000} \, (15,000)$$

INTEREST BASIS

Under this method, each partner is paid interest on his capital investment, and the remaining net income is divided in a fixed ratio or on some other basis.   Thus, a partner's share depends *partially* on his capital investment.

EXAMPLE 9.

Instead of the equal split in Example 8, each partner is to receive 6% interest on his capital balance, the remaining net income to be shared equally.   The entry would be:

Expense and Income Summary   15,000
    Ness, Capital   7,800
    Owen, Capital   7,200

the computation being:

	Ness	Owen	Total
Interest on investment	$1,800	$1,200	$ 3,000
Balance	6,000	6,000	12,000
Totals	$7,800	$7,200	$15,000

SALARY BASIS

The partners may agree to give recognition to contributions in the form of services, while the remaining net income may be divided equally or in a fixed ratio.

EXAMPLE 10.

Assume that the partnership of Ness and Owen (Example 8) agree that a yearly salary allowance of $4,000 be given to Ness and $3,000 to Owen, the balance to be divided equally.   The entry would be:

Expense and Income Summary   15,000
    Ness, Capital   8,000
    Owen, Capital   7,000

the computation being:

	Ness	Owen	Total
Salary	$4,000	$3,000	$ 7,000
Balance	4,000	4,000	8,000
Totals	$8,000	$7,000	$15,000

SALARY-PLUS-INTEREST BASIS

Here, services rendered to the business and capital contribution jointly determine the income division.   Each partner gets a salary, and, at the same time, interest on capital. If any balance remains, it is divided in an agreed ratio.

EXAMPLE 11.

Ness and Owen (Example 8) decide to allow a credit of 6% interest on capital balances, respective salaries of $4,000 and $3,000, and equal division of any remainder. The entry would be:

Expense and Income Summary	15,000	
Ness, Capital		*8,300*
Owen, Capital		*6,700*

which is computed as follows:

	Ness	Owen	Total
Interest	$1,800	$1,200	$ 3,000
Salary	4,000	3,000	7,000
	$5,800	$4,200	$10,000
Balance	2,500	2,500	5,000
Totals	$8,300	$6,700	$15,000

In Example 11, as well as in Examples 9 and 10, the income of the business exceeded the total of the allowances to the partners. However, this may not always be the case. If the net income is less than the total of the allowances, the balance remaining is negative and is divided among the partners as though it were a loss.

EXAMPLE 12.

Ness and Owen (Example 8) decide to allow a credit of 6% interest on capital balances, respective salaries of $8,000 and $6,000, and equal division of the remainder. The entry would be:

Expense and Income Summary	15,000	
Ness, Capital		*8,800*
Owen, Capital		*6,200*

which is computed as follows:

	Ness	Owen	Total
Interest	$1,800	$1,200	$ 3,000
Salary	8,000	6,000	14,000
	$9,800	$7,200	$17,000
Balance	− 1,000	− 1,000	− 2,000
Totals	$8,800	$6,200	$15,000

1.5 LIQUIDATION OF A PARTNERSHIP

If the partners of a firm decide to discontinue the operations of the business, several accounting steps are necessary:

1. The accounts are adjusted and closed.

2. All assets are converted to cash.

3. All creditors are paid in full.

4. Any remaining cash is distributed among the partners according to the balances in their capital accounts (and not according to their P&L ratios).

EXAMPLE 13. Liquidation at a Gain.

After Ness, Owen, and Prey have ceased business operations and adjusted and closed the accounts, the general ledger has the following post-closing trial balance:

Cash	$20,000	
Noncash Assets	65,000	
Liabilities		$10,000
Ness, Capital		15,000
Owen, Capital		25,000
Prey, Capital		35,000
	$85,000	$85,000

Assume for simplicity that all liabilities are paid at one time and that the noncash assets are sold in one transaction. Then, if the sale price is $80,000 and the partners share equally in profits and losses, we have the following liquidation schedule:

	ASSETS	=	LIABILITIES	+	CAPITAL		
	Cash +	Other	Accounts Payable		Ness +	Owen +	Prey
Balances of capital accounts	$ 20,000	$65,000	$10,000		$15,000	$25,000	$35,000
Sales of assets	+ 80,000	− 65,000			+ 5,000	+ 5,000	+ 5,000
Balance after sale	100,000		10,000		20,000	30,000	40,000
Payment of liabilities	− 10,000		− 10,000				
Balance after payment	90,000				20,000	30,000	40,000
Distribution to partners	− 90,000				− 20,000	− 30,000	− 40,000

The entries to record the liquidation are then:

Sale of Assets

Cash	80,000	
Other Assets		65,000
Ness, Capital		5,000
Owen, Capital		5,000
Prey, Capital		5,000

Payment of Liabilities

Liabilities	10,000	
Cash		10,000

Final Distribution to Partners

Ness, Capital	20,000	
Owen, Capital	30,000	
Prey, Capital	40,000	
Cash		90,000

EXAMPLE 14. Liquidation at a Loss.

The data are as in Example 13, except that the noncash assets are now sold for $5,000.

	ASSETS	=	LIABILITIES	+	CAPITAL		
	Cash +	Other	Accounts Payable		Ness +	Owen +	Prey
Balances of capital accounts	$20,000	$65,000	$10,000		$15,000	$25,000	$35,000
Sale of assets	+ 5,000	− 65,000			− 20,000	− 20,000	− 20,000
Balance after sale	25,000		10,000		(5,000)	5,000	15,000
Payment of liabilities	− 10,000		− 10,000				
Balance after payment	15,000				(5,000)	5,000	15,000
Distribution to partners	− 15,000					− 2,500	− 12,500
					(5,000)	2,500	2,500

Notice that in the foregoing liquidation schedule the $60,000 loss on sale of the noncash assets was divided equally among the three partners. However, Ness's capital balance was not sufficient to absorb his share of the loss. This resulted in a debit balance ($5,000) in his capital account and becomes a claim of the partnership against him for that amount. The $5,000 deficit must be borne by the two remaining partners, and thus, in the distribution to partners, Owen and Prey each take an additional loss of $2,500.

The entries to record the liquidation are as follows:

Sale of Assets	Cash	5,000	
	Ness, Capital	20,000	
	Owen, Capital	20,000	
	Prey, Capital	20,000	
	Other Assets		65,000
Payment of Liabilities	Liabilities	10,000	
	Cash		10,000
Distribution to Partners	Owen, Capital	2,500	
	Prey, Capital	12,500	
	Cash		15,000

Since there is a capital deficiency outstanding, one of three different possibilities will arise in the future: (1) Ness pays the deficiency in full; (2) Ness makes a partial payment; (3) Ness makes no payment. The entries corresponding to these possibilities are:

(1) Payment in Full

Cash	5,000	
Ness, Capital		5,000
Owen, Capital	2,500	
Prey, Capital	2,500	
Cash		5,000

(2) Partial Payment of $4,000

Cash	4,000	
Ness, Capital		4,000
Settlement of Ness's deficiency		
Owen, Capital	500	
Prey, Capital	500	
Ness, Capital		1,000
To close out the balance of Ness's account		
Owen, Capital	2,000	
Prey, Capital	2,000	
Cash		4,000
To distribute cash according to capital balances		

(3) No Payment

Owen, Capital	2,500	
Prey, Capital	2,500	
Ness, Capital		5,000

Summary

(1) Partnership and sole proprietorship accounting are alike except in _____.

(2) Noncash assets are recorded at _____ amounts when the partnership is formed.

(3) The book value of the partnership of Acme and Beam is $60,000, with each partner's account showing $30,000. If Caldwell were to purchase Beam's interest for $40,000, the amount credited to Caldwell's equity account would be _____.

(4) In order to reflect higher current prices, certain assets of the partnership will be debited, with the corresponding credit to _____.

(5) A firm's superior earning power is recognized as _____.

(6) If profits and losses are not to be shared equally, the basis of distribution must be stated in the _____.

(7) Salaries and the interest on partners' capital balances are not included on the income statement but are shown on the _____.

(8) When a partnership decides to go out of business, the process of selling the assets, paying the creditors, and distributing the remaining cash to the partners is known as _____.

(9) The final distribution of cash to the partners is based on their _____.

Answers: (1) owners' equity; (2) agreed; (3) $30,000; (4) Asset Revaluation; (5) goodwill; (6) partnership agreement; (7) capital statement; (8) liquidation; (9) capital balances

Solved Problems

1.1. J. Korr and B. Lear have decided to form a partnership. Korr invests the following assets at their agreed valuations, and also transfers his liabilities to the new firm.

Korr's Accounts	Korr's Ledger Balances	Agreed Valuations
Cash	$18,000	$18,000
Accounts Receivable	7,200	7,000
Allowance for Doubtful Accounts	600	500
Merchandise Inventory	12,200	10,000
Equipment	6,000	4,200
Accumulated Depreciation	1,000	
Accounts Payable	3,500	3,500
Notes Payable	3,600	3,600

Lear agrees to invest $26,000 in cash. Record (a) Korr's investment, (b) Lear's investment.

(a)

(b)

SOLUTION

(a)

Cash		18,000	
Accounts Receivable		7,000	
Merchandise Inventory		10,000	
Equipment		4,200	
Allowance for Doubtful Accounts			500
Accounts Payable			3,500
Notes Payable			3,600
J. Korr, Capital			31,600

(b)

Cash		26,000	
B. Lear, Capital			26,000

1.2. The capital accounts of J. Phillips and Ẇ. Schneider have balances of $25,000 each. E. Kurlander joins the partnership. What entry is necessary (a) if Kurlander purchases half of Phillips's investment for $15,000? (b) if Kurlander invests $15,000 in the firm?

(a)

(b)

SOLUTION

(a)

J. Phillips, Capital		12,500	
E. Kurlander, Capital			12,500

(b)

Cash		15,000	
E. Kurlander, Capital			15,000

1.3. W. Schoop and J. Epstein have capital balances of $20,000 and $30,000, respectively, H. Walker and W. Dunn are to be admitted to the partnership — Walker by purchasing half of Epstein's interest for $18,000 and Dunn by investing $10,000, for which he is to receive full equity value ($10,000).

(a) What entry is needed to record the above information?

(b) On a capital basis, what is Dunn's share of profits and losses?

(a)

(b)

SOLUTION

(a)

Cash		10,000	
J. Epstein, Capital		15,000	
H. Walker, Capital			15,000
W. Dunn, Capital			10,000

(b)

W. Schoop, Capital	$20,000	
H. Walker, Capital	15,000	
J. Epstein, Capital	15,000	
W. Dunn, Capital	10,000	
Total Capital	$60,000	

$$\frac{\text{Dunn's Investment}}{\text{Total Capital}} \;=\; \frac{\$10,000}{\$60,000} \;=\; \frac{1}{6}, \text{ or } 16\tfrac{2}{3}\%$$

1.4. The financial position of the partnership of Davidson and Fellows, who share income in the ratio 3 : 2, is shown below.

Davidson-Fellows Company
Balance Sheet
April 30, 197–

ASSETS		LIABILITIES AND CAPITAL	
Current Assets	$ 65,000	Liabilities	$ 50,000
Equipment (net)	125,000	Davidson, Capital	85,000
		Fellows, Capital	55,000
Total Assets	$190,000	Total Liabilities and Capital	$190,000

Both partners agree to admit a new partner, Evans, into the firm. Prepare the necessary entries corresponding to each of the following options:

(a) Evans purchases half of Fellows's interest for $30,000.

(b) Evans invests $70,000 in the partnership and receives a 1/3 interest in capital and income.

(c) The original partners feel that goodwill should be recorded at a value of $20,000. Evans's investment is to gain him a 1/3 interest in capital and income.

(a)

(b)

(c)

SOLUTION

(a)

Fellows, Capital	27,500	
Evans, Capital		27,500

(b)	*Cash*	*70,000*	
	Evans, Capital		*70,000*
(c)	*Goodwill*	*20,000*	
	Davidson, Capital		*12,000*
	Fellows, Capital		*8,000*
	Cash	*80,000*	
	Evans, Capital		*80,000**

* Total worth before admission is $85,000 + $55,000 + $20,000 = $160,000.   To produce three equal parts, Evans has to invest half of this, or $80,000.

1.5.   Before admitting Goldsmith to the partnership, Shapot and Babcock, who share profits and losses equally, decide that (1) Merchandise Inventory, recorded at $26,000, is to be revalued at $29,000; (2) $500 of Accounts Receivable is to be written off. Present journal entries to record the revaluations.

(a)			
(b)			

SOLUTION

(a)	*Merchandise Inventory*	*3,000*	
	Accounts Receivable		*500*
	Asset Revaluation		*2,500*
(b)	*Asset Revaluation*	*2,500*	
	Shapot, Capital		*1,250*
	Babcock, Capital		*1,250*

1.6.   After the assets of the partnership have been adjusted to reflect current prices, the capital balances of L. Benjamin and R. Hochron are each $25,000. However, both partners agree that the partnership is worth $60,000. They decide to admit R. Berechad as an equal partner into their firm for a $30,000 investment. (a) Record the recognition of goodwill. (b) Record Berechad's investment. (c) What is the total capital of the firm?

(a)

(b)

(c)

SOLUTION

(a)	Goodwill		10,000	
	L. Benjamin, Capital			5,000
	R. Hochron, Capital			5,000
(b)	Cash		30,000	
	R. Berechad, Capital			30,000

(c)	L. Benjamin, Capital	$30,000
	R. Hochron, Capital	30,000
	R. Berechad, Capital	30,000
	Total Capital	$90,000

1.7. If in Problem 1.6 R. Berechad invested $20,000 for an equal share of equity, what would the entry be to record his admittance into the firm?

SOLUTION

Cash		20,000	
Goodwill		10,000	
R. Berechad, Capital			30,000

Since the total capital prior to Berechad's admittance was $60,000, an equal share would require an investment of $30,000, as in Problem 1.6. Therefore, the owners must have agreed to recognize the new partner's ability and awarded him capital credit (goodwill) of $30,000 − $20,000 = $10,000.

1.8. Adams, Bentley, and Carson have capital balances of $30,000, $25,000, and $20,000, respectively. Adams devotes three-fourths time; Bentley, half time; and Carson, one-fourth time. Determine their participation in net income of $37,500 if income is divided (a) in the ratio of capital investments, (b) in the ratio of time worked.

(a)	Adams	
	Bentley	
	Carson	
	Net Income	$37,500

(b)	Adams	
	Bentley	
	Carson	
	Net Income	$37,500

SOLUTION

(a) Total capital is $75,000. Hence:

Adams	($30,000/$75,000) × $37,500	=	$15,000
Bentley	($25,000/$75,000) × $37,500	=	12,500
Carson	($20,000/$75,000) × $37,500	=	10,000
Net Income			$37,500

(b) The ratio is $3:2:1$. Hence:

Adams	$3/6 \times \$37,500 =$	$18,750
Bentley	$2/6 \times \$37,500 =$	12,500
Carson	$1/6 \times \$37,500 =$	6,250
Net Income		$37,500

1.9. The capital accounts of W. Dunn and S. Evans have balances of $35,000 and $25,000, respectively. The articles of co-partnership refer to the distribution of net income in the following manner:

(1) Dunn and Evans are to receive salaries of $9,000 and $6,000, respectively.

(2) Each is to receive 6% on his capital account.

(3) The balance is to be divided equally.

If the net income for the firm is $32,000, (a) determine the division of net income and (b) present the entry to close the expense and income summary account.

(a)

	Dunn	Evans	Total
Salary			
Interest			
Balance			
Share of Net Income			

(b)

SOLUTION

(a)

	Dunn	Evans	Total
Salary	$ 9,000	$ 6,000	$15,000
Interest	2,100	1,500	3,600
	$11,100	$ 7,500	$18,600
Balance	6,700	6,700	13,400
Share of Net Income	$17,800	$14,200	$32,000

(b)

Expense and Income Summary	*32,000*	
Dunn, Capital		*17,800*
Evans, Capital		*14,200*

1.10. Redo Problem 1.9 for a net income of $12,000.

(a)

	Dunn	Evans	Total
Salary			
Interest			
Balance			
Share of Net Income			

(b)

SOLUTION

(a)

	Dunn	Evans	Total
Salary	$ 9,000	$ 6,000	$15,000
Interest	2,100	1,500	3,600
	$11,100	$ 7,500	$18,600
Balance	− 3,300	− 3,300	− 6,600
Share of Net Income	$ 7,800	$ 4,200	$12,000

(b)

Expense and Income Summary		12,000	
Dunn, Capital			7,800
Evans, Capital			4,200

1.11. During its first year of operations the partnership Diamond, Ellis, and Frank earned $41,400. Journalize the entries needed to close the expense and income summary account and to allocate the net income to the partners under the following assumptions:

(a) The partners did not agree upon any method for sharing earnings.

(b) The partners agreed to share earnings in the ratio of time invested. Diamond worked full time; Ellis, full time; Frank, half time.

(c) The partners agreed to share earnings in the ratio of their capital investments (Diamond, $25,000; Ellis, $20,000; Frank, $15,000).

(a)

(b)

(c)

SOLUTION

(a)

Expense and Income Summary		41,400	
Diamond, Capital			13,800
Evans, Capital			13,800
Frank, Capital			13,800

If no formal agreement exists, all profits and losses are assumed to be divided equally.

(b) The division ratio is $1 : 1 : \frac{1}{2} = 2 : 2 : 1$.

Expense and Income Summary		41,400	
Diamond, Capital [2/5 × $41,400]			16,560
Evans, Capital [2/5 × $41,400]			16,560
Frank, Capital [1/5 × $41,400]			8,280

(c) The division ratio is 25,000 : 20,000 : 15,000 = 5 : 4 : 3.

Expense and Income Summary	41,400	
Diamond, Capital [5/12 × $41,400]		17,250
Evans, Capital [4/12 × $41,400]		13,800
Frank, Capital [3/12 × $41,400]		10,350

1.12. The abbreviated income statement of James and Kelly for December 31, 197–, appears below:

Sales (net)	$240,000
Less: Cost of Goods Sold	105,000
Gross Profit	$135,000
Less: Expenses	65,000
Net Income	$ 70,000

The profit and loss agreement specifies that:

(1) Interest of 5% is to be allowed on capital balances (James, $25,000; Kelly, $15,000).

(2) Salary allowances to James and Kelly to be $6,000 and $4,000, respectively.

(3) A bonus is to be given to James equal to 20% of net income without regard to interest or salary.

(4) Remaining profits and losses are to be divided in the ratio of capital balances.

(a) Present the distribution of net income.   (b) Present the journal entry required to close the books.

(a)

	James	Kelly	Total
Interest			
Salary			
Bonus			
Balance			
Net Income			

(b)

SOLUTION

(a)

	James	Kelly	Total
Interest	$ 1,250	$ 750	$ 2,000
Salary	6,000	4,000	10,000
Bonus	14,000		14,000
	$21,250	$ 4,750	$26,000
Balance	27,500*	16,500*	44,000
Net Income	$48,750	$21,250	$70,000

* $25,000	James	25/40 × $44,000 = $27,500
15,000	Kelly	15/40 × $44,000 = $16,500
$40,000	Total	

(b)

Expense and Income Summary	70,000	
James, Capital		48,750
Kelly, Capital		21,250

1.13. Kapela, Lesser and Morton, with capital balances of $20,000, $30,000, and $25,000, respectively, decide to terminate their partnership. After selling the noncash assets and paying all debts, there is $75,000 in cash remaining. Assuming that the partners share profits and losses equally, how should this remaining cash be split?

Kapela	
Lesser	
Morton	
Total Cash	$75,000

SOLUTION

Kapela	$20,000
Lesser	30,000
Morton	25,000
Total Cash	$75,000

The final distribution of cash is determined by the capital balances and not by the profit and loss ratio.

1.14. The following "T" accounts show the balances of the partnership of Greenburg and Holand as of June 30, 197–, prior to dissolution

Cash		Merchandise Inventory	
35,000		12,600	

Equipment		Accumulated Depreciation	
15,000			12,000

Prepaid Insurance		Accounts Payable	
1,400			16,000

Greenburg, Capital		Holand, Capital	
	18,000		18,000

The partners share profits and losses equally. The terminating transactions are:

(a) Sold the merchandise for its market value, $16,500.

(b) Realized $1,100 from the surrender of the insurance policies.

(c) Sold the equipment for $2,000.

(d) Distributed the gain to the partners' capital accounts.

(e) Paid all liabilities.

(f) Distributed the remaining cash.

Present journal entries to record the above information.

(a)

(b)

(c)			
(d)			
(e)			
(f)			

SOLUTION

(a)	Cash	16,500	
	Merchandise Inventory		12,600
	Gain or Loss on Realization		3,900
(b)	Cash	1,100	
	Gain or Loss on Realization	300	
	Prepaid Insurance		1,400
(c)	Cash	2,000	
	Accumulated Depreciation	12,000	
	Gain or Loss on Realization	1,000	
	Equipment		15,000
(d)	Gain or Loss on Realization	2,600	
	Greenburg, Capital		1,300
	Holand, Capital		1,300
(e)	Accounts Payable	16,000	
	Cash		16,000
(f)	Greenburg, Capital	19,300	
	Holand, Capital	19,300	
	Cash		38,600

SUMMARY OF TRANSACTIONS

Transaction	Cash	Other Assets	Liabilities	Greenburg, Capital	Holand, Capital
Balance	$35,000	$17,000	$16,000	$18,000	$18,000
(a) − (d)	+ 19,600	− 17,000		+ 1,300	+ 1,300
	$54,600		$16,000	$19,300	$19,300
(e)	− 16,000		− 16,000		
(f)	$38,600			$19,300	$19,300
	− 38,600			− 19,300	− 19,300

1.15. Sochet, Karlin, and Stadler, who divide profits and losses equally, have the following ledger balances as of December 31:

Cash	$36,000	Sochet, Capital	$15,000
Other Assets	18,000	Karlin, Capital	10,000
Liabilities	16,000	Stadler, Capital	13,000

The partners decide to liquidate, and sell their noncash assets at a loss of $6,000. After meeting their obligations, they divide the remaining cash. Present all necessary entries.

(a)	**Loss on realization**		
(b)	**Division of loss**		
(c)	**Payment of liabilities**		
(d)	**Division of remaining cash**		

SOLUTION

(a)	**Loss on realization**		
	Cash	12,000	
	Loss on Realization	6,000	
	Other Assets		18,000
(b)	**Division of loss**		
	Sochet, Capital	2,000	
	Karlin, Capital	2,000	
	Stadler, Capital	2,000	
	Loss on Realization		6,000
(c)	**Payment of liabilities**		
	Liabilities	16,000	
	Cash		16,000
(d)	**Division of remaining cash**		
	Sochet, Capital	13,000	
	Karlin, Capital	8,000	
	Stadler, Capital	11,000	
	Cash		32,000

SUMMARY OF TRANSACTIONS

Transaction	Cash	Other Assets	Liabilities	Sochet, Capital	Karlin, Capital	Stadler, Capital
Balance	$36,000	$18,000	$16,000	$15,000	$10,000	$13,000
(a), (b)	+ 12,000	− 18,000		− 2,000	− 2,000	− 2,000
	$48,000		$16,000	$13,000	$ 8,000	$11,000
(c)	− 16,000		− 16,000			
	$32,000			$13,000	$ 8,000	$11,000
(d)	− 32,000			− 13,000	− 8,000	− 11,000

1.16. Eccleston, Kapela, and Harmin, who share income and losses in the ratio 2:1:1, decide to liquidate their business on April 30. As of that date their post-closing trial balance reads:

Cash	$ 38,000	
Other Assets	82,000	
Liabilities		$ 48,000
Eccleston, Capital		30,000
Kapela, Capital		22,000
Harmin, Capital		20,000
	$120,000	$120,000

Present the entries to record the following liquidating transactions:

(a) Sold the noncash assets for $12,000.

(b) Distributed the loss to the partners.

(c) Paid the liabilities.

(d) Allocated the available cash to the partners.

(e) The partner with the debit balance pays the amount he owes.

(f) Any additional money is distributed.

(a)

(b)

(c)

(d)

(e)

(f)

SOLUTION

(a)	Cash	12,000	
	Loss on Realization	70,000	
	Other Assets		82,000
(b)	Eccleston, Capital	35,000	
	Kapela, Capital	17,500	
	Harmin, Capital	17,500	
	Loss on Realization		70,000
(c)	Liabilities	48,000	
	Cash		48,000
(d)	Kapela, Capital	2,000	
	Cash		2,000
(e)	Eccleston, Capital	5,000	
	Cash		5,000
(f)	Cash	5,000	
	Kapela, Capital		2,500
	Harmin, Capital		2,500

SUMMARY OF TRANSACTIONS

Transaction	Cash	Other Assets	Liabilities	Eccleston, Capital	Kapela, Capital	Harmin, Capital
Balance	$38,000	$82,000	$48,000	$30,000	$22,000	$20,000
(a), (b)	+ 12,000	− 82,000		− 35,000	− 17,500	− 17,500
	$50,000		$48,000	($ 5,000)	$ 4,500	$ 2,500
(c)	− 48,000		− 48,000			
	$ 2,000			($ 5,000)	$ 4,500	$ 2,500
(d)	− 2,000				− 2,000	
				($ 5,000)	$ 2,500	$ 2,500
(e)	+ 5,000			+ 5,000		
	$ 5,000				$ 2,500	$ 2,500
(f)	− 5,000				− 2,500	− 2,500

1.17. The trial balance of Blake and Carson, who share profits and losses equally, is as follows:

Cash	$ 40,000	
Other Assets	60,000	
Accounts Payable		$ 30,000
Blake, Capital		45,000
Carson, Capital		25,000
	$100,000	$100,000

Both partners had decided to admit Davidoff into the partnership, as the business had grown steadily. Prior to Davidoff's admittance, the partners had agreed to record goodwill of $20,000. After this adjustment had been made, Davidoff invested sufficient cash so that he would have a 1/3 interest in the firm. However, the partners could not work together and they decided to liquidate. The business, exclusive of the cash balance but including their liabilities, was sold for $32,000. Assuming that at the time of the sale the balances of the accounts were as they appear above, prepare journal entries to record (a) the recognition of goodwill, (b) the acceptance of Davidoff into the partnership, (c) the sale of the business, (d) the distribution of the loss on realization, (e) the final division of cash.

(a)

(b)

(c)

(d)

(e)

SOLUTION

(a)	Goodwill	20,000	
	Blake, Capital		10,000
	Carson, Capital		10,000
(b)	Cash	45,000	
	Davidoff, Capital		45,000*
	* To produce three equal parts Davidoff must invest one-half		
	of the existing capital ($70,000 + $20,000 goodwill).		
(c)	Cash	32,000	
	Accounts Payable	30,000	
	Loss on Realization	18,000	
	Other Assets		60,000
	Goodwill		20,000
(d)	Blake, Capital	6,000	
	Carson, Capital	6,000	
	Davidoff, Capital	6,000	
	Loss on Realization		18,000
(e)	Blake, Capital	49,000	
	Carson, Capital	29,000	
	Davidoff, Capital	39,000	
	Cash		117,000

SUMMARY OF TRANSACTIONS

Transaction	Cash	Other Assets	Goodwill	Accounts Payable	Blake, Capital	Carson, Capital	Davidoff, Capital
Balance	$ 40,000	$60,000		$30,000	$45,000	$25,000	
(a)			$20,000		+ 10,000	+ 10,000	
	$ 40,000	$60,000	$20,000	$30,000	$55,000	$35,000	
(b)	+ 45,000						$45,000
	$ 85,000	$60,000	$20,000	$30,000	$55,000	$35,000	$45,000
(c), (d)	+ 32,000	− 60,000	− 20,000	− 30,000	− 6,000	− 6,000	− 6,000
	$117,000				$49,000	$29,000	$39,000
(e)	− 117,000				− 49,000	− 29,000	− 39,000

Chapter 2

The Corporation: Organization

2.1 CHARACTERISTICS OF THE CORPORATION

In essence, the corporation is an artificial being, created by law and having a *continuous* existence regardless of its changing membership. The members are the stockholders; they own the corporation but are distinct from it. As a separate legal entity, the corporation has all the rights and responsibilities of a person, such as entering into contracts, suing and being sued in its own name, and buying, selling, or owning property.

2.2 ADVANTAGES OF THE CORPORATE FORM

The corporate form of business in the United States, when compared to the sole proprietorship or partnership, has several important advantages:

(1) *Limited liability of stockholders.* Each stockholder is accountable only for the amount he invests in the corporation. If the company should fail, the creditors cannot ordinarily look beyond the assets of the corporation for settlement of their claims.

(2) *Ready transfer of ownership.* Ownership of a corporation is evidenced by stock certificates; this permits stockholders to buy or sell their interests in a corporation without interfering with the management of the business. Through the medium of organized exchanges, millions of shares of stock change hands each day.

(3) *Continued existence.* The death or incapacity of a partner may dissolve a partnership, but the corporation's existence is independent of the stockholders'.

(4) *Legal entity.* The corporation can sue and be sued, make contracts, buy and sell in its own name. This is in contrast to the sole proprietorship, which must, by law, use individual names in all legal matters.

(5) *Ease of raising capital.* Advantages (1) and (2) above make the corporation an attractive investment for stockholders. Compare this to the partnership, where capital raising is restricted by the number of partners, the amounts of their individual assets, and the prospect of unlimited liability.

2.3 DISADVANTAGES OF THE CORPORATE FORM

TAXATION

Federal and state income taxes, which normally exceed 50% of a corporation's income, constitute the greatest disadvantage of the corporate form. Neither these taxes nor the others outlined below are imposed on the sole proprietorship or the partnership.

Federal income tax. The minimum rate on the first $25,000 of income has varied from 22% to 30% in recent years, and the rate on income in excess of $25,000 has varied from 48% to 52%.

State income tax. The rate varies, the nationwide average being about 6%.

Right to do business.   An annual payment is required by each state for conducting business in that state.

Franchise tax.   This tax is another charge by the state for doing business there.   The nationwide average rate is about 2%.

These are taxes borne directly by the corporation; besides them there are:

Taxes on dividends.   When a corporation has more than 10 stockholders, the stockholders must pay income taxes on any distribution of corporate income made to them (dividends).   This amounts to a *double taxation* of the dividends, since, as a part of corporate earnings, they are already subject to income taxes as described above.

ORGANIZATION COSTS

The corporation comes into existence with the granting of a charter by the state.   For this, the state charges a fee.   In addition, there is the cost of printing stock certificates, and various legal and promoters' fees.   The total amount is charged to Organization Costs and is carried as an intangible asset on the balance sheet.

OTHER DISADVANTAGES

Various departments of the federal and state governments have the right to exercise certain restrictions and to demand financial reports of the corporation – in particular, the annual report.   Vital financial data of the corporation may thereby be disclosed to competitors.

The corporation must operate in accordance with its charter, whereas the sole proprietor or partnership is not so limited.

2.4   CORPORATE TERMINOLOGY

The *stockholder*, as an owner of the business, has the right (*a*) to vote (one vote for every share of stock he holds), (*b*) to share in profits, (*c*) to transfer his ownership, (*d*) to share in the distribution of assets in case of liquidation.

The *board of directors* is elected by the stockholders within the framework of the articles of incorporation.   Their duties include the appointing of corporate officers, determining company policies, and the distribution of profits.

A *share* of stock represents a unit of the stockholders' interest in the business.   The *par value* of a share is an arbitrary amount established in the corporation's charter and printed on the face of each stock certificate.   It bears no relation to the *market value*, i.e. the current purchase or selling price.   There are several categories of stock shares:

Authorized shares are shares of stock which a corporation is permitted to issue (sell) under its articles of incorporation.

Unissued shares are authorized shares which have not yet been offered for sale.

Subscribed shares are shares which a buyer has contracted to purchase at a specific price on a certain date.   The shares will not be issued until full payment has been received.

Treasury stock represents shares which have been issued and later reacquired by the corporation.

Outstanding stock represents shares authorized, issued, and in the hands of stockholders.   (Treasury stock is not outstanding, as it belongs to the corporation and not to the stockholders.)

2.5 EQUITY ACCOUNTING FOR THE CORPORATION

Accounting for the corporation is distingushed from accounting for the sole proprietorship or the partnership by the treatment of owners' (stockholders') equity, which, in the corporation, is separated into *paid-in capital* and *retained earnings*. The reason for this separation is that most states prohibit corporations from paying dividends from other than retained earnings. Paid-in capital is further divided, and so we have three major capital accounts:

Capital Stock. This account shows the par value of the stock issued by the corporation.

Additional Paid-In Capital. Amounts paid in beyond the par value of stock.

Retained Earnings. The accumulated earnings arising from profitable operation of the business.

EXAMPLE 1. Operation at a Profit.

Assume that on January 1 two separate businesses are formed, a sole proprietorship operated by Ira Sochet and a corporation having four stockholders. Assume further that the single owner invested $20,000, while the four stockholders each bought 500 shares of common stock at $10 per share. The entries to record the investments are:

Sole Proprietorship		Corporation	
Cash	*20,000*	*Cash*	*20,000*
Ira Sochet, Capital	*20,000*	*Common Stock*	*20,000*

After a year's operations the net income of each enterprise was $5,000. In the sole proprietorship, the Expense and Income Summary balance is transferred to the capital account; in the corporation, the balance is transferred to Retained Earnings. Thus:

Sole Proprietorship		Corporation	
Expense and Income Summary	*5,000*	*Expense and Income Summary*	*5,000*
Ira Sochet, Capital	*5,000*	*Retained Earnings*	*5,000*

The balance sheets of the two firms are identical except for the owners' equity sections, which appear as follows:

Sole Proprietorship		Corporation	
Ira Sochet, Capital, January 1	$20,000	*Common Stock, $10 par*	
		(2,000 shares authorized and issued)	$20,000
Add: Net Income	5,000	*Retained Earnings*	5,000
Ira Sochet, Capital, December 31	$25,000	*Stockholders' Equity*	$25,000

EXAMPLE 2. Operation at a Loss.

During the second year of operations, both firms in Example 1 lost $7,000, an amount that exceeds the first year's profits. Observe the difference in the two balance sheets:

Sole Proprietorship		Corporation	
Ira Sochet, Capital, January 1	$25,000	*Common Stock, $10 par*	
		(2,000 shares authorized and issued)	$20,000
Deduct: Net Loss	(7,000)	*Deduct: Deficit*	(2,000)*
Ira Sochet, Capital, December 31	$18,000	*Stockholders' Equity*	$18,000

* Retained Earnings

7,000	5,000

The $7,000 was treated as a net loss in the sole proprietorship; in the corporation, it was reduced by the net profit from the first year and titled "Deficit."

2.6 COMMON STOCK

If a corporation issues only one class of stock, it is known as *common stock,* with all shares having the same rights. The ownership of a share of common stock carries with it the right to:

1. Vote in the election of directors and in the making of certain important corporate decisions.
2. Participate in the corporation's profits.
3. Purchase a proportionate part of future stock issues.
4. Share in assets upon liquidation.

2.7 PREFERRED STOCK

In order to appeal to a broader market, the corporation may also issue *preferred stock.* This class of stock does not ordinarily carry voting rights (although such rights are sometimes conferred by a special provision in the charter); however, as its name implies, this stock does take preference over common stock in several respects.

Prior claim against earnings. The board of directors has the power to declare and distribute dividends to the stockholders. In such distributions, the claims of preferred stock are honored before those of common stock. However, the amount of dividends paid to preferred stock is usually limited to a fixed percentage of par value, while no limit is usually placed on the amount paid to common stock. From an accounting viewpoint, the priority in receiving dividends constitutes the most important benefit of preferred stock.

EXAMPLE 3.

Eppy Corporation has outstanding 1,000 shares of preferred stock with a preference of a $5 dividend (5% of $100 par value), and 3,000 shares of common stock. Net income was $20,000 and $40,000 for the first two years of operations. The board of directors has authorized the distribution of all profits.

	Year 1	Year 2
Net profit	$20,000	$40,000
Dividends on preferred (1,000 shares, $5 per share)	5,000	5,000
Balance to common	$15,000	$35,000
Number of common shares	÷ 3,000	÷ 3,000
Common stock dividend per share	$5.00	$11.67

Prior claim to assets. If, upon liquidation of a corporation, the assets that remain after payment of all creditors are not sufficient to return the full amount of the capital contributions of preferred and common stockholders, payment must first be made to preferred stockholders. Any balance would then go to common stockholders.

Preferred stock may also carry the following benefits:

Call privilege. The issuing company will have the right to redeem (call) the stock at a later date for a predetermined price. This call price would be in excess of the original issue price, such as 105% of par value.

Conversion privilege. The stockholder, at his option, may convert preferred stock into common stock. This might be done if the corporation's common stock should become more desirable than the preferred stock because of large earnings (see Example 3).

PARTICIPATION IN EARNINGS

In Example 3, the preferred stock was *nonparticipating*: it did not partake in dividends beyond a certain fixed percentage. *Participating* preferred stock, on the other hand, shares in dividends with common stock, usually as follows:

1. The amount stipulated in the preferred stock agreement is paid to preferred stock.

2. A dividend of the same amount or based on the same percentage rate is paid to common stock.

3. Any additional earnings are divided between preferred and common stock in the manner set forth in the agreement.

If, after Step 1, insufficient earnings remain to allow Step 2, then the remainder is divided equally among the common shares.

EXAMPLE 4.

The data for Eppy Corporation is as in Example 3, except that preferred stock is now fully participating. The distribution of net profit for the first and second year would be as follows:

Net Profit $20,000	**Preferred**	**Common**
To preferred (1,000 shares, $5 per share)	$5,000	. . . .
To common (3,000 shares, $5 per share)	. . . .	$15,000
	$5,000	$15,000
Amount per share	$5	$5

Net Profit $40,000	**Preferred**	**Common**
To preferred (1,000 shares, $5 per share)	$ 5,000	. . . .
To common (3,000 shares, $5 per share)	. . . .	$15,000
	$ 5,000	$15,000
* Balance: 1/4 to preferred	5,000	. . . .
3/4 to common	. . . .	15,000
	$10,000	$30,000
Amount per share	$10	$10

* The balance is divided in the ratio 1 : 3, which is the ratio of 1,000 shares to 3,000 shares.

CUMULATIVE PREFERRED STOCK

To insure the continuity of dividends in the event that there is no dividend declared during some period, the corporation may issue a class of preferred stock for which dividends accumulate. Holders of this *cumulative* preferred stock must be paid their back-dividends (*arrears*) before common stockholders receive any dividends.

EXAMPLE 5.

Eppy Corporation, with 1,000 shares of cumulative preferred stock paying five dollars a share and 3,000 shares of common stock, declares no dividends for the first year. In the second year, all net profits are to be distributed. The net profit for the second year is $40,000.

	First Year	**Second Year**
To preferred (1,000 shares, $5 dividend)	. . . .	$10,000, or $10 per share*
To common (3,000 shares)	. . . .	$30,000, or $10 per share
Net profit		$40,000

* $5 per share for each of two years.

Suppose now that Eppy Corporation did not declare dividends for two years and that the profit for the *third year* was $40,000.

	First Year	Second Year	Third Year
To preferred (1,000 shares, $5 dividend)	....	....	$15,000, or $15 per share*
To common (3,000 shares)	....	....	$25,000, or $8.33 per share
Net profit			$40,000

* $5 per share for each of three years.

Most preferred stock is cumulative, and we shall make this assumption in the remaining sections of this chapter. We shall also assume the stock to be nonparticipating.

2.8 ISSUE OF STOCK

ISSUE AT PAR

When a corporation is organized, the charter will state how many shares of common and preferred stock are authorized. Often more stock is authorized than is intended to be sold immediately. This will enable the corporation to expand in the future without applying to the state for permission to issue more shares. When stock is sold for cash and issued immediately, the entry to record the security has the usual form: Cash is debited and the particular security is credited.

EXAMPLE 6.

Carey Corporation, organized on January 1 with an authorization of 10,000 shares of common stock ($40 par), issues 8,000 shares at par for cash. The entry to record the stockholders' investment and the receipt of cash is:

Cash	320,000	
Common Stock		320,000

If, in addition, Carey Corporation issues 1,000 shares of preferred 5% stock ($100 par) at par, the combined entry would be:

Cash	420,000	
Preferred Stock		100,000
Common Stock		320,000

A corporation may accept property other than cash in exchange for stock. If this occurs, the assets should be recorded at fair market value, usually as determined by the board of directors of the company.

EXAMPLE 7.

In exchange for 1,000 shares of $100-par common stock, Walker Corporation receives, at fair market value, machinery worth $50,000, and land and buildings worth $30,000 and $20,000 respectively. The transaction is recorded as:

Machinery	50,000	
Land	30,000	
Buildings	20,000	
Common Stock		100,000

ISSUE AT A PREMIUM OR A DISCOUNT

The market price of stock is influenced by many factors, such as:

- potential earning power
- general business conditions and other prospects
- financial condition and earnings record
- dividend record

Stock will be sold at a price above par if investors are willing to pay the excess, or *premium*. The premium is not profit to the corporation but rather part of the investment of the stockholders.

EXAMPLE 8.

Carey Corporation issues 8,000 shares of its authorized 10,000 shares of common stock ($40 par) for $45 a share. The entry to record the transaction is:

Cash	360,000	
Common Stock		320,000
Premium on Common Stock		40,000

If the purchaser will not pay par value, the corporation may issue the stock at a price below par. The difference between par value and the lower price is called the *discount*.

EXAMPLE 9.

Carey Corporation issues 1,000 shares of 5% preferred stock ($100 par) at 98.

Cash	98,000	
Discount on Preferred Stock	2,000	
Preferred Stock		100,000

EXAMPLE 10.

Based on Examples 8 and 9, the stockholders' equity section of the balance sheet of Carey Corporation is as follows:

Paid-In Capital		
Preferred Stock, 5%, $100 par		
(1,000 shares authorized and issued)	$100,000	
Less: Discount on Preferred Stock	2,000	$ 98,000
Common Stock, $40 par		
(10,000 shares authorized, 8,000 shares issued)	$320,000	
Premium on Common Stock	40,000	360,000
Total Paid-In Capital		$458,000
Retained Earnings		22,000*
Stockholders' Equity		$480,000

* assumed

2.9 BOOK VALUE

The *book value* per share of stock is obtained by dividing the stockholders' equity amount by the number of shares outstanding. It thus represents the amount that would be distributed to each share of stock if the corporation were to be dissolved.

Individual book values for common and preferred stock are defined by separating the stockholders' equity amount into two parts and dividing each part by the corresponding number of shares. All premiums and discounts, as well as retained earnings or deficits, go to common stock only. (See Example 12.)

EXAMPLE 11.

Suppose that the balance sheet reads:

Common Stock, $40 par	
(10,000 shares authorized, 8,000 shares issued)	*$320,000*
Retained Earnings	*22,000*
Stockholders' Equity	*$342,000*

Then we would have:

$$\text{Book value} = \frac{\$342,000}{8,000 \text{ shares}} = \$42.75 \text{ per share}$$

EXAMPLE 12.

For the data in Example 10, the allocation of the total equity between preferred and common stock would be

Total equity	$480,000
Allocation to preferred stock	100,000
Balance to common stock	$380,000

and the book values would be

$$\text{Book value of preferred} = \frac{\$100,000}{1,000 \text{ shares}} = \$100 \text{ per share}$$

$$\text{Book value of common} = \frac{\$380,000}{8,000 \text{ shares}} = \$47.50 \text{ per share}$$

Summary

(1) The rights to vote and to share in the profits of the company rest with the _____.

(2) The greatest disadvantage of the corporate form of business is the _____ on income.

(3) The value established for stock is called _____.

(4) Shares of stock which a corporation is allowed to sell are called _____.

(5) The profit and loss of the corporation is recorded in the _____ account.

(6) If a corporation issues only one class of stock, it is known as _____.

(7) To achieve a broader market and a more attractive issue price, preferred stock may _____ in profits beyond the specified rate.

(8) To insure the right to unbroken dividends, _____ stock may be issued.

(9) The amount paid in excess of par by a purchaser of newly issued stock is called a _____, while the amount paid below par is known as a _____.

(10) Past dividends owed to preferred stockholders are called dividends in _____.

Answers: (1) stockholders; (2) tax; (3) par value; (4) authorized shares; (5) retained earnings; (6) common stock; (7) participate; (8) cumulative preferred; (9) premium, discount; (10) arrears

Solved Problems

2.1. Two separate business organizations, a partnership and a corporation, are formed on January 1, 1974:

(1) The initial investments of the partners, Blue and Gray, are $25,000 and $20,000, respectively.

(2) The Green Corporation has five stockholders, each owning 90 shares of $100-par common.

At the end of the calendar year, the net income of each company was $15,000. (a) For each organization show the proper entry to close the expense and income account. (b) Prepare a capital statement for the partnership and a stockholders' equity statement for the corporation, as of December 31, 1974.

(a) **Partnership entry**

Corporation entry

(b) *Partnership Capital Statement*

Stockholders' Equity Statement

SOLUTION

(a)

Partnership entry	Expense and Income Summary	15,000	
	Blue, Capital		7,500*
	Gray, Capital		7,500*
* Profits and losses are to be divided equally if no other distribution is specified.			
Corporation entry	Expense and Income Summary	15,000	
	Retained Earnings		15,000

(b)

Partnership Capital Statement

	Blue	Gray	Total
Capital, Jan. 1, 1974	$25,000	$20,000	$45,000
Add: Net Income	7,500	7,500	15,000
Capital, Dec. 31, 1974	$32,500	$27,500	$60,000

Stockholders' Equity Statement

Common Stock, $100 par	
(450 shares authorized and issued)	$45,000
Retained Earnings	15,000
Stockholders' Equity	$60,000

2.2.   Redo Problem 2.1 assuming that each business suffers a loss of $18,000 in the second
year of operations.

(a)

Partnership entry		
Corporation entry		

(b)

Partnership Capital Statement

Stockholders' Equity Statement

SOLUTION

(a)

Partnership entry	Blue, Capital	9,000	
	Gray, Capital	9,000	
	Expense and Income Summary		18,000
Corporation entry	Retained Earnings	18,000	
	Expense and Income Summary		18,000

(b)

Partnership Capital Statement

	Blue	Gray	Total
Capital, Jan. 1, 1975	$32,500	$27,500	$60,000
Less: Net Loss	9,000	9,000	18,000
Capital, Dec. 31, 1975	$23,500	$18,500	$42,000

Stockholders' Equity Statement

Common Stock, $100 par	
(450 shares authorized and issued)	$45,000
Less: Deficit*	(3,000)
Stockholders' Equity	$42,000

* Retained Earnings (Dec. 31, 1974)	$15,000
Less: Net Loss (Dec. 31, 1975)	18,000
	($3,000)

2.3.   The board of directors' policy is to distribute *all* profits earned in a year to preferred
and common stockholders.   During the first three years of operations, the corporation
earned $68,000, $180,000, and $320,000.   There are outstanding 10,000 shares of 6%,
$100-par preferred stock and 40,000 shares of common stock. Determine the amount
per share applicable to common stock for each of the three years.

	Year 1	Year 2	Year 3

SOLUTION

	Year 1	Year 2	Year 3
Net profit (after taxes)	$68,000	$180,000	$320,000
Dividend on preferred stock	60,000	60,000	60,000
Balance to common stock	$ 8,000	$120,000	$260,000
Common dividend per share	$0.20	$3.00	$6.50

2.4. The Agin Corporation has outstanding 5,000 shares of 6%, $100-par participating preferred stock and 20,000 shares of common stock. The preferred stock is entitled to equal participation with common *per share* in any dividend distribution that exceeds both the regular preferred dividend and a $6 per share common dividend. Find the dividend per share on preferred stock and common stock if net profit is (a) $110,000, (b) $200,000.

(a)

	Preferred	Common

(b)

	Preferred	Common

SOLUTION

(a)

	Preferred	Common
Preferred dividend		
($100 par, 6%, 5,000 shares)	$30,000	. . . .
To common stock (20,000 shares)	. . . .	$80,000
	$30,000	$80,000
Dividend per share	$6	$4

Common stock did not receive its full dividend, $6 × 20,000 = $120,000, because there was not sufficient net income after the payment of the regular preferred dividend. In this case preferred stock receives its stated dividend and common stock the balance.

(b)

	Preferred	Common
Preferred dividend		
($100 par, 6%, 5,000 shares)	$30,000	....
Common dividend (20,000 shares at $6)	....	$120,000
	$30,000	$120,000
Balance ($50,000)	10,000*	40,000**
	$40,000	$160,000
Dividend per share	$8	$8

$$* \quad \frac{5,000}{5,000 + 20,000} \times \$50,000 \qquad ** \quad \frac{20,000}{5,000 + 20,000} \times \$50,000$$

2.5. The outstanding stock of the Roland Corporation consists of 10,000 shares of 5%, $100-par cumulative preferred stock and 20,000 shares of $50-par common stock. The company pays out as dividends *all* of its net income. Annual earnings for the last four years are $30,000 (first year of operations), $40,000, $90,000 and $210,000. Determine the distribution per share on each class of stock for each of the four years.

	Total	Preferred	Common
Year 1			
Year 2			
Year 3			
Year 4			

SOLUTION

	Total	Preferred	Common
Year 1	$ 30,000	$3.00	....
Year 2	40,000	4.00	....
Year 3	90,000	8.00*	$0.50
Year 4	210,000	5.00	8.00

* In order to guarantee the continuation of dividends to preferred stock, no distribution may be made to common stockholders if any dividends are in arrears to preferred stockholders. Since there are arrears for Years 1 and 2, the computation for Year 3 is:

Arrears for Year 1	$20,000	($50,000 − $30,000)
Arrears for Year 2	10,000	($50,000 − $40,000)
Regular dividend for Year 3	50,000	
	$80,000	
Distribution per preferred share	$8.00	

2.6. The Glatt Company has outstanding 5,000 shares of $100-par, 6% preferred stock and 10,000 shares of $50-par common stock. Complete the table below under each of the following assumptions: (a) preferred stock is noncumulative and nonparticipating; (b) preferred stock is cumulative and nonparticipating; (c) preferred stock is noncumulative and participates equally per share after common stock receives $5 per share dividend.

(a)

Year	Total Dividends	Paid to Preferred	Total Arrears	Dividend per Share Preferred	Paid to Common	Dividend per Share Common
1975	$ 10,000					
1976	25,000					
1977	40,000					
1978	80,000					
1979	200,000					

(b)

Year	Total Dividends	Paid to Preferred	Total Arrears	Dividend per Share Preferred	Paid to Common	Dividend per Share Common
1975	$ 10,000					
1976	25,000					
1977	40,000					
1978	80,000					
1979	200,000					

(c)

Year	Total Dividends	Paid to Preferred	Total Arrears	Dividend per Share Preferred	Paid to Common	Dividend per Share Common
1975	$ 10,000					
1976	25,000					
1977	40,000					
1978	80,000					
1979	200,000					

SOLUTION

(a)

Year	Total Dividends	Paid to Preferred	Total Arrears	Dividend per Share Preferred	Paid to Common	Dividend per Share Common
1975	$ 10,000	$10,000	....	$2.00	....	....
1976	25,000	25,000	....	5.00	....	....
1977	40,000	30,000	....	6.00	$ 10,000	$ 1.00
1978	80,000	30,000	....	6.00	50,000	5.00
1979	200,000	30,000	....	6.00	170,000	17.00

(b)

Year	Total Dividends	Paid to Preferred	Total Arrears	Dividend per Share Preferred	Paid to Common	Dividend per Share Common
1975	$ 10,000	$10,000	$20,000	$2.00	....	....
1976	25,000	25,000	25,000	5.00	....	....
1977	40,000	40,000	15,000	8.00	....	....
1978	80,000	45,000	....	9.00	$ 35,000	$ 3.50
1979	200,000	30,000	....	6.00	170,000	17.00

(c)

Year	Total Dividends	Paid to Preferred	Total Arrears	Dividend per Share Preferred	Paid to Common	Dividend per Share Common
1975	$ 10,000	$10,000	....	$ 2.00	....	....
1976	25,000	25,000	....	5.00	....	....
1977	40,000	30,000	....	6.00	$ 10,000	$ 1.00
1978	80,000	30,000	....	6.00	50,000	5.00
*1979	200,000	70,000	....	14.00	130,000	13.00

* In 1979 preferred stockholders receive a normal dividend of $30,000 and common stockholders a normal dividend of $50,000. The balance, $200,000 − ($30,000 + $50,000) = $120,000, is divided equally among the 15,000 preferred and common shares. Thus, each share gets an additional $8, as shown below.

	Preferred	Common	Total
Normal dividend	$30,000	$ 50,000	$ 80,000
Participating dividend	40,000 [5,000 × $8]	80,000 [10,000 × $8]	120,000
	$70,000	$130,000	$200,000

2.7.   On January 1, the Greene Corporation issued for cash 5,000 shares of its authorized 10,000 shares of $10-par common stock. Three months later it was decided to issue another 5,000 shares of common stock at par and also 1,000 shares of 5%, $100-par preferred stock. What entries are required to record the January and April transactions?

January 1			
April 1			

SOLUTION

January 1	Cash		50,000	
	Common Stock			50,000
April 1	Cash		150,000	
	Common Stock			50,000
	Preferred Stock			100,000

2.8. In Problem 2.7 present the stockholders' equity section (*a*) as of January 31, (*b*) as of April 30.

(*a*)

(*b*)

SOLUTION

(*a*)

Paid-In Capital		
Common Stock, $10 par		
(10,000 shares authorized, 5,000 shares issued)	$ 50,000	
Stockholders' Equity		$ 50,000

(*b*)

Paid-In Capital		
Preferred Stock, 5%, $100 par		
(1,000 shares authorized and issued)	$100,000	
Common Stock, $10 par		
(10,000 shares authorized and issued)	100,000	
Stockholders' Equity		$200,000

2.9. Rund Corporation issues 2,000 shares of 6%, $50-par preferred stock at $48 and 5,000 shares of $25-par common stock at $30. (*a*) Present the entry needed to record the above information. (*b*) Present the stockholders' equity section.

(*a*)

(b)

SOLUTION

(a)

Cash	246,000	
Discount on Preferred Stock	4,000	
Preferred Stock		100,000
Common Stock		125,000
Premium on Common Stock		25,000

(b)

Paid-In Capital			
Preferred Stock, 6%, $50 par	$100,000		
Less: Discount on Preferred Stock	4,000	$ 96,000	
Common Stock, $25 par	125,000		
Add: Premium on Common Stock	25,000	150,000	
Stockholders' Equity		$246,000	

2.10. Boaches Inc. receives in exchange for 3,000 shares of $100-par preferred stock and 2,000 shares of $50-par common stock the following fixed assets:

	Cost	Fair Market Value
Building	$200,000	$125,000
Land	100,000	80,000
Machinery	150,000	150,000
Equipment	60,000	45,000

Provide the entry to record the above information.

SOLUTION

Building	125,000	
Land	80,000	
Machinery	150,000	
Equipment	45,000	
Preferred Stock		300,000
Common Stock		100,000

2.11. The Tobak Corporation agrees to issue 10,000 shares of common stock in exchange for equipment valued at $250,000. Present the required journal entry if par value of the common stock is (a) $25, (b) $20, (c) $30.

(a)

(b)

(c)

SOLUTION

(a)	Equipment	250,000	
	Common Stock		250,000
(b)	Equipment	250,000	
	Common Stock		200,000
	Premium on Common Stock		50,000
(c)	Equipment	250,000	
	Discount on Common Stock	50,000	
	Common Stock		300,000

2.12. On January 1, P. C. Sloan, Inc. was organized with an authorization of 5,000 shares of preferred 6% stock, $100 par, and 10,000 shares of $25-par common stock.

(a) Record the following transactions:

January 10:   Sold half of the common stock at $28 for cash

January 15:   Issued 2,000 shares of preferred and 1,000 shares of common at par in exchange for land and building with fair market values of $140,000 and $85,000 respectively

March 6:   Sold the balance of the preferred stock for cash at $105

(b) Present the stockholders' equity section of the balance sheet as of March 6.

(a) January 10

January 15

March 6

(b)

SOLUTION

(a)	January 10	Cash	140,000	
		Common Stock		125,000
		Premium on Common Stock		15,000

January 15	Land		140,000	
	Building		85,000	
	Preferred Stock			200,000
	Common Stock			25,000
March 6	Cash		315,000	
	Preferred Stock			300,000
	Premium on Preferred Stock			15,000

(b)

Paid-In Capital		
Preferred Stock, 6%, $100 par		
(5,000 shares authorized and issued)	$500,000	
Add: Premium on Preferred Stock	15,000	$515,000
Common Stock, $25 par		
(10,000 shares authorized, 6,000 shares issued)	$150,000	
Add: Premium on Common Stock	15,000	165,000
Total Paid-In Capital		$680,000

2.13. Corporations A and B each have 10,000 shares of common stock outstanding. Assuming that the two stocks have the same book value (Sec. 2.9), complete the following table:

	Corporation A	Corporation B
Assets	$350,000	?
Liabilities	100,000	$ 70,000
Common Stock	200,000	175,000
Retained Earnings	?	?

SOLUTION

	Corporation A	Corporation B
Assets	$350,000	$320,000***
Liabilities	100,000	70,000
Common Stock	200,000	175,000
Retained Earnings	50,000*	75,000**

* ASSETS   =   LIABILITIES + STOCKHOLDERS' EQUITY
  $350,000   = $100,000   +   ($200,000 + ?)

** Because the book values of the common stock in both corporations are identical, Corporation B must have the same total for stockholders' equity: $250,000 ($175,000 + $75,000)

*** ASSETS   =   LIABILITIES + STOCKHOLDERS' EQUITY
       ?   = $70,000   + $250,000

2.14. The corporation's equity accounts appear below:

Preferred Stock, 5%, $100 par	
(5,000 shares authorized, 3,000 shares issued)	$300,000
Discount on Preferred Stock	30,000
Common Stock, $50 par	
(10,000 shares authorized, 4,000 shares issued)	200,000
Premium on Common Stock	10,000
Retained Earnings (credit balance)	35,000

In order to secure additional funds, the board of directors approved the following proposals:

(1) To borrow $100,000, with an 8% mortgage.

(2) To sell the remaining common stock at par.

(3) To issue the balance of the preferred stock in exchange for equipment valued at $185,000.

Prepare (a) journal entries for the transactions, (b) the stockholders' equity section.

(a)

(1)

(2)

(3)

(b)

SOLUTION

(a)

(1)	Cash	100,000	
	Mortgage Payable		100,000
(2)	Cash	300,000	
	Common Stock		300,000
(3)	Equipment	185,000	
	Discount on Preferred Stock	15,000	
	Preferred Stock		200,000

(b)

Paid-In Capital:		
Preferred Stock, 5%, $100 par (5,000 shares authorized and issued)	$500,000	
Less: Discount on Preferred Stock	45,000	$ 455,000
Common Stock, $50 par (10,000 shares authorized and issued)	$500,000	
Add: Premium on Common Stock	10,000	$ 510,000
Total Paid-In Capital		$ 965,000
Retained Earnings		35,000
Total Stockholders' Equity		$1,000,000

2.15. Based on the balances of the accounts below, prepare a classified balance sheet.

Accounts Receivable	82,000	Goodwill	40,000
Accounts Payable	22,000	Income Tax Payable	16,000
Accumulated Depreciation, Building	14,000	Land	50,000
Accumulated Depreciation, Equipment	62,000	Merchandise Inventory	102,000
Allowance for Uncollectible Accounts	6,000	Mortgage Payable	124,000
Building	124,000	Notes Payable	28,000
Cash	245,000	Preferred Stock, 6%, $100 par	
Common Stock, $50 par		(2,000 shares authorized	
(10,000 shares authorized,		and issued)	200,000
5,000 shares issued)	250,000	Premium on Common Stock	25,000
Discount on Preferred Stock	20,000	Prepaid Insurance	16,000
Equipment	148,000	Retained Earnings	80,000

ASSETS

Current Assets

Total Current Assets
Fixed Assets

Total Fixed Assets
Intangible Assets

Total Assets

LIABILITIES

Current Liabilities

Total Current Liabilities
Long-Term Liabilities

Total Liabilities

STOCKHOLDERS' EQUITY

Paid-In Capital

Total Paid-In Capital
Retained Earnings
Total Stockholders' Equity
Total Liabilities and Stockholders' Equity

SOLUTION

ASSETS

Current Assets		
Cash		$245,000
Accounts Receivable	$82,000	
Less: Allowance for Uncollectible Accounts	6,000	76,000
Merchandise Inventory		102,000
Prepaid Insurance		16,000
Total Current Assets		$439,000

(cont. page 42)

ASSETS (cont.)

Fixed Assets			
Equipment	$148,000		
Less: Accumulated Depreciation, Equipment	62,000	$ 86,000	
Building	$124,000		
Less: Accumulated Depreciation, Building	14,000	110,000	
Land		50,000	
Total Fixed Assets			$246,000
Intangible Assets			
Goodwill			40,000
Total Assets			$725,000

LIABILITIES

Current Liabilities			
Accounts Payable	$22,000		
Notes Payable	28,000		
Income Tax Payable	16,000		
Total Current Liabilities		$ 66,000	
Long-Term Liabilities			
Mortgage Payable		124,000	
Total Liabilities			$190,000

STOCKHOLDERS' EQUITY

Paid-In Capital			
Preferred Stock, 6%, $100 par			
(2,000 shares authorized and issued)	$200,000		
Less: Discount on Preferred Stock	20,000	$180,000	
Common Stock, $50 par (10,000 shares			
authorized, 5,000 shares issued)	$250,000		
Add: Premium on Common Stock	25,000	275,000	
Total Paid-In Capital			$455,000
Retained Earnings			80,000
Total Stockholders' Equity			$535,000
Total Liabilities and Stockholders' Equity			$725,000

2.16. Determine the equity per share of preferred and of common stock, if the balance sheet shows:

(a)

Preferred Stock, $100 par	$200,000
Common Stock, $25 par	100,000
Premium on Common Stock	10,000
Retained Earnings	40,000

(b)

Preferred Stock, $100 par	$200,000
Premium on Preferred Stock	10,000
Common Stock, $25 par	100,000
Retained Earnings (deficit)	(40,000)

(a)

Preferred Stock	Common Stock

(b)

Preferred Stock	Common Stock

SOLUTION

(a)

Preferred Stock		Common Stock	
$200,000	To preferred stock	$100,000	Common stock
		10,000	Premium
$100.00	Per share	40,000	Retained earnings
		$150,000	To common stock
		$37.50*	Per share

* $150,000 ÷ 4,000 shares. The number of shares outstanding is determined by dividing the value of the stock, $100,000, by its par value, $25.

(b)

Preferred Stock		Common Stock	
$200,000	To preferred stock	$100,000	Common stock
		10,000*	Premium
$100.00	Per share	(40,000)	Deficit
		$ 70,000	To common stock
		$17.50	Per share

* The premium on preferred stock is allocated to common stock when computing equity per share.

2.17. The capital accounts of the Sullivan Corporation are as follows:

Preferred Stock, 7%, $100 par	$1,000,000
Common Stock, $50 par	500,000
Premium on Common Stock	50,000
Retained Earnings	100,000

Dividends are in arrears for the current year and the previous year. Find the equity per share of each class of stock if (a) preferred stock is entitled to par plus unpaid cumulative dividends regardless of the availability of retained earnings; (b) preferred stock is entitled to par plus unpaid cumulative dividends to the extent of retained earnings.

(a)

Preferred Stock	Common Stock

(b)

Preferred Stock	Common Stock

SOLUTION

(a)

Preferred Stock		Common Stock	
$1,000,000	Preferred stock	$500,000	Common stock
140,000*	Dividends in arrears	50,000	Premium
$1,140,000	To preferred stock	100,000	Retained earnings
$114	Per share	(140,000)	Arrears
		$510,000	To common stock
		$51	Per share

* 10,000 shares × $7 per share per year × 2 years

(b)

Preferred Stock		Common Stock	
$1,000,000	Preferred stock	$500,000	Common stock
100,000*	Dividends in arrears	50,000	Premium on common stock
$1,100,000	To preferred stock	100,000	Retained earnings
$110	Per share	(100,000)	Arrears
		$550,000	To common stock
		$55	Per share

* Dividends in arrears amount to $140,000 but can be paid only to the extent of retained earnings ($100,000).

2.18. Below are data from four different corporations, labeled (a) through (d). Determine for each corporation the equity per share of preferred and common stock.

(a)

Preferred Stock, 6%, $100 par	$400,000
Premium on Preferred Stock	40,000
Common Stock, $25 par	250,000
Discount on Common Stock	20,000
Retained Earnings	100,000

(b)

Preferred Stock, 6%, $100 par	$500,000
Common Stock, $25 par	100,000
Premium on Common Stock	10,000
Retained Earnings	40,000

The corporation is being dissolved and preferred stock is entitled to receive $110 upon liquidation.

(c)

Preferred Stock, 7%, $100 par	$500,000
Common, Stock, $50 par	500,000
Retained Earnings	50,000

Dividends on preferred stock are in arrears for three years, including the present year. Preferred stock is entitled to par plus payment of dividends in arrears up to the extent of retained earnings.

(d)

Preferred Stock, 7%, $100 par	$500,000
Premium on Preferred Stock	20,000
Common Stock, $50 par	500,000
Discount on Common Stock	10,000
Retained Earnings	70,000

Dividends on preferred stock are in arrears for three years, including the present year. Preferred stock is entitled to par plus payment of dividends in arrears regardless of the availability of retained earnings.

(a)   **Preferred Stock**   **Common Stock**

_____

(b)   **Preferred Stock**   **Common Stock**

_____

(c)   **Preferred Stock**   **Common Stock**

_____

(d)   **Preferred Stock**   **Common Stock**

_____

SOLUTION

(a)

	Preferred Stock		**Common Stock**
$400,000	To preferred stock	$250,000	Common stock
$100	Per share	40,000	Premium on preferred stock
		(20,000)	Discount on common stock
		100,000	Retained earnings
		$370,000	To common stock
		$37	Per share

(b)

	Preferred Stock		**Common Stock**
$550,000	To preferred stock	$100,000	Common stock
$110	Per share	10,000	Premium
		40,000	Retained earnings
		(50,000)	Preferred liquidation
		$100,000	To common stock
		$25	Per share

(c)

	Preferred Stock		**Common Stock**
$500,000	Preferred stock	$500,000	Common stock
50,000	Dividends in arrears	50,000	Retained earnings
$550,000	To preferred stock	(50,000)	Arrears
$110	Per share	$500,000	To common stock
		$50	Per share

(d)

Preferred Stock		Common Stock	
$500,000	Preferred stock	$500,000	Common stock
105,000	Dividends in arrears	20,000	Premium on preferred
$605,000	To preferred stock	(10,000)	Discount on common
$121.00	Per share	70,000	Retained earnings
		(105,000)	Arrears
		$475,000	To common stock
		$47.50	Per share

Chapter 3

The Corporation:
Subscriptions, Treasury Stock, and Retained Earnings

3.1 STOCK SUBSCRIPTIONS

In the examples in Chapter 2, it was assumed that capital stock is paid for in full immediately upon issuance. This is indeed the case when the corporation sells the stock in the open market or through an underwriter (who pays the corporation in full and then resells to investors at a higher price). On occasion, however, stock may be purchased on an installment plan (*subscription basis*). The buyer signs a subscription stating the number of shares he wishes to purchase and the method of installment payment. The subscription is treated as any other receivable: the account Stock Subscriptions Receivable is debited when the subscription is received and is credited as the subscriber makes payments. Any balance in Stock Subscriptions Receivable at the end of the year is classified on the balance sheet as a current asset.

When the number of subscribers is large, a separate *subscribers' ledger* is established with an account for each subscriber and with Stock Subscriptions Receivable as the control account. This control account operates in the same manner as does Accounts Receivable for the accounts receivable ledger.

Stock bought on subscription is not actually issued by the corporation until final payment has been received. Therefore, a *temporary* account, Capital Stock Subscribed, is used to record the par value of the subscribed stock. This account will be credited at the time the subscription is received and debited when final payment is made and the stock issued. If a balance sheet is prepared prior to the issuance of the stock, Capital Stock Subscribed will appear in the stockholders' equity section.

If the subscription is sold for a price above or below par, Stock Subscriptions Receivable is debited for the subscription price rather than for par value. Capital Stock Subscribed is credited at par, while the difference between the subscription price and par is debited to the discount account (if the subscription price is below par) or credited to the premium account (if the subscription price exceeds par).

In case the corporation offers more than one class of stock for subscription, each class has its own subscriptions receivable and stock subscribed accounts.

EXAMPLE 1.

The Phillips Corporation received various subscriptions for a total of 5,000 shares of $10-par common stock. The subscription price was $12 per share, with a down payment of 50% of this price. Three months later the balance was paid and the stock issued.

Entry 1	Common Stock Subscriptions Receivable	60,000	
	Common Stock Subscribed		50,000
	Premium on Common Stock		10,000
	To record subscriptions to 5,000 shares of $10-par common stock at $12		
	Cash	30,000	
	Common Stock Subscriptions Receivable		30,000
	To record receipt of 50% down payment on the subscription price		

47

Entry 2

Cash	30,000	
Common Stock Subscriptions Receivable		30,000

To record final payment of the subscription price

Entry 3

Common Stock Subscribed	50,000	
Common Stock		50,000

Issued stock certificates (5,000 shares at $10 par)

The above transactions have the same final effect in the accounts as if the stock had originally been purchased in full for cash:

Cash

(1) 30,000		
(2) 30,000		

Common Stock Subscriptions Receivable

(1) 60,000	30,000 (1)	
	30,000 (2)	

Common Stock Subscribed

(3) 50,000	50,000 (1)

Premium on Common Stock

	10,000 (1)

Common Stock

	50,000 (3)

Trial Balance

Cash	$60,000	
Premium on Common Stock		$10,000
Common Stock		50,000
	$60,000	$60,000

3.2 DEFAULT ON SUBSCRIPTION

There is always the possibility that a subscriber may pay part of his subscription price but not fulfill his obligation. No one method for the accounting of this default prevails, as each corporation must act within the laws of the state of its incorporation. In some states the subscriber will forfeit the amount he has paid, to compensate the corporation for any damages. This income becomes part of capital and must be shown in an account describing the transaction; for example, Capital from Forfeited Subscriptions. In other states, however, the subscriber who defaults is entitled to a refund or to a number of shares based upon the amount he had paid.

3.3 TREASURY STOCK

Shares of a corporation's issued stock that have been reacquired by the corporation are known as *treasury stock*. A corporation may want to reacquire some of its outstanding stock:

1. to have shares available for resale to its employees in stock options or stock purchase plans
2. to have shares available for use in the acquisition of other companies
3. to keep the price of its stock stable

The differences and similarities between treasury stock and unissued stock should be noted. Treasury stock had at one time been owned by stockholders, whereas unissued stock has never been in stockholders' possession. On the other hand:

1. Both types of stock are equity items rather than assets. (Treasury stock cannot be an asset, as a corporation cannot own itself.)

2. To calculate outstanding stock, both are subtracted from authorized stock.

3. There are no voting rights or dividend distributions for either type.

Most states limit the amount of treasury stock that a corporation may acquire. This is done for the protection of the creditors, whose claims might be jeopardized if a great deal of the corporation's assets had been converted into treasury stock.

DONATION OF TREASURY STOCK

If a company finds itself in need of cash, it may ask its stockholders to give shares of stock back to the company to be resold. As there is no cost involved when the company reacquires the donated stock, and as assets, liabilities, and equity are unaffected, the only entry needed to record the acquisition is a memorandum indicating the number of shares reacquired. As this reacquired stock (treasury stock) is sold, Cash is debited and Donated Capital credited for the amount of the proceeds. When the corporation resells its treasury stock to the public, the par value of the stock is not recognized, and any proceeds received will be charged directly to Donated Capital.

EXAMPLE 2.

Before a donation of stock, the financial position of Sunco Corporation is as follows:

Sunco Corporation
Balance Sheet
October 1, 197–

ASSETS		STOCKHOLDERS' EQUITY		
Cash	$ 25,000	Paid-In Capital		
Other Assets	235,000	Common Stock, $25 par (10,000		
		shares authorized and issued)		$250,000
		Retained Earnings		10,000
Total Assets	$260,000	Stockholders' Equity		$260,000

The corporation (1) receives 1,000 shares of donated stock from its stockholders, (2) sells 600 shares of treasury stock at $30 per share, then (3) sells 300 shares at $20 per share.

Entry 1   Memo: Received 1,000 shares common stock, $25 par, as donation

Entry 2   Cash   18,000
                  Donated Capital   18,000

Entry 3   Cash   6,000
                  Donated Capital   6,000

Summary

Cash		Donated Capital	
Bal. 25,000		18,000	(2)
(2) 18,000		6,000	(3)
(3) 6,000			

The new financial position of Sunco Corporation appears as follows:

Sunco Corporation
Balance Sheet
October 15, 197–

ASSETS		STOCKHOLDERS' EQUITY	
Cash	$ 49,000	Paid-In Capital	
Other Assets	235,000	Common Stock, $25 par (10,000	
		shares authorized and issued, less	
		100 shares donated treasury stock)	$250,000
		Donated Capital	24,000
		Total Paid-In Capital	$274,000
		Retained Earnings	10,000
Total Assets	$284,000	Stockholders' Equity	$284,000

PURCHASE OF TREASURY STOCK

Subject to certain legal restrictions (see Sec. 3.4, page 51), a corporation may acquire treasury stock by buying its own shares from stockholders. Under the most common accounting method, the reacquired stock is recorded at cost, with Treasury Stock debited for its purchase price and Cash credited. The price at which the stock was originally bought and its par value are ignored.

When the stock is resold to the public, Treasury Stock is credited for the purchase price paid by the corporation, while the difference between selling and purchase price is recorded in the account Paid-In Capital from Sale of Treasury Stock. When the balance sheet is prepared, any balance in the treasury stock account is subtracted from the total stockholders' equity.

EXAMPLE 3.

Before a purchase of treasury stock, the balance sheet reads:

Sunco Corporation
Balance Sheet
October 1, 197–

ASSETS		STOCKHOLDERS' EQUITY	
Cash	$ 25,000	Paid-In Capital	
Other Assets	235,000	Common Stock, $25 par (10,000	
		shares authorized and issued)	$250,000
		Retained Earnings	10,000
Total Assets	$260,000	Stockholders' Equity	$260,000

The corporation (1) buys 500 shares of its outstanding stock at 30, (2) sells 200 shares of treasury stock at 40, then (3) sells 200 shares at 25.

Entry 1	Treasury Stock	15,000	
	Cash		15,000
Entry 2	Cash	8,000	
	Treasury Stock		6,000
	Paid-In Capital from Sale of Treasury Stock		2,000
Entry 3	Cash	5,000	
	Paid-In Capital from Sale of Treasury Stock	1,000	
	Treasury Stock		6,000

Summary

Cash		Treasury Stock		Paid-In Capital from Sale of Treasury Stock	
Bal. 25,000	15,000 (1)	(1) 15,000	6,000 (2)	(3) 1,000	2,000 (2)
(2) 8,000			6,000 (3)		
(3) 5,000					

In the adjustment of the balance sheet, the $1,000 credit balance in Paid-In Capital from Sale of Treasury Stock is treated in the same manner as a premium on common stock. (A debit balance would be treated as a discount.)

Sunco Corporation
Balance Sheet
December 31, 197–

ASSETS		**STOCKHOLDERS' EQUITY**	
Cash	$ 23,000	Paid-In Capital	
Other Assets	235,000	Common Stock, $25 par (10,000	
		shares authorized and issued)	$250,000
		Paid-In Capital from Sale of	
		Treasury Stock	1,000
		Total Paid-In Capital	$251,000
		Retained Earnings	10,000
		Total	$261,000
		Less: Treasury Stock (100 shares at cost)	3,000
Total Assets	$258,000	Stockholders' Equity	$258,000

The result of the treasury stock transactions was to reduce the number of outstanding common shares by 100 (the number of treasury shares kept by the corporation).

3.4 RETAINED EARNINGS

Retained earnings are the accumulated earnings of a corporation that have not been distributed to stockholders. Normally the retained earnings account will have a credit balance, but a debit balance (deficit) results if accumulated losses have exceeded accumulated profits. This deficit would be deducted from the total of the stockholders' equity accounts in the balance sheet.

Retained earnings may be specifically reserved (*appropriated*), or they may be free (*unappropriated*) for distribution as dividends. When an appropriation account is established, the retained earnings account is debited and the appropriation account credited. This has the effect of reducing the balance of unappropriated retained earnings by the amount put into the appropriation account. The following appropriations are frequently made:

Appropriation for contingencies. This account would be created to set up a reserve to meet unforeseen happenings—for instance, the event that future earnings might be insufficient to allow the normal payment of dividends.

Appropriation for expansion. The corporation may have plans to expand operations or build more facilities. It might, in the future, sell additional stock to obtain the assets needed or it might float bonds.

Appropriation for treasury stock. In most states, an amount equal to the cost of the treasury stock held by the corporation must be set aside out of retained earnings. Like the payment of a cash dividend, a purchase of treasury stock reduces both corporate assets and stockholders' equity. Thus, the restriction on retained earnings serves to protect the corporation's creditors and other concerned parties.

Appropriation for bonded indebtedness. A corporation may borrow money by issuing bonds (see Sec. 4.1) and, as an inducement, may agree to protect the loan by making an annual restriction of dividends.

EXAMPLE 4.

The Barker Corporation has retained earnings of $60,000. The board of directors decides to set up a fund of $5,000 annually out of earnings, to meet unforeseen happenings.

| **Entry 1** | *Retained Earnings* | 5,000 | |
| | *Appropriation for Contingencies* | | 5,000 |

The board also decides to set up an appropriation of $20,000 a year for the next five years for plant expansion.

| **Entry 2** | *Retained Earnings* | 20,000 | |
| | *Appropriation for Expansion* | | 20,000 |

The corporation buys some of its own stock for $10,000; this calls for a restriction of retained earnings, limiting the distribution of dividends.

| **Entry 3** | *Retained Earnings* | 10,000 | |
| | *Appropriation for Treasury Stock* | | 10,000 |

When, at a later date, the corporation sells $8,000 of its treasury stock, part of the appropriation for treasury stock becomes unnecessary.

| **Entry 4** | *Appropriation for Treasury Stock* | 8,000 | |
| | *Retained Earnings* | | 8,000 |

The corporation decides to borrow, through an issue of bonds, $75,000 over a ten-year period. Equal annual appropriations of $7,500 would be made over the life of the bonds.

| **Entry 5** | *Retained Earnings* | 7,500 | |
| | *Appropriation for Bonded Indebtedness* | | 7,500 |

Summary

Retained Earnings		*Appropriation for Contingencies*	*Appropriation for Expansion*
(1) 5,000	Bal. 60,000	5,000 (1)	20,000 (2)
(2) 20,000	8,000 (4)		
(3) 10,000			
(5) 7,500			

Appropriation for Treasury Stock		*Appropriation for Bonded Indebtedness*
(4) 8,000	10,000 (3)	7,500 (5)

Retained Earnings Statement
Barker Corporation
December 31, 197–

Appropriated:		
For Contingencies	$ 5,000	
For Expansion	20,000	
For Treasury Stock	2,000	
For Bonded Indebtedness	7,500	
Total Appropriated Retained Earnings		$34,500
Unappropriated Retained Earnings		25,500
Total Retained Earnings		$60,000

3.5 DIVIDENDS

A *dividend* is a distribution to stockholders by a corporation's board of directors. Dividends are ordinarily made from retained earnings. (In the event of liquidation, distributions may be made from paid-in capital.)   Unless otherwise stated we will be concerned with distributions from retained earnings only.   The distribution may be in cash, other assets, promissory notes (script), or the corporation's own stock. In this section we confine ourselves to distributions of cash or of stock.

CASH DIVIDENDS

The cash dividend is the most common type of dividend; it is normally stated in terms of dollars and cents per share.   (Sometimes, if the dividend is on preferred stock, it is stated as a percentage of par.)   A cash dividend can be declared only if (*a*) there is sufficient cash; (*b*) there is sufficient unappropriated retained earnings; and (*c*) there has been a positive vote by the board of directors.   When a dividend is declared, it becomes a current liability of the corporation.

There are three different dates associated with the declaration of a dividend:

(1)   **Date of declaration.**   On this date the board of directors votes to declare the dividend.

(2)   **Date of record.**   Any person listed as a stockholder on this date is legally entitled to receive the dividend.

(3)   **Date of payment.**   On this date payment is made to stockholders of record [see (2)].

A journal entry is made on the date of declaration, reducing the stockholders' equity and recording the liability.   No entry is needed for the date of record.   A second entry, on the date of payment, records the payment.

EXAMPLE 5.

On December 15 the board of directors declares a dividend of $2 per share on 20,000 shares of outstanding common stock, to stockholders of record as of January 2.   Payment is to be made on January 10.

December 15	Retained Earnings	40,000	
	Cash Dividend Payable		40,000
January 2	Memo: $2 per share dividend on 20,000 shares		
January 10	Cash Dividend Payable	40,000	
	Cash		40,000

STOCK DIVIDENDS

A stock dividend is a pro rata distribution of stock to stockholders; it requires a transfer of retained earnings to paid-in capital.   From an accounting viewpoint, the number of shares to be distributed by the corporation must be less than 25% of the number of shares outstanding before the distribution.   Anything greater than 25% would be a *stock split*.

To maintain a consistent dividend policy the corporation may issue a stock dividend in place of cash when it is necessary or desirable to conserve cash.   Unlike a cash dividend, *a stock dividend provides no income to stockholders and affects neither corporate assets nor owners' equity in the corporation* (see Examples 6 and 7).   However, it does sustain the stockholders' confidence in the company.

EXAMPLE 6.

The balances in the stockholders' equity accounts of the Nuco Corporation, as of December 1, are:

Paid-In Capital	
Common Stock, $100 par (15,000 shares authorized, 10,000 shares issued)	$1,000,000
Premium on Common Stock	120,000
Total Paid-In Capital	$1,120,000
Retained Earnings	430,000
Stockholders' Equity	$1,550,000

On December 24 the board of directors declare a 10% stock dividend distributable to the shareholders of record as of January 2, for payment January 18. If the market value of the stock on December 24 is $120 per share, the following entries will be made to record the dividend declaration and payment:

December 24	Retained Earnings	120,000*	
	Common Stock Dividend Distributable		100,000
	Premium on Common Stock		20,000
	* 1,000 shares (10% × 10,000 shares) at $120 per share.		
January 2	Memo: 1,000 shares stock dividend at $120 per share		
January 18	Common Stock Dividend Distributable	100,000	
	Common Stock		100,000

In effect, the above transactions transfer $120,000 from Retained Earnings to Paid-In Capital and increase the number of shares outstanding by 1,000.

If a balance sheet is prepared between the date of declaration (December 24) and the date of payment (January 18), then the amount of the stock dividend distributable is shown in the Paid-In Capital section:

Paid-In Capital	
Common Stock, $100 par (15,000 shares authorized, 10,000 shares issued)	$1,000,000
Premium on Common Stock	140,000
Common Stock Dividend Distributable	100,000
Total Paid-In Capital	$1,240,000
Retained Earnings	310,000
Stockholders' Equity	$1,550,000

EXAMPLE 7.

Bill Schneider owned 100 shares in the Nuco Corporation. His holdings before and after the transactions of Example 6 are displayed below.

NUCO CORPORATION	Prior to Dividend	After Payment of Dividend
Common stock	$1,000,000	$1,100,000
Premium on common stock	120,000	140,000
Total	$1,120,000	$1,240,000
Retained earnings	430,000	310,000
Stockholders' equity	$1,550,000	$1,550,000
Number of shares outstanding	÷ 10,000	÷ 11,000
Book value per share	$155	$140.91
BILL SCHNEIDER		
Number of shares owned	100	110
Book value of shares	$15,500	$15,500
Percent of corporation owned	1%	1%

Before the stock dividend, Schneider owned 100/10,000, or 1%, of the corporation, with a book value of $15,500. After January 12, when the stock dividend was paid, he owned 110/11,000, or 1%, and his holdings were still valued at $15,500. The stock dividend transactions had no effect on either Schneider's books or the corporation's capital. Though a stock dividend might appear to be beneficial for both the corporation and the individual stockholder, neither benefits, as no shift in equity or assets occurs.

EFFECT ON RETAINED EARNINGS

The retained earnings account is affected whether a cash or stock dividend is declared.

EXAMPLE 8.

The accounts below show changes that affect retained earnings. The retained earnings statement for the end of the period appears directly below these accounts.

Retained Earnings

June 30	Semiannual Dividend	8,000	Jan. 1	Balance	100,000
Dec. 31	Semiannual Dividend	8,000	Dec. 31	Net Income	60,000
Dec. 31	Stock Dividend	12,000	Dec. 31	Appropriation for Contingencies	10,000
Dec. 31	Appropriation for Expansion	20,000			

Appropriation for Expansion		*Appropriation for Contingencies*	
	Jan. 1 Bal. 35,000	Dec. 31 10,000	Jan. 1 Bal. 25,000
	Dec. 31 20,000		

Statement of Retained Earnings

Appropriated:			
For Expansion			
Balance, January 1	$35,000		
Add: Appropriation in December	20,000	$ 55,000	
For Contingencies			
Balance, January 1	$25,000		
Deduct: Transfer to Retained Earnings	10,000	15,000	
Appropriated Retained Earnings			$ 70,000
Unappropriated:			
Balance, January 1		$100,000	
Add: Net Income	$60,000		
Transfer from Appropriation for Contingencies	10,000	70,000	
		$170,000	
Deduct: Cash Dividends Declared	$16,000		
Stock Dividends Declared	12,000		
Transfer to Appropriation for Expansion	20,000	48,000	
Unappropriated Retained Earnings			$122,000
Total Retained Earnings			$192,000

Summary

(1) When a person agrees to pay over a period of time for stock purchased, the sale is said to be on _____.

(2) Stock Subscriptions Receivable is a _____ on the balance sheet, while Capital Stock Subscribed is part of _____.

(3) Issued stock later reacquired by the corporation is known as _____.

(4) Treasury stock may be acquired by either _____ or _____.

(5) The nondistributed accumulated earnings of a corporation are known as _____ _____.

(6) If accumulated losses exceed accumulated profits, the result is a _____.

(7) Retained earnings put in reserve are called _____; otherwise, they are called _____.

(8) The date of _____ determines which stockholders receive a dividend.

(9) A distribution to stockholders of a corporation is known as a _____.

(10) Dividends are most commonly in the form of _____, but on occasion dividends may be declared in _____.

Answers: (1) subscription; (2) current asset, stockholders' equity; (3) treasury stock; (4) donation, purchase; (5) retained earnings; (6) deficit; (7) appropriated, unappropriated; (8) record; (9) dividend; (10) cash, stock

Solved Problems

3.1. Identify each account in the table below by inserting its balance (debit or credit) in the appropriate column.

Account	Asset	Liability	Equity	Income	Expense
Appropriation for Contingencies			Credit		
Cash Dividend Payable					
Common Stock					
Common Stock Subscriptions Receivable					
Common Stock Subscribed					
Discount on Preferred Stock					
Donated Capital					
Expense and Income Summary					
Organization Costs					
Paid-In Capital from Sale of Treasury Stock					
Premium on Common Stock					
Retained Earnings					
Stock Dividend Distributable					
Treasury Stock					

SOLUTION

Account	Asset	Liability	Equity	Income	Expense
Appropriation for Contingencies			Credit		
Cash Dividend Payable		Credit			
Common Stock			Credit		
Common Stock Subscriptions Receivable	Debit				
Common Stock Subscribed			Credit		
Discount on Preferred Stock			Debit		
Donated Capital			Credit		
Expense and Income Summary				Credit	
Organization Costs	Debit				
Paid-In Capital from Sale of Treasury Stock			Credit		
Premium on Common Stock			Credit		
Retained Earnings			Credit		
Stock Dividend Distributable			Credit		
Treasury Stock			Debit		

3.2. On September 1 the Stevens Corporation received subscriptions at $14 to 50,000 shares of $10-par common stock, collecting one-half of the subscription price immediately. Three months later the remainder was received and the stock issued. Present entries to record the transactions.

September 1		
December 1		

SOLUTION

September 1	Common Stock Subscriptions Receivable	700,000	
	Common Stock Subscribed		500,000
	Premium on Common Stock		200,000
	Cash	350,000	
	Common Stock Subscriptions Receivable		350,000
December 1	Cash	350,000	
	Common Stock Subscriptions Receivable		350,000
	Common Stock Subscribed	500,000	
	Common Stock		500,000

The final effect on the accounts is as if the stock had originally been purchased in full for cash:

Cash		Common Stock Subscribed	
Sept. 1 350,000		Dec. 1 500,000	Sept. 1 500,000
Dec. 1 350,000			

Common Stock Subscriptions Receivable		Common Stock
Sept. 1 700,000	Sept. 1 350,000	Dec. 1 500,000
	Dec. 1 350,000	

Premium on Common Stock

Sept. 1 200,000

3.3. Using the information in Problem 3.2, present the asset and equity sections of the balance sheet (a) as of September 2, (b) as of December 2.

(a)

ASSETS	STOCKHOLDERS' EQUITY

(b)

ASSETS	STOCKHOLDERS' EQUITY

SOLUTION

(a)

ASSETS		STOCKHOLDERS' EQUITY	
Cash	$350,000	Paid-In Capital	
Common Stock		Common Stock Subscribed	$500,000
Subscriptions Receivable	350,000	Premium on Common Stock	200,000
Total Assets	$700,000	Total Stockholders' Equity	$700,000

(b)

ASSETS		STOCKHOLDERS' EQUITY	
Cash	$700,000	Paid-In Capital	
		Common Stock	$500,000
		Premium on Common Stock	200,000
Total Assets	$700,000	Total Stockholders' Equity	$700,000

3.4. On its first day of operations the Caren Company completed several transactions that culminated in the following account balances:

Caren Company
Trial Balance
January 31, 1975

Cash	$ 60,000	
Common Stock Subscriptions Receivable	120,000	
Equipment	80,000	
Land	68,000	
Building	72,000	
Mortgage Payable		$140,000
Preferred Stock, 5%, $100 par		50,000
Premium on Preferred Stock		10,000
Common Stock, $40 par		80,000
Common Stock Subscribed		100,000
Premium on Common Stock		20,000
	$400,000	$400,000

Prepare all entries to record the above stock transactions, assuming that (1) land and building were secured by a mortgage; (2) common stock was issued at par in exchange for the equipment; (3) no cash was received on the common stock subscribed.

(a)

(b)

(c)

(d)

SOLUTION

(a)	Cash		60,000	
		Preferred Stock		50,000
		Premium on Preferred Stock		10,000
(b)	Common Stock Subscriptions Receivable		120,000	
		Common Stock Subscribed		100,000
		Premium on Common Stock		20,000
(c)	Equipment		80,000	
		Common Stock		80,000
(d)	Land		68,000	
	Building		72,000	
		Mortgage Payable		140,000

3.5. Prepare in general journal form the entries required for the transactions below:

> March 1: Englefield Corporation received 5,000 shares of donated common stock from its stockholders (15,000 shares had been issued at par value of $20)
>
> May 1: Sold 3,000 shares of treasury stock at $25 per share
>
> July 1: Sold the remaining shares of treasury stock at $15

(a) March 1

(b) May 1

(c) July 1

SOLUTION

(a)	March 1	Memo*: Receipt of 5,000 shares of donated common stock		
	*There is no entry needed, as no cost is involved when the company acquires treasury stock by donation.			
(b)	May 1	Cash	75,000	
		Donated Capital		75,000
(c)	July 1	Cash	30,000	
		Donated Capital		30,000

3.6. From the information in Problem 3.5 prepare the stockholders' equity section as of (a) March 31, (b) May 31, (c) July 31.

(a)

(b)

(c)

SOLUTION

(a) | Paid-In Capital | |
Common Stock, $20 par (15,000 shares authorized and issued,	
less 5,000 shares of donated treasury stock)	$300,000
Stockholders' Equity	$300,000

(b) | Paid-In Capital | |
Common Stock, $20 par (15,000 shares authorized and issued,	
less 2,000 shares of donated treasury stock)	$300,000
Donated Capital	75,000
Stockholders' Equity	$375,000

(c) | Paid-In Capital | |
Common Stock, $20 par (15,000 shares authorized and issued)	$300,000
Donated Capital	105,000
Stockholders' Equity	$405,000

3.7. Suppose that in Problems 3.5 and 3.6 the 5,000 shares of treasury stock had been purchased for $120,000 instead of being donated. (a) What entries would be required? (b) Prepare the stockholders' equity section as of March 31, May 31, and July 31.

(a)

March 1		

May 1		

July 1		

(b) **March 31**

May 31

_____

July 31

_____

SOLUTION

(a)

March 1	Treasury Stock		120,000	
	Cash			120,000
May 1	Cash		75,000	
	Treasury Stock			72,000*
	Paid-In Capital from Sale of			
	Treasury Stock			3,000
* (3,000/5,000) × $120,000				
July 1	Cash		30,000	
	Paid-In Capital from Sale of Treasury Stock		18,000	
	Treasury Stock			48,000*
* (2,000/5,000) × $120,000				

(b)

March 31

Paid-In Capital

Common Stock, $20 par (15,000 shares authorized and issued)	$300,000
Less: Treasury Stock	120,000
Stockholders' Equity	$180,000

May 31

Paid-In Capital

Common Stock, $20 par (15,000 shares authorized and issued)	$300,000
Paid-In Capital from Sale of Treasury Stock	3,000
Total Paid-In Capital	$303,000
Less: Treasury Stock	48,000
Stockholders' Equity	$255,000

July 31

Paid-In Capital

Common Stock, $20 par (15,000 shares authorized and issued)	$300,000
Less: Paid-In Capital from Sale of Treasury Stock	15,000
Stockholders' Equity	$285,000

3.8. The board of directors of the Kotin Corporation presented to the stockholders for their approval a plan to expand facilities at a cost of $1,000,000. This sum was to come from:

(a) Issuing 5,000 shares of preferred stock, $50 par, at par.

(b) Borrowing $450,000 from the bank.

(c) A donation of 10% of all common stock outstanding (100,000 shares authorized and issued, par value $20). It is assumed that this treasury stock will be sold for $30 per share.

Prepare entries for the transactions.

(a)

(b)

(c)

SOLUTION

(a)	Cash	250,000	
	Preferred Stock		250,000
(b)	Cash	450,000	
	Notes Payable		450,000
(c)	Memo: Received 10,000 shares common stock as a donation		
	Cash	300,000	
	Donated Capital		300,000

3.9. Below is the stockholders' equity section of the balance sheet as of April 30.

Paid-In Capital		
Preferred Stock, 5%, $100 par (20,000 shares authorized, 15,000 shares issued)	$1,500,000	
Premium on Preferred Stock	40,000	$1,540,000
Common Stock, $50 par (100,000 shares authorized, 60,000 shares issued)	3,000,000	
Premium on Common Stock	100,000	3,100,000
Total Paid-In Capital		$4,640,000
Retained Earnings		500,000
Stockholders' Equity		$5,140,000

During the next eight months, selected transactions are:

May 10: Received subscriptions to 5,000 shares of preferred stock at $102, collecting half of the subscription price

July 15: Purchased 10,000 shares of treasury common for $400,000

Sept. 10: Received 25% of the subscription price on the preferred stock

Oct. 25: Sold 6,000 shares of treasury common for $300,000

Dec. 10: Received the balance due on preferred stock subscribed and issued the shares

Dec. 20: Sold 3,000 shares of treasury common for $100,000

Prepare all entries necessary to record the above information.

May 10		
July 15		
Sept. 10		
Oct. 25		
Dec. 10		
Dec. 20		

SOLUTION

May 10	*Preferred Stock Subscriptions Receivable*	510,000	
	Preferred Stock Subscribed		500,000
	Premium on Preferred Stock		10,000
	Cash	255,000	
	Preferred Stock Subscriptions Receivable		255,000
July 15	*Treasury Stock*	400,000	
	Cash		400,000
Sept. 10	*Cash*	127,500	
	Preferred Stock Subscriptions Receivable		127,500
Oct. 25	*Cash*	300,000	
	Treasury Stock $[(6,000/10,000) \times \$400,000]$		240,000
	Paid-In Capital from Sale of Treasury Stock		60,000
Dec. 10	*Cash*	127,500	
	Preferred Stock Subscriptions Receivable		127,500
	Preferred Stock Subscribed	500,000	
	Preferred Stock		500,000
Dec. 20	*Cash*	100,000	
	Paid-In Capital from Sale of Treasury Stock	20,000	
	Treasury Stock		120,000

3.10. Based on the information in Problem 3.9 prepare the stockholders' equity section of the balance sheet as of (*a*) July 31, (*b*) December 31.

(*a*)

(*b*)

SOLUTION

(*a*)

Paid-In Capital		
Preferred Stock, 5%, $100 par (20,000 shares		
authorized, 15,000 shares issued)	$1,500,000	
Premium on Preferred Stock	50,000	$1,550,000
Preferred Stock Subscribed		500,000
Common Stock, $50 par (100,000 shares		
authorized, 60,000 shares issued)	3,000,000	
Premium on Common Stock	100,000	3,100,000
Total Paid-In Capital		$5,150,000
Retained Earnings		500,000
Total		$5,650,000
Less: Treasury Stock (10,000 shares at cost)		400,000
Total Stockholders' Equity		$5,250,000

(b)   *Paid-In Capital*

Preferred Stock, 5%, $100 par (20,000 shares		
authorized and issued)	$2,000,000	
Premium on Preferred Stock	50,000	$2,050,000
Common Stock, $50 par (100,000 shares		
authorized, 60,000 shares issued)	3,000,000	
Premium on Common Stock	100,000	3,100,000
Paid-In Capital from Sale of Treasury Stock		40,000*
Total Paid-In Capital		$5,190,000
Retained Earnings		500,000
Total		$5,690,000
Less: Treasury Stock (1,000 shares at cost)		40,000
Total Stockholders' Equity		$5,650,000

*   *Paid-In Capital from Sale of Treasury Stock*

Dec. 20 20,000	*Oct. 25 60,000*

3.11. What effect (increase, decrease, no effect) do the following transactions have on assets, liabilities, and stockholders' equity?

	Assets	Liabilities	Stockholders' Equity
Receipt of subscription to stock at par			
Receipt of cash for stock subscription			
Issue of stock fully subscribed			
Receipt of donated stock			
Sale of donated stock			
Purchase of treasury stock			
Sale of treasury stock above par			
Declaration of cash dividend			
Payment of cash dividend			
Declaration of stock dividend			
Payment of stock dividend			
Setting date of record of cash dividend			
Increasing appropriation for expansion			
Decreasing appropriation for contingencies			

SOLUTION

	Assets	Liabilities	Stockholders' Equity
Receipt of subscription to stock at par	Increase	No effect	Increase
Receipt of cash for stock subscription	No effect	No effect	No effect
Issue of stock fully subscribed	No effect	No effect	No effect
Receipt of donated stock	No effect	No effect	No effect
Sale of donated stock	Increase	No effect	Increase
Purchase of treasury stock	Decrease	No effect	Decrease
Sale of treasury stock above par	Increase	No effect	Increase
Declaration of cash dividend	No effect	Increase	Decrease
Payment of cash dividend	Decrease	Decrease	No effect
Declaration of stock dividend	No effect	No effect	No effect
Payment of stock dividend	No effect	No effect	No effect
Setting date of record of cash dividend	No effect	No effect	No effect
Increasing appropriation for expansion	No effect	No effect	No effect
Decreasing appropriation for contingencies	No effect	No effect	No effect

3.12. The retained earnings accounts of Brandon Company appear below.

Appropriation for Contingencies	*Appropriation for Plant Expansion*	*Retained Earnings*
60,000	110,000	240,000

During the month of December the board of directors decided to:

(*a*) increase the appropriation for contingencies *by* $20,000

(*b*) decrease the appropriation for plant expansion *to* $60,000

(*c*) establish an appropriation for bonded indebtedness, with an annual deposit of $10,000

(*d*) declare cash dividends of $70,000

Present entries to record the decisions of the board.

(*a*)

(*b*)

(*c*)

(*d*)

SOLUTION

(*a*)	*Retained Earnings*	20,000	
	Appropriation for Contingencies		20,000
(*b*)	*Appropriation for Plant Expansion*	50,000	
	Retained Earnings		50,000
(*c*)	*Retained Earnings*	10,000	
	Appropriation for Bonded Indebtedness		10,000
(*d*)	*Retained Earnings*	70,000	
	Cash Dividend Payable		70,000

3.13. Prepare a retained earnings statement for Brandon Company (Problem 3.12).

Brandon Company
Statement of Retained Earnings
December 31, 197—

Appropriated Retained Earnings

(continued next page)

Unappropriated Retained Earnings

Total Retained Earnings

SOLUTION

Brandon Company
Statement of Retained Earnings
December 31, 197—

Appropriated Retained Earnings			
Appropriation for Contingencies, Balance	$ 60,000		
Add: Appropriation Increase	20,000	$ 80,000	
Appropriation for Plant Expansion, Balance	110,000		
Less: Appropriation Decrease	50,000	60,000	
Appropriation for Bonded Indebtedness		10,000	
Total Appropriated Retained Earnings			$150,000
Unappropriated Retained Earnings			
Balance	240,000		
Add: Transfer from Appropriation			
for Plant Expansion	50,000	290,000	
Less: Transfer to Appropriation			
for Contingencies	20,000		
Transfer to Appropriation			
for Bonded Indebtedness	10,000		
Cash Dividends Declared	70,000	100,000	
Total Unappropriated Retained Earnings			190,000
Total Retained Earnings			$340,000

3.14. A $45,000 cash dividend was declared by the Bowes Corporation. The dates involved in the cash dividend transactions are November 5, December 14, and January 6. (a) What is the significance of each date and what entry is made on it? (b) What legal obligation does the declaration of the dividend carry?

(a)   **November 5.**

December 14.

January 6.

(b)

SOLUTION

(a)

November 5. Date of declaration		
Retained Earnings	45,000	
Cash Dividend Payable		45,000
December 14. Date of record		
Memo: Stockholders owning shares on this		
date will receive the cash dividend		
January 6. Date of payment		
Cash Dividend Payable	45,000	
Cash		45,000

(b)   The board of directors of a corporation do not legally have to declare a dividend, even though sufficient cash and unappropriated retained earnings exist. However, if they do decide to declare a cash dividend, it will become a current liability of the corporation and must be paid.

3.15.   The stockholders' equity section of the Willard Corporation's balance sheet shows:

> *Paid-In Capital*
> *Common Stock, $100 par (10,000 shares*
> *authorized, 8,000 shares issued)* $800,000
> *Premium on Common Stock*   40,000 $ 840,000
> *Retained Earnings*   200,000
> *Total Stockholders' Equity* $1,040,000

The board of directors declares an annual cash dividend of $7 per share, and, in addition, a 10% stock dividend. At the time of declaration, the fair market value of the common stock to be issued is $120. Present (a) the entry to record the declaration of the cash dividend, (b) the entry to record the declaration of the stock dividend, (c) the stockholders' equity section after the completion of the above transactions and the payment of the stock dividend.

(a)

(b)

(c)

SOLUTION

(a)

Retained Earnings	56,000	
Cash Dividend Payable		56,000

(b)

Retained Earnings	96,000	
Stock Dividend Distributable		80,000
Premium on Common Stock		16,000

(c)	Paid-In Capital		
	Common Stock, $100 par (10,000 shares authorized, 8,800 shares issued)	$880,000	
	Premium on Common Stock	56,000	$936,000
	Retained Earnings		48,000
	Total Stockholders' Equity		$984,000

3.16. Redo (a) and (b) of Problem 3.15 if 1,000 shares of common stock had been reacquired by purchase.

(a)

(b)

SOLUTION

(a)	Retained Earnings	49,000	
	Cash Dividend Payable		49,000*
(b)	Retained Earnings	84,000	
	Stock Dividend Distributable		70,000*
	Premium on Common Stock		14,000

* Dividends are neither declared nor paid on treasury stock, whether donated or purchased.

3.17. The accounts below bear on the retained earnings of Ivy Industries during the year.

Appropriation for Plant Expansion		Appropriation for Contingencies	
	Jan. 1 Bal. 40,000	Dec. 31 5,000	Jan. 1 Bal. 70,000
	Dec. 31 10,000		

Retained Earnings

March 31	Quarterly Dividend	5,000	Jan. 1	Bal.	205,000
June 30	Quarterly Dividend	5,000	Dec. 31	Appr. for Contingencies	5,000
Sept. 30	Quarterly Dividend	5,000	Dec. 31	Net Income	65,000
Dec. 31	Quarterly Dividend	5,000			
Dec. 31	Appr. for Plant Expansion	10,000			

Prepare a retained earnings statement as of December 31.

Ivy Industries
Statement of Retained Earnings
December 31, 197—

Appropriated Retained Earnings

(continued next page)

Unappropriated Retained Earnings

SOLUTION

Ivy Industries
Statement of Retained Earnings
December 31, 197—

Appropriated Retained Earnings			
Appropriation for Plant Expansion, Jan. 1 Balance	$40,000		
Add: Appropriation, Dec. 31	10,000	50,000	
Appropriation for Contingencies, Jan. 1 Balance	70,000		
Less: Transfer to Retained Earnings	5,000	65,000	
Total Appropriated Retained Earnings			$115,000
Unappropriated Retained Earnings			
Balance, Jan. 1		205,000	
Add: Transfer from Appropriation for			
Contingencies	5,000		
Net Income	65,000	70,000	
		275,000	
Less: Cash Dividend Declared	20,000		
Transfer to Appropriation for			
Plant Expansion	10,000	30,000	
Total Unappropriated Retained Earnings			245,000
Total Retained Earnings			$360,000

Chapter 4

The Corporation: Bonds

4.1 BOND CHARACTERISTICS

A corporation may obtain funds by selling stock or by borrowing through long-term obligations. An issue of bonds is a form of long-term debt in which the corporation agrees to pay interest periodically and to repay the principal at a stated future date.

Bond denominations are commonly multiples of $1,000. A bond issue normally has a term of ten or twenty years, although some issues may have longer lives. The date at which a bond is to be repaid is known as the *maturity date*. In an issue of *serial bonds* the maturity dates are spread in a series over the term of the issue. This relieves the corporation from the impact of total payment at one date.

4.2 SECURITY

MORTGAGES

One method for protecting the investor in bonds is to back the bonds by mortgages on the corporation's property. These are *chattel mortgages*, if placed on movable items such as equipment and machinery, or else *real estate mortgages*.

TRUST INDENTURES

A trustee, usually a trust company or large bank, is chosen by the corporation to safeguard the investors' interest. In an agreement (*indenture*) between the trustee and the corporation, the trustee certifies that the bonds are existent and are genuine. He also promises to hold collateral to be used for the issue, and to collect money from the corporation to pay interest and eventually the principal.

Collateral trust bonds are bonds backed by investments held by the issuing corporation. These investments (securities of other corporations) can be sold by the trustee if the corporation defaults on the payment of either interest or principal.

Sinking fund bonds. The issuing corporation deposits annual amounts with the trustee. Together with earnings on sinking fund investments, these deposits add up to the amount due at maturity.

EXAMPLE 1.

A one-million-dollar issue of ten-year sinking fund bonds does not require the issuing corporation to set aside $100,000 a year for ten years. The deposit per year can be much smaller because of substantial interest earned through compounding. (More on sinking fund bonds is found in Sec. 4.9.)

UNSECURED BONDS

If a firm does not need security to back its bonds, the bonds are known as *debentures*; they are based on the general credit of the company. United States Government bonds are an example.

4.3 PAYMENT OF INTEREST. OPTIONS

Bonds are divided into two categories according to the way interest is paid.

(1) *Registered bonds.*   A registered bond states the name of the owner on the face of the bond.   The corporation maintains a register or list of the bond owners and forwards payments to them as interest becomes due.

(2) *Coupon bonds.*   This type of bond has no evidence of ownership.   Interest is paid to the party who presents a dated coupon attached to the bond.

Certain bonds carry options for conversion or recall.

Convertible bonds.   These are bonds that may be exchanged at a future date for other securities of the issuing corporation, at the option of the *bondholder*. (See Sec. 4.8.)

Callable bonds.   These are bonds that may be recalled before they mature, at the option of the *issuing corporation*.   (See Sec. 4.8.)

4.4   FUNDING BY STOCK VERSUS FUNDING BY BONDS

The major differences between stocks and bonds may be summarized as follows:

	Stocks	Bonds
Representation	Ownership in the corporation	A debt of the corporation
Inducement to holders	Dividends	Interest
Accounting treatment	Dividends are a distribution of profits	Interest is an expense
	Stocks are equity	Bonds are a long-term liability
Repayment	....	On a predetermined date

These differences give rise to alternative methods of financing, as in Examples 2 and 3 below.

EXAMPLE 2.

The board of directors of a new company has decided that $1,000,000 is needed to begin operations. The controller presents three different methods of financing:

	Method 1 (Common Stock)	Method 2 (Preferred and Common Stock)	Method 3 (Bonds, Preferred and Common Stock)
Bonds, 5%	....	....	$ 500,000
Preferred stock, 6%	....	$ 500,000	250,000
Common stock, $100 par	$1,000,000	500,000	250,000
Total	$1,000,000	$1,000,000	$1,000,000

Subsequent profits before interest on bonds and before taxes are estimated at $300,000; taxes are estimated at 50%.

	Method 1	Method 2	Method 3
Profit	$300,000	$300,000	$300,000
Less: Interest on bonds	....	....	25,000
Net income before taxes	$300,000	$300,000	$275,000
Less: Income taxes	150,000	150,000	137,500
Net income	$150,000	$150,000	$137,500
Less: Dividends on preferred stock	....	30,000	15,000
Common stock balance	$150,000	$120,000	$122,500
Number of common shares	÷ 10,000*	÷ 5,000**	÷ 2,500***
Earnings per common share	$15	$24	$49

* $1,000,000/$100   ** $500,000/$100   *** $250,000/$100

For the common stockholders, Method 3 (called *debt and equity funding*) is clearly the best. It gives greater earnings because (1) bond interest is deducted for income tax purposes; (2) bonds are marketed at an interest rate which is lower than the dividend rate on preferred stock.

EXAMPLE 3.

As the amount of profit becomes smaller, Method 1 of Example 2 becomes the best financing method. Assume that the same three methods of funding are under consideration for an anticipated net income of $60,000 before interest and taxes.

	Method 1	Method 2	Method 3
Profit	$60,000	$60,000	$60,000
Less: Interest on bonds	....	....	25,000
Net income before taxes	$60,000	$60,000	$35,000
Less: Income taxes	30,000	30,000	17,500
Net income	$30,000	$30,000	$17,500
Less: Dividends on preferred stock	....	30,000	15,000
Common stock balance	$30,000	....	$ 2,500
Earnings per common share	$3	0	$1

4.5 RECORDING AUTHORIZED BOND TRANSACTIONS

A corporation's charter may require that a bond issue receive the prior approval of the stockholders. When the necessary approvals are received and the bonds issued, a memorandum entry will be made to record the authorization.

EXAMPLE 4.

On December 15, 1974, the Phillips Corporation authorizes the issue of $100,000 in 5%, 10-year bonds, with interest payable semiannually on June 30 and December 31. A memorandum entry should be made.

Memo: $100,000 in 5%, 10-year bonds authorized

On January 1, 1975, $75,000 of the $100,000 authorized bond issue is sold to the public. (The reason for authorizing more than the amount issued is that if additional funds are needed later, no other type of financing will be required.)

Cash	75,000	
Bonds Payable		75,000

The balance sheet presentation of the above information would be:

Long-Term Liabilities
5%, 10-Year Bonds Payable Authorized	$100,000	
Less: Unissued	25,000	
Issued		$75,000

If, at a later date, the corporation decides to sell the remaining authorized bonds, the entry to record this additional sale would be:

Cash	25,000	
Bonds Payable		25,000

and the balance sheet liability section would then show a long-term liability of $100,000 for 5%, 10-year bonds payable, authorized and issued.

4.6 PREMIUM AND DISCOUNT ON BONDS

Just as the par value of stock does not measure its market value, the face value of a bond does not represent its market value. The rate of interest which bonds pay helps determine how much investors are willing to pay for the bonds.

EXAMPLE 5.

A corporation may issue bonds carrying an interest rate of $4\frac{1}{2}\%$, while similar bonds on the market pay 5%. Thus investors may not be willing to pay *face* value for the bonds. Conversely, if bonds on the market are paying only 4%, investors may be willing to pay more than the face value of the bonds.

The interest rate paid by the corporation on its bonds depends upon (1) the security that the corporation offers, (2) its credit standing, and (3) the current level of bond interest rates. When the corporation issues bonds, it states the rate of interest it will pay (*contract rate*). In the period of time between the authorization and the sale of the bond issue, market interest rates may have deviated from the contract rate. Because of this, bonds may be sold at a price above or below their face value.

The difference between the proceeds from the sale of the bonds and their face value is recorded as Premium on Bonds Payable (if issue price exceeds face value) or Discount on Bonds Payable (if issue price is less than face value).

Premium or discount is reflected in the price of bonds, which is stated as a percentage of face value.

EXAMPLE 6.

A $1,000 bond issued "at 105" costs $1,050 ($1,000 × 105%); issued "at 98," the same bond costs $980 ($1,000 × 98%).

EXAMPLE 7.   Issue at a Premium.

When a corporation offers an issue with the contract rate higher than the market rate, buyers will normally pay a premium for the bonds. Suppose that on January 1 the Phillips Corporation sells a $100,000 issue of 10-year, 5% bonds at 104 ($104,000), with interest payable semiannually on June 30 and December 31. The entry to record the sale would be:

January 1	Cash	104,000	
	Bonds Payable		100,000
	Premium on Bonds Payable		4,000

The entries to record the semiannual interest payments would be:

June 30	Interest Expense	2,500	
	Cash		2,500
December 31	Interest Expense	2,500	
	Cash		2,500

Although the interest expense account has a balance of $5,000, this is not the true amount of interest expense for the year. The $4,000 premium received by the corporation should not be treated as income but rather as interest collected in advance, in adjustment of the contract rate. Thus, the interest expense each year should be reduced by $4,000/10 = $400. The adjusting entry needed to record this spreading out (amortization) of the premium over the life of the bond would be:

December 31	Premium on Bonds Payable	400	
	Interest Expense		400
	To amortize 1/10 of the premium		

and the balance of the interest expense account as of December 31 will be:

Interest Expense

June 30 Interest 2,500	Dec. 31 Premium 400
Dec. 31 Interest 2,500	

Immediately after the sale of the bonds the balance sheet of the Phillips Corporation shows unamortized premium of $4,000:

> *Long-Term Liabilities*
>   *Bonds Payable, 5%, 10-year* $100,000
>   *Add: Unamortized Premium*   4,000 $104,000

EXAMPLE 8.   Issue at a Discount.

If a corporation offers a rate of interest below the market rate, buyers will normally pay less than face value for the bonds. Assume that the Schneider Corporation offers a $1,000,000 issue of 6%, 10-year bonds, with interest paid annually on December 31. Since the prevailing rate is more than 6%, the highest bid for the bonds, $970,000, was less than face value. If the corporation accepts the bid, the entry would be:

> *Cash*   970,000
> *Discount on Bonds Payable*   30,000
>   *Bonds Payable*   1,000,000

The $30,000 discount is treated as extra interest expense, so that it is amortized over the 10-year life of the bonds (compare Example 7). Hence the entry to record the interest payment each year would be:

> *December 31*   *Interest Expense*   60,000
>   *Cash*   60,000
>   *To record interest charges (6% × $1,000,000)*

and the adjusting entry would be:

> *December 31*   *Interest Expense*   3,000
>   *Discount on Bonds Payable*   3,000
>   *To amortize 1/10 of the discount*

The annual charges to Interest Expense will then appear as:

> *Interest Expense*
>
> *Dec. 31 Interest*   60,000
> *Dec. 31 Discount*   3,000

Immediately after the sale of the bonds the corporation's balance sheet shows unamortized discount of $30,000:

> *Long-Term Liabilities*
>   *Bonds Payable, 6%, 10-year* $1,000,000
>   *Deduct: Unamortized Discount*   30,000 $970,000

4.7   ACCRUED INTEREST

At times bonds are sold between interest payment dates. This means that a purchaser of the bonds will be charged for the interest that has accrued since the last interest payment. He will, however, recover the accrued interest at the next payment date, when he will receive interest for the *full* period. This procedure frees the corporation from keeping a record of each bond sold and its accrued interest.

EXAMPLE 9.

Assume that on January 1 a corporation authorizes $1,000,000 of 6% bonds on which interest is payable on January 1 and July 1. The bonds are not sold to the public until February 1.

February 1	*Cash*		1,005,000	
		Bond Interest Expense		5,000*
		Bonds Payable		1,000,000

$$* \ \$1,000,000 \times 6\% \ = \ \$60,000$$
$$\$60,000 \div 12 \ months \ = \ \$5,000 \ per \ month$$

On July 1, five months later, the semiannual interest payment will be made for the *full* six months. This will include both the five months' interest earned by the bondholders and the one month's interest that was collected in advance.   The entry to record the payment would be:

July 1	*Bond Interest Expense*	30,000	
	Cash		30,000

The $25,000 balance in the interest expense account is shown below:

Interest Expense	
July 1 30,000	Feb. 1 5,000

We have, till now, assumed that interest was paid in January and July of the same year.   However, as the interest period may not coincide with the accounting period, an adjusting entry for accrued interest may be required at the end of each accounting period.

EXAMPLE 10.

On March 1, 1974, the M. Bradley Corporation issues $100,000 of 6%, 10-year bonds, with interest payable semiannually on March 1 and September 1.

March 1	*Cash*	100,000	
	Bonds Payable		100,000
	To record the sale of bonds		
September 1	*Interest Expense*	3,000	
	Cash		3,000
	To record semiannual interest		
December 31	*Interest Expense*	2,000	
	Interest Payable		2,000*
	To record adjustment of interest payable		

$$* \ September \ 1 \ to \ December \ 31 \ = \ 4 \ months$$
$$4/6 \times \$3,000 \ = \ \$2,000$$

When the interest is paid on March 1 of the following year, the entry to record the payment would be:

March 1, 1975	*Interest Expense*	1,000	
	Interest Payable	2,000	
	Cash		3,000

The above entry is made if no reversing entry occurred.   If the reversing entry method is used, the following entries would be required instead:

January 1, 1975	*Interest Payable*	2,000	
	Interest Expense		2,000
	Reversing entry required for interest payable		
March 1, 1975	*Interest Expense*	3,000	
	Cash		3,000
	To record interest payment		

4.8 REDEMPTION OF BONDS

CALLABLE BONDS

Many bonds are issued with the notice that they may be redeemed at the option of the corporation within a specific period of time and at a price specified, usually above face value. This is done because corporations may, at times, find themselves in a market where interest rates are declining. To profit from this situation, the corporation may sell new bonds carrying the lower interest rate and use the funds to redeem the original, higher-paying issue.

EXAMPLE 11.

The Wakefield Corporation exercises its option by calling in all of its bonds for $103,000. The ledger balances prior to the redemption were:

Bonds Payable		*Premium on Bonds Payable*	
	100,000	1,800	6,000

The entry to record the recall of the bonds would be:

Bonds Payable	100,000	
Premium on Bonds Payable	4,200	
Cash		103,000
Gain on Redemption of Bonds		1,200

EXAMPLE 12.

The Wakefield Corporation (see Example 11) decides to call in only 25% of its outstanding bonds. The entry to record the redemption would be:

Bonds Payable	25,000	
Premium on Bonds Payable	1,050	
Cash		25,750
Gain on Redemption of Bonds		300

CONVERTIBLE BONDS

An option offered to the bondholder is the right to exchange his bonds for a specific number of common stock shares. Convertible bonds offer the purchaser security in the initial stage of ownership, with the option of taking more risks if the company prospers. In other words, if the market price of common stock increases, the bondholder can convert to common stock and share in the increase.

EXAMPLE 13.

The R. Tobey Corporation has $100,000 in convertible bonds outstanding, with $6,000 of related unamortized premiums. The bonds are convertible at the rate of 30 shares of $25-par common stock for each $1,000 bond. Assuming that all bonds have been presented for conversion, the entry is:

Bonds Payable	100,000	
Premium on Bonds	6,000	
Common Stock		75,000*
Premium on Common Stock		31,000**

$$* \ 100 \ bonds \ \times \ 30 \ \frac{shares}{bond} \ \times \ \$25 \ per \ share$$

$$** \ \$100,000 + \$6,000 - \$75,000$$

4.9 BOND SINKING FUNDS. RESTRICTION OF DIVIDENDS

A *sinking fund* is created under the supervision of a trustee for the purpose of accumulating funds for the payment of bonds at maturity. The trustee invests the cash in the sinking fund in securities whose income, together with periodic payments into the fund by the corporation, is expected to produce an amount sufficient to retire the bonds when they mature. The new accounts to be established when a bond sinking fund is created include *Sinking Fund Cash* (cash of the corporation transferred to the sinking fund), *Sinking Fund Investments* (investments purchased with sinking fund cash), and *Sinking Fund Income* (income from the sinking fund investments).

EXAMPLE 14.

A corporation issues $100,000 of 6%, 10-year bonds and agrees to deposit with a sinking fund trustee equal amounts for the ten years so that the accumulated amount will be sufficient to retire the bonds at maturity. The following sinking fund transactions are representative:

Annual deposit into the sinking fund

Sinking Fund Cash	8,200	
Cash		8,200

[A yearly deposit of $10,000 ($100,000 ÷ 10 years) is not needed, as substantial interest will be earned.]

Purchase of securities

Sinking Fund Investments	8,200	
Sinking Fund Cash		8,200

Income from investments

Sinking Fund Cash	500	
Sinking Fund Income		500

Sale of securities

Sinking Fund Cash	91,000	
Sinking Fund Investments		89,000
Gain on Sale of Investments		2,000

Payment at maturity

Bonds Payable	100,000	
Sinking Fund Cash		100,000

With this last entry, the sinking fund is closed. If the final balance of Sinking Fund Cash had been more than $100,000, the excess would be returned to the cash account; if the amount had been less than $100,000, additional cash would be needed to retire the bonds.

To prevent a corporation from using all its assets either to pay out sinking fund deposits or for the payment of earnings, a trustee may restrict the dividends of the corporation while the bonds are outstanding. One way of doing this would be to require that the corporation appropriate retained earnings each year equal to the sinking fund requirements.

EXAMPLE 15.

For the bond issue of Example 14, the entry to record the annual appropriation would be:

Retained Earnings	10,000	
Appropriation for Bonded Indebtedness		10,000

At maturity the appropriation would be returned to the unappropriated retained earnings account:

| Appropriation for Bonded Indebtedness | 100,000 | |
| Retained Earnings | | 100,000 |

4.10 REVIEW OF EQUITY AND DEBT FINANCING

In the last three chapters we have examined accounting areas of the corporation involving equity (stock) and debt (bond) financing.   The balance sheet below illustrates the reporting of the types of financial information which have been discussed.

Cashier Corporation
Balance Sheet
December 197–

ASSETS

Current Assets		
Cash	$ 25,000	
Securities (market value, $52,000) at Cost	46,000	
Accounts Receivable	$112,000	
Less: Allowance for Doubtful Accounts	3,300	108,700
Merchandise Inventory (First-In-First-Out)		104,200
Common Stock Subscriptions Receivable		25,000
Prepaid Expenses		6,000
Total Current Assets		$314,900
Long-Term Investments		
Bond Sinking Fund	$ 35,000	
XYZ Common Stock	15,000	
Total Long-Term Investments		50,000
Fixed Assets		
Building	$200,000	
Less: Accumulated Depreciation	120,000	80,000
Equipment	100,000	
Less: Accumulated Depreciation	30,000	70,000
Land	100,000	
Total Fixed Assets		250,000
Intangible Assets		
Goodwill	20,000	
Organization Costs	40,000	
Total Intangible Assets		60,000
Total Assets		$674,900

LIABILITIES

Current Liabilities		
Accounts Payable	$ 60,000	
Notes Payable	40,000	
Income Tax Payable	21,000	
Total Current Liabilities		$121,000
Long-Term Liabilities		
Sinking Fund, 6%, 10-Year Bonds	$100,000	
Add: Unamortized Premium	8,000	108,000
Total Liabilities		$229,000

(continued next page)

STOCKHOLDERS' EQUITY

Paid-In Capital			
Common Stock, $50 par (10,000 shares authorized, 6,000 shares issued)	$300,000		
Premium on Common Stock	10,000		
Common Stock Subscribed	50,000		
Total Paid-In Capital		$360,000	
Retained Earnings			
Appropriated Retained Earnings			
For Bonded Indebtedness	$25,000		
For Contingencies	15,000	$ 40,000	
Unappropriated Retained Earnings		45,900	
Total Retained Earnings		85,900	
Total Stockholders' Equity			$445,900
Total Liabilities and Stockholders' Equity			$674,900

Summary

(1) Most bonds are issued in units of $_____.

(2) The market price of a bond is commonly given as a _____ of the face value.

(3) A bond that is repaid by means of annual deposits is known as a _____ bond.

(4) Bonds that may be exchanged at a future date at the option of the bondholder are termed _____ bonds, while bonds that may be recalled at the option of the corporation are termed _____ bonds.

(5) Bond premium (or discount) appears in the balance sheet as an addition to (or deduction from) _____.

(6) Bonds sold between interest payment dates are said to be sold plus _____.

(7) A mortgage placed on movable items is known as a _____.

(8) An account used to restrict dividends while bonds are outstanding is _____ _____.

(9) A bond based on the general credit of the company is known as a _____.

(10) Capital stock is known as _____ capital, while bonds are termed _____ capital.

Answers: (1) 1,000; (2) percentage; (3) sinking fund; (4) convertible, callable; (5) Bonds Payable; (6) accrued interest; (7) chattel mortgage; (8) Appropriation for Bonded Indebtedness; (9) debenture; (10) equity, debt

Solved Problems

4.1. Match the items in Column A with the appropriate phrases from Column B.

Column A	Column B
1. Trust indentures	a) Bonds backed by investments held by the issuing corporation
2. Serial bonds	
3. Sinking fund bonds	b) Corporation deposits annual amounts to make up the amount due at maturity
4. Chattel mortgages	
5. Collateral trust bonds	c) A trustee is chosen by the corporation to safeguard investors' interest
6. Registered bonds	d) Mortgages placed on movable items
7. Callable bonds	e) Bonds mature in different years
8. Convertible bonds	f) Bondholder has option to exchange bonds for other securities
	g) Corporation has option to call in bonds
	h) Owner's name is stated on the face of the bond

SOLUTION

1. c   2. e   3. b   4. d   5. a   6. h   7. g   8. f

4.2. Three companies have the following structures:

	G Company	H Company	I Company
Bonds Payable, 5%	$1,000,000	$ 600,000	. . . .
Preferred Stock, 6%, $100 par	. . . .	600,000	$1,000,000
Common Stock, $100 par	1,000,000	800,000	1,000,000
Total	$2,000,000	$2,000,000	$2,000,000

Assuming a tax rate of 50% of income, determine the earnings per share of common stock if the net income of each company before bond interest and taxes was (a) $140,000; (b) $500,000.

(a)

	G Company	H Company	I Company

(b)

	G Company	H Company	I Company

SOLUTION

(a)

	G Company	H Company	I Company
Income	$140,000	$140,000	$140,000
Less: Bond interest	50,000	30,000	....
Income before taxes	90,000	110,000	140,000
Less: Tax (50%)	45,000	55,000	70,000
Net income	$ 45,000	$ 55,000	$ 70,000
Less: Preferred dividend	....	36,000	60,000
To common stock	$ 45,000	$ 19,000	$ 10,000
Number of common shares	÷ 10,000	÷ 8,000	÷ 10,000
Earnings per share	$4.50	$2.38	$1.00

(b)

	G Company	H Company	I Company
Income	$500,000	$500,000	$500,000
Less: Bond interest	50,000	30,000	....
Income before taxes	450,000	470,000	500,000
Less: Tax (50%)	225,000	235,000	250,000
Net income	$225,000	$235,000	$250,000
Less: Preferred dividend	....	36,000	60,000
To common stock	$225,000	$199,000	$190,000
Number of common shares	÷ 10,000	÷ 8,000	÷ 10,000
Earnings per share	$22.50	$24.88	$19.00

4.3. Shapot Industries has 12,000 shares of common stock outstanding. The board decides to expand existing facilities at a projected cost of $3,000,000. *Method I*: Issue of $3,000,000 in common stock, $50 par. *Method II*: Issue of $1,500,000 in preferred stock, 6%, $100 par, and $1,500,000 in common stock, $50 par. *Method III*: Issue of $1,500,000 in 6% bonds, $750,000 in preferred stock, 6%, $100 par, and $750,000 in common stock, $50 par. Assuming that the net income before bond interest and taxes (50%) will be increased to $300,000, find the earnings per share of common stock under each method.

	Method I	Method II	Method III

SOLUTION

	Method I	Method II	Method III
Income	$300,000	$300,000	$300,000
Less: Bond interest	....	....	90,000
Income before taxes	300,000	300,000	210,000
Less: Taxes	150,000	150,000	105,000
Net income	$150,000	$150,000	$105,000
Less: Preferred dividend	....	90,000	45,000
To common stock	$150,000	$ 60,000	$ 60,000
Number of common shares	÷ 72,000	÷ 42,000	÷ 27,000
Earnings per share	$2.08	$1.43	$2.22

4.4.   Rework Problem 4.3 for an expected income of $180,000.

	Method I	Method II	Method III

SOLUTION

	Method I	Method II	Method III
Income	$180,000	$180,000	$180,000
Less: Bond interest	....	....	90,000
Income before taxes	180,000	180,000	90,000
Less: Taxes	90,000	90,000	45,000
Net income	$ 90,000	$ 90,000	$ 45,000
Less: Preferred dividend	....	90,000	45,000
To common stock	90,000	....	....
Number of common shares	÷ 72,000		
Earnings per share	$1.25	....	....

4.5.   On January 1 Savin Corporation authorizes $1,000,000 in 6%, 20-year bonds. On February 1 it issues half of them and three months later issues the balance.

(*a*) Present the entries needed to record the above information.

(*b*) Present the liabilities section of the balance sheet as of (1) February 28, (2) May 31.

(*a*)   *January 1*

February 1

May 1

(*b*)   (1)

(2)

SOLUTION

(*a*)   *January 1*   (*No entry. Memorandum noting authorization of $1,000,000 in 6%, 20-year bonds.*)

February 1	Cash		500,000	
	Bonds Payable			500,000
May 1	Cash		500,000	
	Bonds Payable			500,000

(b)	(1)	Long-Term Liabilities		
		20-year, 6% Bonds Payable Authorized	$1,000,000	
		Less: Unissued	500,000	
		Total Issued		$ 500,000
	(2)	Long-Term Liabilities		
		20-year, 6% Bonds Payable Authorized and Issued		$1,000,000

4.6. On January 1, Saperstein Inc. issued $100,000 in 20-year, 5% bonds at 104, interest payable semiannually on June 30 and December 31. Present entries to record (a) sale of the bonds, (b) payment of interest on June 30, (c) payment of interest on December 31, (d) amortization of the premium.

(a)	January 1		
(b)	June 30		
(c)	December 31		
(d)	December 31		

SOLUTION

(a)	January 1	Cash	104,000	
		Bonds Payable		100,000
		Premium on Bonds Payable		4,000
(b)	June 30	Interest Expense	2,500	
		Cash		2,500
(c)	December 31	Interest Expense	2,500	
		Cash		2,500
(d)	December 31	Premium on Bonds Payable	200*	
		Interest Expense		200

* $4,000 premium ÷ 20 years

4.7. Based on the information in Problem 4.6, present the liabilities section of the balance sheet as of (a) January 31, (b) December 31.

(a)

(b)

SOLUTION

(a)	Long-Term Liabilities		
	Bonds Payable, 5%, 20-year	$100,000	
	Add: Unamortized Premium	4,000	$104,000
(b)	Long-Term Liabilities		
	Bonds Payable, 5%, 20-year	$100,000	
	Add: Unamortized Premium	3,800	$103,800

4.8. Assume that Saperstein Inc. (Problem 4.6) issued the bonds at 96 instead of 104. Present the entries to record (a) sale of the bonds, (b) payment of interest on June 30, (c) payment of interest on December 31, (d) amortization of the discount.

(a)	January 1		
(b)	June 30		
(c)	December 31		
(d)	December 31		

SOLUTION

(a)	January 1	Cash	96,000	
		Discount on Bonds Payable	4,000	
		Bonds Payable		100,000
(b)	June 30	Interest Expense	2,500	
		Cash		2,500
(c)	December 31	Interest Expense	2,500	
		Cash		2,500
(d)	December 31	Interest Expense	200	
		Discount on Bonds Payable		200*

* $4,000 discount ÷ 20 years

4.9. Based on the information in Problem 4.8, present the liabilities section of the balance sheet as of (a) January 31, (b) December 31.

(a)

(b)

SOLUTION

(a)	Long-Term Liabilities		
	Bonds Payable	100,000	
	Less: Unamortized Discount	4,000	$96,000
(b)	Long-Term Liabilities		
	Bonds Payable	100,000	
	Less: Unamortized Discount	3,800	$96,200

4.10. On January 1 the Stevens Company authorized the issuance of $100,000 in 10-year, 6% bonds paying interest semiannually on June 30 and December 31, but it did not sell them until March 1 of that year. Prepare entries to record (a) the authorization, (b) the sale, (c) the first interest payment, (d) the second interest payment.

(a)

(b)

(c)

(d)

SOLUTION

(a)	Memo: Authorized $100,000 in 10-year, 6% bonds with		
	semiannual interest payable June 30 and December 31		
(b)	Cash	101,000	
	Bonds Payable		100,000
	Interest Expense		1,000*

* $100,000 × 6% per year × 2/12 year

The purchaser of a bond will be charged for the interest that has accrued during January and February. This interest, however, will be repaid to him (see the following entry).

| (c) | Interest Expense | 3,000 | |
| | Cash | | 3,000 |

Payment is made for the full 6 months (4 months' interest earned by purchaser and 2 months' interest collected in advance).

| (d) | Interest Expense | 3,000 | |
| | Cash | | 3,000 |

4.11. During 1975 and 1976, Beckworth Industries had the following transactions:

1975   March 31:   Issued $100,000 in 10-year, 6% bonds at 105. Interest to be paid semiannually on March 31 and September 30

September 30:   Paid the semiannual interest on bonds payable

December 31:   Recorded the accrued interest on bonds payable

December 31:   Closed the interest expense account

1976   January 1:   Reversed the adjusting entry for accrued interest

March 31:   Paid the semiannual interest

September 30:   Paid the semiannual interest

December 31:   Recorded the accrued interest on bonds payable

December 31:   Recorded the amortization of premium on bonds

December 31:   Closed the interest expense account

Prepare entries to record the foregoing transactions.

1975	March 31			
	Sept. 30			
	Dec. 31			
	Dec. 31			
	Dec. 31			
1976	Jan. 1			
	March 31			
	Sept. 30			
	Dec. 31			
	Dec. 31			
	Dec. 31			

SOLUTION

1975	March 31	Cash	105,000	
		Bonds Payable		100,000
		Premium on Bonds Payable		5,000
	Sept. 30	Interest Expense	3,000	
		Cash		3,000
	Dec. 31	Interest Expense	1,500	
		Interest Payable		1,500*

* 3 months' interest

	Dec. 31	Premium on Bonds Payable	375**	
		Interest Expense		375

** March 31 to December 31 $= \frac{9}{12}$ year; $\frac{\$5,000 \; premium}{10 \; years} \times \frac{9}{12}$ year $= \$375$

	Dec. 31	Expense and Income Summary	4,125	
		Interest Expense		4,125
1976	Jan. 1	Interest Payable	1,500	
		Interest Expense		1,500
	March 31	Interest Expense	3,000	
		Cash		3,000
	Sept. 30	Interest Expense	3,000	
		Cash		3,000
	Dec. 31	Interest Expense	1,500	
		Interest Payable		1,500
	Dec. 31	Premium on Bonds Payable	500	
		Interest Expense		500
	Dec. 31	Expense and Income Summary	5,500	
		Interest Expense		5,500

4.12. Prior to redeeming its obligations at 104, Gallagher Company had the following ledger balances:

Bonds Payable		Discount on Bonds Payable	
	1,000,000	40,000	25,000

(a) Present the entry necessary to record the redemption.

(b) If it were decided to redeem only half the bonds, what entry would be needed?

(a)

(b)

SOLUTION

(a)	Bonds Payable	1,000,000	
	Loss on Redemption of Bonds	55,000	
	Cash		1,040,000
	Discount on Bonds Payable		15,000
(b)	Bonds Payable	500,000	
	Loss on Redemption of Bonds	27,500	
	Cash		520,000
	Discount on Bonds Payable		7,500

4.13. The Whalstom Corporation has the following balances in its ledger regarding its convertible bonds:

Bonds Payable		Premium on Bonds Payable	
	1,000,000	50,000	60,000

All bondholders exercise their option and convert their holdings at the ratio of 16 shares of $50-par common stock for each $1,000 bond. Present the entry for the conversion.

SOLUTION

Bonds Payable	1,000,000	
Premium on Bonds Payable	10,000	
Common Stock		800,000*
Premium on Common Stock		210,000

* 1,000 bonds $\times \dfrac{16}{1} \times$ $50

4.14. The Davis Company issues $2,000,000 in 5%, 10-year, sinking fund bonds and agrees to deposit annually with a trustee equal amounts sufficient to retire the bond issue at maturity. Transactions for three selected years appear below.

1975	January 1:	Sold the bonds at 103
	December 31:	Deposited $176,000 in the bond sinking fund
1980	March 21:	Purchased securities with sinking fund cash for $100,000
	December 31:	Deposited $176,000 in the bond sinking fund
	December 31:	Received $5,620 of income on sinking fund securities
1984	October 20:	Sold the sinking fund securities for $108,000
	December 31:	Paid the bonds at maturity. At this time the sinking fund cash account has a balance of $2,024,000

Present entries to record all information relating to the bond issue.

1975	Jan. 1			
	Dec. 31			
1980	March 21			
	Dec. 31			
	Dec. 31			
1984	Oct. 20			
	Dec. 31			

SOLUTION

1975	Jan. 1	Cash [$2,000,000 × 103%]	2,060,000	
		Bonds Payable		2,000,000
		Premium on Bonds Payable		60,000
	Dec. 31	Sinking Fund Cash	176,000	
		Cash		176,000
1980	March 21	Sinking Fund Securities	100,000	
		Sinking Fund Cash		100,000
	Dec. 31	Sinking Fund Cash	176,000	
		Cash		176,000
	Dec. 31	Sinking Fund Cash	5,620	
		Sinking Fund Income		5,620
1984	Oct. 20	Sinking Fund Cash	108,000	
		Sinking Fund Securities		100,000
		Gain on Sale of Securities		8,000
	Dec. 31	Bonds Payable	2,000,000	
		Cash	24,000	
		Sinking Fund Cash		2,024,000

4.15. Below are the balance sheet accounts and balances for Stevemarc Corporation as of December 31, 197–. Prepare a classified balance sheet.

Accounts Receivable	$ 128,400
Accounts Payable	102,000
Accumulated Depreciation, Building	120,000
Accumulated Depreciation, Equipment	26,000
Allowance for Doubtful Accounts	4,600
Appropriation for Plant Expansion	68,000
Appropriation for Treasury Stock	42,000
Bonds (6%, 10-year debentures)	1,000,000
Building	696,700
Cash	1,655,000
Common Stock, $25 par (40,000 shares authorized, 30,000 shares issued)	750,000
Common Stock Subscribed	100,000
Common Stock Subscriptions Receivable	60,000
Discount on Preferred Stock	60,000
Equipment	216,000
Goodwill	125,000
Land	30,000
Merchandise Inventory	442,500
Notes Receivable	75,000
Notes Payable	38,000
Organization Costs	15,000
Paid-In Capital from Sale of Treasury Stock	22,000
Premium on Bonds Payable	36,000
Premium on Common Stock	15,000
Preferred Stock, 6%, $100 par (20,000 shares authorized, 10,000 shares issued)	1,000,000
Prepaid Expenses	32,000
Taxes Payable	24,000
Treasury Stock (at cost)	42,000
Unappropriated Retained Earnings	230,000

Stevemarc Corporation

Balance Sheet

December 31, 197—

ASSETS

Current Assets

Fixed Assets

(continued next page)

Intangible Assets

Total Assets

LIABILITIES
Current Liabilities

Long-Term Liabilities

Total Liabilities

STOCKHOLDERS' EQUITY
Paid-In Capital

Retained Earnings

Total Stockholders' Equity

Total Liabilities and Stockholders' Equity

SOLUTION

ASSETS
Current Assets

Cash		$1,655,000
Accounts Receivable	$ 128,400	
Less: Allowance for Doubtful Accounts	4,600	123,800
Notes Receivable		75,000
Merchandise Inventory		442,500
Common Stock Subscriptions Receivable		60,000
Prepaid Expenses		32,000
Total Current Assets		$2,388,300

(continued next page)

Fixed Assets			
Building	696,700		
Less: Accumulated Depreciation,			
Building	120,000	576,700	
Equipment	216,000		
Less: Accumulated Depreciation,			
Equipment	26,000	190,000	
Land		30,000	
Total Fixed Assets			796,700
Intangible Assets			
Goodwill		125,000	
Organization Costs		15,000	
Total Intangible Assets			140,000
Total Assets			$3,325,000

LIABILITIES

Current Liabilities			
Accounts Payable	$ 102,000		
Notes Payable	38,000		
Taxes Payable	24,000		
Total Current Liabilities		$ 164,000	
Long-Term Liabilities			
Bonds (6%, 10-year debentures)	1,000,000		
Add: Premium on Bonds Payable	36,000		
Total Long-Term Liabilities		1,036,000	
Total Liabilities			$1,200,000

STOCKHOLDERS' EQUITY

Paid-In Capital			
Preferred Stock, 6%, $100 par (20,000 shares			
authorized, 10,000 shares issued)	$1,000,000		
Less: Discount on Preferred Stock	60,000	$ 940,000	
Common Stock, $25 (40,000 shares			
authorized, 30,000 shares issued)	750,000		
Add: Premium on Common Stock	15,000	765,000	
Common Stock Subscribed		100,000	
From Sale of Treasury Stock		22,000	
Total Paid-In Capital			$1,827,000
Retained Earnings			
Appropriated Retained Earnings			
For Plant Expansion	68,000		
For Treasury Stock	42,000		
Total Appropriated Retained Earnings		110,000	
Unappropriated Retained Earnings		230,000	
Total Retained Earnings			340,000
Total			2,167,000
Less: Treasury Stock (at cost)			42,000
Total Stockholders' Equity			$2,125,000
Total Liabilities and Stockholders' Equity			$3,325,000

Examination I

Chapters 1-4

1. Giddy and Handelman have decided to form a partnership. Giddy invests the following business assets at their agreed valuations, and transfers his liabilities to the new firm.

	Giddy's Ledger Balances	Agreed Valuations
Cash	$10,000	$10,000
Accounts Receivable	8,200	7,200
Allowance for Doubtful Accounts	600	300
Merchandise Inventory	20,200	15,000
Equipment	8,000	6,200
Accumulated Depreciation	1,000	
Accounts Payable	5,500	5,500
Notes Payable	2,600	2,600

Handelman agrees to invest $30,000 in cash. What entries are needed to record the investments of Giddy and Handelman?

2. The abbreviated income statement of Rothchild and Quick for December 31, 197–, is as follows:

Sales (net)	$350,000
Less: Cost of Goods Sold	110,000
Gross Income	240,000
Less: Expenses	140,000
Net Income	$100,000

The profit and loss agreement specifies that:

(1) Interest of 5% is to be allowed on capital balances (Rothchild, $50,000; Quick, $25,000).

(2) Salary allowances to Rothchild and Quick to be $8,000 and $7,000, respectively.

(3) A bonus is to be given to Rothchild equal to 20% of net income without regard to interest or salary.

(4) Remaining profits and losses are to be divided equally.

(a) Present the distribution of net income. (b) Present the journal entry required to close the books.

3. Able, Baker, and Con, who share income and losses in the ratio of 2:1:1, decide to liquidate their business on May 31. As of that date, their post-closing trial balance reveals the following balances:

Cash	$ 48,000	
Other Assets	72,000	
Liabilities		$ 40,000
Able, Capital		30,000
Baker, Capital		30,000
Con, Capital		20,000
	$120,000	$120,000

Present the entries to record the following liquidating transactions:

(*a*) Sold the noncash assets for $10,000.

(*b*) Distributed the loss to the partners.

(*c*) Paid the liabilities.

(*d*) Allocated the available cash to the partners.

(*e*) The partner with the debit balance pays the amount he owes.

(*f*) Any additional money is distributed.

4. The outstanding stock of the Russie Corporation consists of 10,000 shares of 6%, $100-par cumulative preferred stock and 30,000 shares of $50-par common stock. The company pays out as dividends all of its net income. Over the last four years the company's earnings record has been: first year, $20,000; second year, $50,000; third year, $120,000; fourth year, $210,000. Determine the dividend per share on each class of stock for each of the four years.

5. The Agin Corporation agrees to issue 20,000 shares of common stock in exchange for equipment valued at $500,000. What journal entry must be made if the par value is (*a*) $25? (*b*) $20? (*c*) $30?

6. On January 1 the Rakosi Corporation was organized with an authorization of 10,000 shares of preferred 6% stock, $100 par, and 20,000 shares of common stock, $25 par. Record the following transactions:

> January 10:   Sold half of the common stock at $30 for cash
>
> January 15:   Issued 3,000 shares of preferred stock and 1,000 shares of common stock at par in exchange for land and building with fair market values of $200,000 and $125,000, respectively
>
> March 16:   Sold the balance of the preferred stock at $105 for cash

7. On September 1 the Marc Corporation received subscriptions to 50,000 shares of $10-par common stock at $16, collecting one-half of the subscription price immediately. Three months later the balance due was received and the stock issued. (*a*) Present the necessary entries. (*b*) Present the balance sheet as of September 30.

8. The board of directors of the Anit Corporation presented to the stockholders a plan to expand facilities at a cost of $1,000,000. This sum was to come from:

(*a*) an issue of 10,000 shares of preferred stock at par ($50)

(*b*) a loan of $200,000 by the bank

(*c*) a donation of 10% of all common stock outstanding (100,000 shares authorized and issued, par value $20)

Prepare entries to record the transactions above, assuming that the treasury stock in (*c*) was sold for $30 per share.

9. The retained earnings accounts of Weis Company appear below.

Appropriation for Contingencies	*Appropriation for Plant Expansion*	*Retained Earnings*
80,000	100,000	320,000

During the month of December the board of directors decided to:

(*a*) increase the appropriation for contingencies *by* $30,000

(*b*) decrease the appropriation for plant expansion *to* $90,000

(*c*) establish an appropriation for bonded indebtedness requiring an annual deposit of $20,000

(*d*) declare cash dividends of $80,000

Present entries to record the decisions of the board.

10. Three companies have the following financial structures.

	G Company	H Company	I Company
Bonds payable, 6%	$1,000,000	$ 500,000	....
Preferred stock, 7%, $100 par	....	500,000	$1,000,000
Common stock, $50 par	1,000,000	1,000,000	1,000,000
Total	$2,000,000	$2,000,000	$2,000,000

Assuming a tax rate of 50% of income, determine the earnings per share for common stock of each company, if the net income of each before bond interest and taxes was (a) $100,000, (b) $500,000.

11. On January 1, Thomas Inc. issued $100,000 in 10-year, 6% bonds at 102, interest payable semiannually on June 30 and December 31. Present entries to record (a) sale of the bonds, (b) payment of interest on June 30, (c) payment of interest on December 31, (d) amortization of the premium.

12. The board of directors of the Philip Company decides to issue $1,000,000 in 6%, 20-year sinking fund bonds and to deposit annually with a trustee equal amounts sufficient to retire the bond issue at maturity. Transactions for three separate years appear below.

1975	Jan. 1:	Sold the bonds at 102
	Dec. 31:	Deposited $46,000 in the bond sinking fund
1980	Mar. 21:	Purchased securities with sinking fund cash for $95,000
	Dec. 31:	Deposited $46,000 in the bond sinking fund
	Dec. 31:	Received $2,600 of income on sinking fund securities
1994	Oct. 20:	Sold the sinking fund securities for $100,000
	Dec. 31:	Paid the bonds at maturity; at this time the sinking fund cash account has a balance of $1,120,000

Present entries to record all information relating to the bond issue.

Answers to Examination I

1.

Cash	10,000	
Accounts Receivable	7,200	
Merchandise Inventory	15,000	
Equipment	6,200	
Allowance for Doubtful Accounts		300
Accounts Payable		5,500
Notes Payable		2,600
Giddy, Capital		30,000
Cash	30,000	
Handelman, Capital		30,000

2. (a)

	Rothchild	Quick	Total
Interest	$ 2,500	$ 1,250	$ 3,750
Salary	8,000	7,000	15,000
Bonus	20,000	....	20,000
	$30,500	$ 8,250	$ 38,750
Balance	30,625	30,625	61,250
Net income	$61,125	$38,875	$100,000

(b)	*Expense and Income Summary*		100,000	
	Rothchild, Capital			61,125
	Quick, Capital			38,875

3. (a)	*Cash*		10,000	
	Loss on Realization		62,000	
	Other Assets			72,000
(b)	*Able, Capital*		31,000	
	Baker, Capital		15,500	
	Con, Capital		15,500	
	Loss on Realization			62,000
(c)	*Liabilities*		40,000	
	Cash			40,000
(d)	*Baker, Capital*		14,000	
	Con, Capital		4,000	
	Cash			18,000
(e)	*Able, Capital*		1,000	
	Cash			1,000
(f)	*Cash*		1,000	
	Baker, Capital			500
	Con, Capital			500

SUMMARY OF TRANSACTIONS

Transaction	Cash	Other Assets	Liabilities	Able, Capital	Baker, Capital	Con, Capital
Balance	$48,000	$72,000	$40,000	$30,000	$30,000	$20,000
(a), (b)	+ 10,000	− 72,000		− 31,000	− 15,500	− 15,500
	$58,000		$40,000	($1,000)	$14,500	$ 4,500
(c)	− 40,000		− 40,000			
	$18,000			($1,000)	$14,500	$ 4,500
(d)	− 18,000				− 14,000	− 4,000
				($1,000)	$ 500	$ 500
(e)	+ 1,000			+ 1,000		
	$ 1,000				$ 500	$ 500
(f)	− 1,000				− 500	− 500

4.	Total Distributed	Per Share Preferred	Per Share Common
First year	$ 20,000	$ 2.00	....
Second year	50,000	5.00	....
Third year	120,000	11.00	$0.33
Fourth year	210,000	6.00	5.00

5. (a)	*Equipment*	500,000	
	Common Stock		500,000
(b)	*Equipment*	500,000	
	Common Stock		400,000
	Premium on Common Stock		100,000
(c)	*Equipment*	500,000	
	Discount on Common Stock	100,000	
	Common Stock		600,000

6.   January 10   Cash   300,000
                        Common Stock   250,000.
                        Premium on Common Stock   50,000

      January 15   Land   200,000
                    Building   125,000
                        Preferred Stock   300,000
                        Common Stock   25,000

      March 16   Cash   735,000
                        Preferred Stock   700,000
                        Premium on Preferred Stock   35,000

7. (a) September 1   Common Stock Subscriptions Receivable   800,000
                          Common Stock Subscribed   500,000
                          Premium on Common Stock   300,000

         September 1   Cash   400,000
                          Common Stock Subscriptions Receivable   400,000

         December 1   Cash   400,000
                          Common Stock Subscriptions Receivable   400,000

         December 1   Common Stock Subscribed   500,000
                          Common Stock   500,000

    (b)   **ASSETS**   **STOCKHOLDERS' EQUITY**

         Cash $400,000   Paid-In Capital
         Common Stock Subscriptions   Common Stock Subscribed $500,000
            Receivable   400,000   Premium on Common Stock   300,000
         Total Assets $800,000   Total Stockholders' Equity $800,000

8. (a)   Cash   500,000
                        Preferred Stock   500,000

    (b)   Cash   200,000
                        Notes Payable   200,000

    (c)   Memo: Received 10,000 shares of common stock as a donation
                     Cash   300,000
                        Donated Capital   300,000

9. (a)   Retained Earnings   30,000
              Appropriation for Contingencies   30,000

    (b)   Appropriation for Plant Expansion   10,000
              Retained Earnings   10,000

    (c)   Retained Earnings   20,000
              Appropriation for Bonded Indebtedness   20,000

    (d)   Retained Earnings   80,000
              Cash Dividend Payable   80,000

10. (a)

	G Company	H Company	I Company
Income	$100,000	$100,000	$100,000
Less: Bond interest	60,000	30,000	. . . .
	$ 40,000	$ 70,000	$100,000
Less: Tax (50%)	20,000	35,000	50,000
Net income	$ 20,000	$ 35,000	$ 50,000
Less: Preferred dividend	. . . .	35,000	50,000
To common	$ 20,000	0	0
Per share distribution	$1	0	0

(b)

	G Company	H Company	I Company
Income	$500,000	$500,000	$500,000
Less: Bond interest	60,000	30,000	. . . .
	$440,000	$470,000	$500,000
Less: Tax (50%)	220,000	235,000	250,000
Net income	$220,000	$235,000	$250,000
Less: Preferred dividend	. . . .	35,000	70,000
To common	$220,000	$200,000	$180,000
Per share distribution	$11	$10	$9

11. (a) *January 1*   *Cash*   102,000

                                   Bonds Payable   100,000
                                   Premium on Bonds Payable   2,000

(b) *June 30*   *Interest Expense*   3,000
                                   Cash   3,000

(c) *December 31*   *Interest Expense*   3,000
                                   Cash   3,000

(d) *December 31*   *Premium on Bonds Payable*   200
                                   Interest Expense   200

12. **1975**   *Jan. 1*   *Cash*   1,020,000

                                   Bonds Payable   1,000,000
                                   Premium on Bonds Payable   20,000

        Dec. 31   *Sinking Fund Cash*   46,000
                                   Cash   46,000

1980   *Mar. 21*   *Sinking Fund Securities*   95,000
                                   Sinking Fund Cash   95,000

        Dec. 31   *Sinking Fund Cash*   46,000
                                   Cash   46,000

        Dec. 31   *Sinking Fund Cash*   2,600
                                   Sinking Fund Income   2,600

1994   *Oct. 20*   *Sinking Fund Cash*   100,000
                                   Sinking Fund Securities   95,000
                                   Gain on Sale of Securities   5,000

        Dec. 31   *Bonds Payable*   1,000,000
                    Cash   120,000
                                   Sinking Fund Cash   1,120,000

Chapter 5

Manufacturing Accounting

5.1 MANUFACTURING ACCOUNTS

A merchandising company provides services or buys and sells articles without changing their form. A manufacturing company, by contrast, converts raw materials into finished goods, in the process incurring labor and overhead costs. Because of this difference in nature, a manufacturing company requires additional asset and expense accounts. These may be summarized as follows:

Inventories. Instead of the single inventory account used by a merchandising company, a manufacturing company will need three separate inventory accounts: Raw Materials (or Direct Materials), Work in Process, and Finished Goods.

Plant and equipment (fixed assets). The equipment used in manufacturing is varied, numerous, and costly. Thus it is desirable to maintain a subsidiary plant ledger in which the individual items are recorded and to have a general ledger account, Plant and Equipment, to control the subsidiary ledger.

Research and development costs. Success in manufacturing is usually related to substantial research and introduction of new products. Consequently, intangible assets, such as patents and the cost of research and development, are shown on the financial statements of many manufacturing companies.

Manufacturing or production cost. As described in Sec. 5.2, manufacturing cost is made up of the cost of raw materials, direct labor costs, and factory overhead. Each of these three elements requires an account. If there are two or more products, subsidiary records may be used to list the production costs by product. For factory overhead a separate account is set up for each type of expense, such as depreciation, repairs, or taxes.

5.2 ANALYSIS OF MANUFACTURING COST

Each unit of finished goods includes the three elements of manufacturing cost — raw materials, direct labor, and factory overhead.

RAW MATERIALS

This represents the *cost* of raw materials that become part of the finished product. Purchases of raw materials go into inventory, from which goods are issued and placed in production. The cost of raw materials used is obtained by adding the beginning inventory to the purchases for the period to arrive at the total raw materials available for use. Of this amount, part is used during, and part is on hand at the end of, the period. By taking a physical count at the end of the period the final inventory can be determined; the balance is presumed to have been used. The cost of raw materials is the invoice cost, plus transportation-in, less any returns or allowances received from the vendor.

EXAMPLE 1.

Raw Materials Inventory	Transportation-In
Jan. 1 20,000	5,000
Dec. 31 23,000	

Raw Materials Purchases	Raw Materials Returns
75,500	5,000

From the above ledger accounts, the cost of raw materials used is computed as follows:

Beginning Inventory		$20,000
Purchases	$75,500	
Less: Returns and Allowances	5,000	70,500
Transportation-In		5,000
Raw Materials Available for Use		$95,500
Less: Ending Inventory		23,000
Cost of Raw Materials Used		$72,500

DIRECT LABOR

This represents the amount of wages paid to factory employees who work *directly on the product*; it is charged to Work in Process. Included are the wages of machine operators, assemblers, and others. The work of employees such as supervisors, janitors, and time-keepers is indirect labor and their wages are included in factory overhead.

EXAMPLE 2.

At the end of the month, labor costs are summarized and posted to the general ledger, usually according to direct and indirect costs, as shown by the following entry:

Work in Process	20,000	
Factory Overhead	6,000	
Wages Payable		26,000

FACTORY OVERHEAD

This includes all factory costs other than raw materials and direct labor. Each overhead item is recorded in an individual account, but a single predetermined overhead rate is used in computing estimates and bids for jobs and for recording costs. If actual cost exceeds estimated cost, factory overhead is *underapplied*; otherwise it is *overapplied*. This simplifying procedure enables management to determine the total cost of a job as soon as the job is finished and to find out if the job resulted in a profit or a loss.

5.3 INVENTORIES

To calculate manufacturing cost and the cost of goods sold, it is generally necessary to find the amount of inventory at the end of the period. This amount is determined by (1) the *unit cost,* or manufacturing cost per item, and (2) the number of units on hand.

EXAMPLE 3.

Assume that the unit cost of this month's production of alarm clocks was $6.52 for 1,000 clocks. Assume also that at the beginning of the month there were on hand 200 clocks that had been produced last month at a unit cost of $6.20, and 100 clocks that had been produced two months previously at $5.80 a clock. If 400 clocks were sold during the month, the cost of the clocks sold would be $2,472 by the FIFO method or $2,608 by the LIFO method.

PERIODIC INVENTORY METHOD

Under the periodic method the costs of individual sales are not recorded, and to find the amount of the closing inventory it is necessary to count and price the items on hand at the end of the period. If units of a product were on hand at the beginning of the period and additional units were produced during the period, the sum of the two is the number of units available for sale during the period. Of this number, some units were sold and some are still on hand. In most cases it is easier to count the items on hand at the end of the period and to apply a cost using LIFO, FIFO, or some other costing basis (see Chapter 11 of *Schaum's Outline of Accounting I*). The amount so obtained is then subtracted from the total goods available for sale to derive the amount of Cost of Goods Sold.

The periodic inventory method, while much simpler than keeping track of hundreds or thousands of receipts and issues throughout the period, also has some disadvantages. It is time-consuming, and since it is applied only at intervals, usually once a year, there are sometimes errors in counting, pricing, or compiling the total.

PERPETUAL INVENTORY METHOD

Continuous individual records are usually maintained to keep closer control of high-priced manufactured items or to assure that a sufficient quantity of raw materials is on hand for production. For expensive products, especially where there are not a great many transactions, it is desirable to know at all times how many units have been sold and how many are on hand—and also how many should be on hand. In the case of automobiles or large appliances, each unit will carry a serial number which appears on the purchase invoice. It is then a simple matter to list from purchase invoices the serial numbers of those units that were not sold and should be on hand. If any unit is missing, it is usually easy to trace by serial number the receipt, shipment, or location of the particular item.

Critical raw materials do not bear serial numbers. However, it is necessary to keep perpetual records of receipts, issues, and quantity on hand to prevent shortages which might halt production and be very costly.

5.4 WORKSHEET

As in nonmanufacturing companies, the financial statements can be prepared more quickly and accurately if a worksheet is used. The form of the worksheet for a manufacturing company is derived from the form for a merchandising company by merely adding a pair of columns to provide the data needed for the statement of Cost of Goods Manufactured (see Sec. 5.5). The preparation of the worksheet is illustrated in Problem 5.7.

5.5 COST OF GOODS MANUFACTURED

The *cost of goods manufactured* is the manufacturing cost (raw materials + direct labor + factory overhead) of the products *finished* during the period. It is to be distinguished from *total manufacturing cost*, which also includes work in process.

As illustrated in Example 4 below, the balance of Cost of Goods Manufactured is carried in the manufacturing summary account, from which it is transferred to Expense and Income Summary. To keep the income statement from becoming overly long, a separate Statement of Cost of Goods Manufactured is prepared. This statement expands upon the manufacturing summary, providing the additional operating details required by management. Two or more periods may be included on the statement to show the changes from one period to another.

EXAMPLE 4.

For the Chamberlain Manufacturing Company, the development of the Statement of Cost of Goods Manufactured is shown on page 102.

Chamberlain Manufacturing Company
Manufacturing Summary
year ended December 31, 197–

197–			197–		
Dec. 31	Work in Process Inv., Jan. 1	15,000	Dec. 31	Work in Process Inv., Dec. 31	12,500
	Raw Materials Inv., Jan. 1	20,000		Raw Materials Inv., Dec. 31	23,000
	Purchases and Transportation	75,500		Bal. to Exp. and Inc. Summ.	174,300 ←
	Direct Labor	57,500			209,800
	Factory Overhead	41,800			
		209,800			

Chamberlain Manufacturing Company
Expense and Income Summary
year ended December 31, 197–

197–			197–		
Dec. 31	Finished Goods Inv., Jan. 1	27,600	Dec. 31	Finished Goods Inv., Dec. 31	32,500
	From Manufacturing Summ.	174,300 ←		Cost of Goods Sold	169,400
		201,900			201,900

Chamberlain Manufacturing Company
Statement of Cost of Goods Manufactured
year ended December 31, 197–

Work in Process Inventory, January 1, 197–			$ 15,000
Raw Materials			
Inventory, January 1, 197–		$20,000	
Purchases	$75,500		
Less: Returns and Allowances	5,000	70,500	
Transportation-In		5,000	
Raw Materials Available for Use		$95,500	
Less: Inventory, December 31, 197–		23,000	
Cost of Raw Materials Used		$72,500	
Direct Labor		57,500	
Factory Overhead			
Indirect Labor	$12,200		
Heat, Light, and Power	10,500		
Property Taxes	2,250		
Insurance	1,500		
Depreciation	11,500		
Miscellaneous	3,850		
Total Factory Overhead		41,800	
Total Manufacturing Cost			171,800
Total Work in Process During Period			$186,800
Less: Work in Process Inventory, December 31, 197–			12,500
Cost of Goods Manufactured			$174,300

5.6　INCOME STATEMENT

The income statement for a manufacturing company is similar to that for a merchandising company, except for the terminology in the cost of goods sold section. Below is shown a comparison of the terms.

Merchandising Company	Manufacturing Company
BEGINNING INVENTORY OF MERCHANDISE	BEGINNING INVENTORY OF FINISHED GOODS
+	+
PURCHASES OF MERCHANDISE	COST OF GOODS MANUFACTURED
−	−
ENDING INVENTORY OF MERCHANDISE	ENDING INVENTORY OF FINISHED GOODS
=	=
COST OF GOODS SOLD	COST OF GOODS SOLD

In most cases the caption in the income statement for manufacturing costs is shown as "Cost of Goods Manufactured (see Exhibit A)." Thus, attention is directed to the cost statement which supports the total figure shown in the income statement.

EXAMPLE 5.

In the income statement of the Chamberlain Manufacturing Company (Example 4), the sales and cost of goods sold sections would appear as:

Chamberlain Manufacturing Company
Income Statement
year ended December 31, 197–

Sales		$256,700
Cost of Goods Sold		
Finished Goods Inventory, January 1, 197–	$ 27,600	
Cost of Goods Manufactured (see Exhibit A)	174,300	
Goods Available for Sale	$201,900	
Less: Finished Goods Inventory, December 31, 197–	32,500	
Cost of Goods Sold		169,400

Here, "Exhibit A" is the statement shown in Example 4.

5.7　JOINT PRODUCTS AND BY-PRODUCTS

Where two or more products are obtained from a common process, they are usually referred to as *joint products* if all are of significant value. A product is referred to as a *by-product* if it has limited value in relation to the principal product. Generally a by-product is merely incidental to the manufacture of the principal product.

JOINT PRODUCTS

Typical of joint products are gasoline, kerosene, and naphtha, which are all obtained from the refining of crude oil. Generally, one joint product cannot be produced without the others, and only the total revenue of the entire group and the total production cost are relevant. However, for inventory purposes it is necessary to make an allocation of costs among the joint products. The usual method of allocating cost is on the sales value of the various products.

EXAMPLE 6.

Assume that 5,000 units of Product A and 20,000 units of Product B were produced at a total cost of $30,000.

Joint Product	Units Produced	Unit Sales Price	Sales Value	Percent of Total
A	5,000	$4.00	$20,000	40%
B	20,000	1.50	30,000	60%
			$50,000	

Allocation of Joint Cost

A	40%	$12,000
B	60%	18,000
		$30,000

Unit Cost

A: $12,000 ÷ 5,000 units = $2.40

B: 18,000 ÷ 20,000 units = .90

     $30,000

BY-PRODUCTS

An example of a by-product would be leftover material such as sawdust in a lumber mill. Generally, the sales value of the by-product, less any processing or selling costs, is deducted from Work in Process of the principal product and transferred to a finished goods account.

EXAMPLE 7.

Assume that costs accumulated in Work in Process, Production Department was $18,600, including the by-product, Product B, with an estimated value of $400. The entry would be as follows:

Finished Goods, Product B   400

       Work in Process, Production Department   400

The accounts would appear as below:

Work in Process, Production Department		*Finished Goods, Product B*	
18,600	400	400	

Summary

(1) The three kinds of manufacturing costs included in finished goods are _____ _____, _____, and _____.

(2) Indirect materials, indirect labor, factory manager's salary, machinery repairs are all examples of _____.

(3) The three inventory accounts for a manufacturing business are _____, _____, and _____.

(4) The value of inventory is determined through counting and pricing under the _____ method, and through individual records under the _____ method.

(5) The manufacturing summary account is amplified in the _____ _____.

(6) To calculate _____ , we add the opening work in process inventory, the direct materials placed in production, and the direct labor and factory overhead for the period, and then subtract the ending work in process inventory.

(7) The total production cost of two joint products would usually be divided between them in the ratio of their _____ .

Answers: (1) direct materials, direct labor, factory overhead; (2) factory overhead; (3) finished goods, work in process, materials; (4) periodic, perpetual; (5) Statement of Cost of Goods Manufactured; (6) cost of goods manufactured; (7) sales values

Solved Problems

5.1. The Robert Benson Company manufactures one product, Egypt Balm, which is processed in four departments. During December $56,700 of direct materials was put into production and $68,500 of direct labor was incurred in Department 1. The factory overhead rate is 75% of direct labor cost. Work in process in Department 1 was $36,200 at the beginning of the month and $32,600 at the end of the month. Prepare general journal entries to record (*a*) direct materials, (*b*) direct labor, (*c*) factory overhead, and (*d*) cost of the production transferred to Department 2.

(a)

(b)

(c)

(d)

SOLUTION

(a)	Work in Process, Department 1	56,700	
	Materials		56,700
(b)	Work in Process, Department 1	68,500	
	Wages Payable		68,500
(c)	Work in Process, Department 1	51,375	
	Factory Overhead, Department 1		51,375
(d)	Work in Process, Department 2	180,175	
	Work in Process, Department 1		180,175

5.2. The W. F. Pierce Company expects that for Department 2 the total factory overhead cost for the coming year will be $75,000 and total direct labor cost will be $60,000. The actual costs for January were $7,000 and $5,000, respectively. (*a*) Compute the estimated factory overhead rate based on direct labor cost. (*b*) Show the entry applying factory overhead to January costs. (*c*) Find the balance of Factory Overhead, Department 2 at January 31. (*d*) Is the overhead overapplied or underapplied?

SOLUTION

(*a*) Estimated overhead rate: $75,000 ÷ $60,000 = 125% of direct labor cost.

(b)   Work in Process, Department 2   6,250
                        Factory Overhead, Department 2   6,250*
                   * $5,000 × 125%

(c) $7,000 (actual overhead) − $6,250 (estimated overhead) = $750 (debit balance)

(d) Underapplied, since the amount applied was less than the actual amount.

5.3. The James Harold Manufacturing Company has the following accounts in its pre-closing trial balance at December 31:

Direct Materials Purchases	$ 75,700	Finished Goods Inventory	$ 85,000
Direct Materials Inventory	29,500	Sales	360,000
Direct Labor	113,500	Selling Expense (control)	18,000
Factory Overhead (control)	76,000	General Expense (control)	12,000
Work in Process Inventory	35,000		

Inventories at December 31 were:

Direct Materials	$31,400
Work in Process	28,200
Finished Goods	80,000

Prepare a Statement of Cost of Goods Manufactured.

SOLUTION

Work in Process Inventory, January 1, 197–		$ 35,000
Direct Materials		
Inventory, January 1, 197–	$ 29,500	
Purchases	75,700	
Available for Use	$105,200	
Less: Inventory, December 31, 197–	31,400	
Put in Production	$ 73,800	
Direct Labor	113,500	
Factory Overhead	76,000	
Total Manufacturing Costs		263,300
Total Work in Process During Period		$298,300
Less: Work in Process Inventory, December 31, 197–		28,200
Cost of Goods Manufactured		$270,100

5.4. Based on the data in Problem 5.3, show the journal entries for December 31 needed (*a*) to adjust the inventory accounts, (*b*) to close the accounts to Manufacturing Summary, (*c*) to close Manufacturing Summary.

(*a*)

(*b*)

(*c*)

SOLUTION

(*a*)	Manufacturing Summary	64,500	
	Work in Process Inventory		35,000
	Direct Materials Inventory		29,500
	Work in Process Inventory	28,200	
	Direct Materials Inventory	31,400	
	Manufacturing Summary		59,600
	Expense and Income Summary	85,000	
	Finished Goods Inventory		85,000
	Finished Goods Inventory	80,000	
	Expense and Income Summary		80,000
(*b*)	Manufacturing Summary	265,200	
	Direct Materials Purchases		75,700
	Direct Labor		113,500
	Factory Overhead		76,000
(*c*)	Expense and Income Summary	270,100	
	Manufacturing Summary		270,100

5.5. The account Work in Process, Department B for the Lanuto Electric Company shows dollar charges and units of products completed as follows:

Work in Process, Department B

From Department A	8,600	By-product M (1,000 units)
Direct Labor	17,777	Joint Product X (6,000 units)
Factory Overhead	22,223	Joint Product Y (8,000 units)

The value of M is $0.60 a unit; X sells for $12 a unit and Y sells for $3 a unit. Work in Process has no inventory at either the beginning or the end of the period. (*a*) Allocate the costs to the three products. (*b*) Compute the unit cost for each joint product.

SOLUTION

(*a*)

Total cost to be allocated	$48,600
Less: Value of by-product M (1,000 × $0.60)	600
Cost to be allocated to joint products	$48,000

Joint Product	**Sales Value**
X (6,000 units @ $12)	$72,000
Y (8,000 units @ $3)	24,000
Total sales value	$96,000

Cost of X: $\dfrac{72,000}{96,000} \times \$48,000 = \$36,000$

Cost of Y: $\dfrac{24,000}{96,000} \times \$48,000 = \$12,000$

Allocation Summary

M	$ 600
X	36,000
Y	12,000
Total cost	$48,600

(*b*) Unit cost of X: $36,000 ÷ 6,000 units = $6.00

      Unit cost of Y: $12,000 ÷ 8,000 units = $1.50

5.6. At the end of the first month of the current fiscal year P & T Mahoney Company has the following trial balance:

Cash	$ 34,750	
Marketable Securities	15,000	
Accounts Receivable	41,300	
Allowance for Doubtful Accounts		$ 2,200
Finished Goods, Product A	32,400	
Finished Goods, Product B	56,200	
Work in Process, Department 1	22,900	
Work in Process, Department 2	22,600	
Materials	25,400	
Prepaid Expenses	5,800	
Machinery and Equipment	115,700	
Accumulated Depreciation, Machinery and Equipment		35,000
Buildings	257,000	
Accumulated Depreciation, Buildings		55,000
Land	50,000	
Accounts Payable		48,600
Wages Payable		6,500
Income Tax Payable		4,200
Mortgage Note Payable (due 1990)		75,000

Common Stock, $25 par		$350,000
Retained Earnings		85,400
Sales		175,800
Cost of Goods Sold	$115,600	
Factory Overhead, Department 1	300	
Factory Overhead, Department 2	50	
Factory Overhead, Department 3		100
Selling Expenses	24,600	
General Expenses	13,500	
Interest Expense	650	
Interest Income		150
Income Tax	4,200	
	$837,950	$837,950

Prepare (a) an income statement, (b) a balance sheet.

(a)

P & T Mahoney Company
Income Statement
month ended January 31, 197—

(b)

P & T Mahoney Company
Balance Sheet
January 31, 197—

ASSETS

Current Assets

Total Current Assets
Plant Assets

Total Plant Assets

(continued on next page)

Deferred Charge			
Total Assets			
LIABILITIES			
Current Liabilities			
Total Current Liabilities			
Long-Term Liabilities			
Total Liabilities			
STOCKHOLDERS' EQUITY			
Stockholders' Equity			
Total Liabilities and Stockholders' Equity			

SOLUTION

(a)

Sales		$175,800
Less: Cost of Goods Sold		115,600
Gross Profit on Sales		$ 60,200
Operating Expenses		
Selling Expenses	$24,600	
General Expenses	13,500	38,100
Income from Operations		$ 22,100
Other Expenses (net)		
Interest Expense	$ 650	
Less: Interest Income	150	500
Income Before Income Tax		$ 21,600
Income Tax		4,200
Net Income		$ 17,400

(b) **ASSETS**

	Cost	Accumulated Depreciation	Book Value	
Current Assets				
Cash			$ 34,750	
Marketable Securities			15,000	
Accounts Receivable	$41,300			
Less: Allowance for Doubtful Accounts	2,200		39,100	
Inventories				
Finished Goods	$88,600			
Work in Process	45,500			
Materials	25,400		159,500	
Prepaid Expenses			5,800	
Total Current Assets				$254,150
Plant Assets				
Mach. & Equip.	$115,700	$35,000	$ 80,700	
Buildings	257,000	55,000	202,000	
Land	50,000		50,000	
Total Plant Assets	$422,700	$90,000		$332,700
Deferred Charge				
Factory Overhead Underapplied				250
Total Assets				$587,100

LIABILITIES

Current Liabilities		
Accounts Payable	$ 48,600	
Wages Payable	6,500	
Income Tax Payable	4,200	
Total Current Liabilities		$ 59,300
Long-Term Liabilities		
Mortgage Note Payable (due 1990)		75,000
Total Liabilities		$134,300

STOCKHOLDERS' EQUITY

Common Stock, $25 par	$350,000	
Retained Earnings	102,800*	
Stockholders' Equity		452,800
Total Liabilities and Stockholders' Equity		$587,100

* Balance per trial balance	$ 85,400
Net income for January	17,400
Balance, January 31	$102,800

5.7. Shown below is the trial balance for Van Horn Chemicals, Inc. (For account groups for which subsidiary ledgers are maintained, only the control balances are listed.)

Cash	$ 44,750	
Accounts Receivable	35,300	
Allowance for Doubtful Accounts		$ 1,250
Finished Goods	60,300	
Work in Process	25,600	
Direct Materials	22,100	
Prepaid Expenses (control)	7,500	
Plant Assets (control)	545,450	
Accumulated Depreciation, Plant Assets		138,400
Accounts Payable		32,500
Common Stock, $15 par		450,000
Retained Earnings		50,500
Sales		510,000
Direct Materials Purchases	160,800	
Direct Labor	145,000	
Factory Overhead (control)	46,750	
Selling Expenses (control)	41,000	
General Expenses (control)	35,600	
Interest Expense	500	
Income Tax	12,000	
	$1,182,650	$1,182,650

Adjustments data for the current year are as follows:

(1) Prepaid insurance of $4,000 has expired during the year, 80% being applicable to factory operations and 20% to general operations.

(2) An analysis of accounts receivable shows that the Allowance for Doubtful Accounts should be $2,000.

(3) Unpaid payroll amounts at the end of the year are: direct labor, $2,200; factory supervision, $300.

(4) Depreciation for the year was $20,000, chargeable 90% to factory operations and 10% to general operations.

(5) Inventories at December 31, 197–, are: Finished Goods, $43,100; Work in Process, $31,500; Direct Materials, $27,600.

(6) The opening inventories are to be closed out to the appropriate summaries.

(7) The estimated federal income tax for the year is $15,000.

Prepare (*a*) a ten-column worksheet, (*b*) a Statement of Cost of Goods Manufactured, (*c*) an income statement.

SOLUTION

(*a*) See Fig. 5-1 opposite.

(*b*)

Van Horn Chemicals, Inc.
Statement of Cost of Goods Manufactured
year ended December 31, 197–

Work in Process Inventory, January 1		$ 25,600
Direct Materials		
Inventory, January 1	$ 22,100	
Purchases	160,800	
Available for Use	$182,900	
Less: Inventory, December 31	27,600	
Cost Put in Production	$155,300	
Direct Labor	147,200	
Factory Overhead	68,250	
Total Manufacturing Costs		370,750
Total Work in Process During Period		$396,350
Less: Work in Process Inventory, December 31		31,500
Cost of Goods Manufactured		$364,850

(*c*)

Van Horn Chemicals, Inc.
Income Statement
year ended December 31, 197–

Sales		$510,000
Cost of Goods Sold		
Finished Goods Inventory, January 1	$ 60,300	
Cost of Goods Manufactured	364,850	
Goods Available for Sale	$425,150	
Less: Finished Goods Inventory, December 31	43,100	
Cost of Goods Sold		382,050
Gross Profit on Sales		$127,950
Operating Expenses		
Selling Expenses	$ 41,000	
General Expenses	39,150	
Total Operating Expenses		80,150
		$ 47,800
Other Expense		
Interest Expense		500
Income Before Income Tax		$ 47,300
Income Tax		15,000
Net Income		$ 32,300

VAN HORN CHEMICALS, INC.   Worksheet   Year Ending   December 31, 197 –

ACCOUNTS	TRIAL BALANCE Debit	TRIAL BALANCE Credit	ADJUSTMENTS Debit	ADJUSTMENTS Credit	COST OF GOODS MANUFACTURED Debit	COST OF GOODS MANUFACTURED Credit	INCOME STATEMENT Debit	INCOME STATEMENT Credit	BALANCE SHEET Debit	BALANCE SHEET Credit
Cash	44750								44750	
Accounts Receivable	35300								35300	
Allowance for Doubtful Accounts		1250		(3) 750						2000
Finished Goods	66300		(5) 43100	(6) 60300					43100	
Work in Process	25600		(5) 31500	(6) 25600					31500	
Direct Materials	27600		(5) 27600	(6) 22100					27600	
Prepaid Expenses (Control)	7500			(1) 4000					3500	
Plant Assets (Control)	545450								545450	
Accumulated Dep. Plant Assets		138400		(4) 20000						158400
Accounts Payable		32500								32500
Income Tax Payable				(7) 3000						3000
Accrued Liabilities				(3) 2500						2500
Common Stock $15 par		450000								450000
Retained Earnings		50500								50500
Income Summary			(6) 60300	(5) 43100			60300	43100		
Manufacturing Summary			(6) 25600	(5) 31500	25600	31500				
"			(6) 22100	(5) 27600	22100	27600				
Sales		510000						510000		
Direct Materials Purchases	160800				160800					
Direct Labor	145000		(3) 2200		147200					
Factory Overhead (control)	46750		(10) 3200		68250					
"			(3) 300							
"			(4) 18000							
Selling Expenses (Control)	41000		(2) 800				41000			
General Expenses (Control)	35600		(2) 750				39750			
"			(4) 2000							
Interest Expense	500						500			
Income Tax	12000		(7) 3000				15000			
	1182650	1182650	240450	240450						
Cost of Goods Manufactured					423950	364850	364850			
					423950	423950	529900	553100	698900	32300
							32300		32300	
Net Income							553100	553100	731200	731200

Fig. 5-1

5.8. On December 1 the Kuezek Auto Company had the following inventory balances: Materials, $25,000; Work in Process, $40,000; Finished Goods, $20,000. Representative transactions for the month of December are:

(1)   Materials were purchased for $18,500.

(2)   Parts in the amount of $20,000 were issued from the storeroom for production.

(3)   Requisitions for indirect materials and supplies amounted to $2,500.

(4)   Labor costs for December were $28,000, including salesmen's salaries of $5,000 and office salaries of $3,000. Income taxes of $2,500 and social security taxes of $1,500 were deducted.

(5)   Miscellaneous manufacturing expenses during the month were $7,500.

(6)   The factory overhead rate is 75% of direct labor cost.

(7)   The cost of production completed in December was $65,500 and finished goods inventory at December 31 was $8,100.

(8)   Sales, all on account, for the month were $95,600.

Prepare journal entries (a) to record the above transactions, (b) to close the various accounts to Expense and Income Summary and to close the net income to Retained Earnings.

(a)	(1)		
	(2)		
	(3)		
	(4)		
	(5)		
	(6)		
	(7)		
	(8)		
(b)			

SOLUTION

(a)	(1)	Materials	18,500	
		Accounts Payable		18,500
	(2)	Work in Process	20,000	
		Materials		20,000
	(3)	Factory Overhead Control	2,500	
		Materials		2,500
	(4)	Work in Process (Direct Labor)	20,000	
		Selling Expenses Control (Salesmen's Salaries)	5,000	
		General Expenses Control (Office Salaries)	3,000	
		Federal Income Taxes Withheld		2,500
		Social Security Taxes Withheld		1,500
		Cash		24,000
	(5)	Factory Overhead Control	7,500	
		Accounts Payable		7,500
	(6)	Work in Process	15,000	
		Factory Overhead Applied		15,000
	(7)	Finished Goods	65,500	
		Work in Process		65,500
	(8)	Accounts Receivable	95,600	
		Sales		95,600
		Cost of Goods Sold	77,400*	
		Finished Goods		77,400

* Finished goods inventory, December 1	$20,000
December production	65,500
Goods available for sale	$85,500
Less: Finished goods inventory, December 31	8,100
	$77,400

(b)	Sales	95,600	
	Expense and Income Summary		95,600
	Expense and Income Summary	85,400	
	Cost of Goods Sold		77,400
	Selling Expenses		5,000
	General Expenses		3,000
	Expense and Income Summary	10,200	
	Retained Earnings		10,200

5.9. The Cameo Baking Company produces Cameo Crispies and Cameo Creamies. Initially materials are put into process in Department A and on completion are transferred to Department B, where further materials are added. After processing in Department B the finished goods are ready for sale. The two service departments are Maintenance & Repair and Factory Office. Manufacturing transactions for January are:

(1) Materials purchased on account, $15,000.

(2) Materials issued from inventory: Department A, $13,600 (of which $11,000 is direct materials); Department B, $10,050 (of which $8,650 is direct materials); Maintenance & Repair, $600.

(3) Miscellaneous costs and expenses payable: Department A, $700; Department B, $450; Maintenance & Repair, $350; Factory Office, $235.

(4)   Labor costs: Department A, $8,850 (of which $8,250 is direct costs); Department B, $6,400 (of which $6,000 is direct costs); Maintenance & Repair, $950; Factory Office, $750.

(5)   Prepaid expenses used up: Department A, $80; Department B, $60; Maintenance & Repair, $150; Factory Office, $65.

(6)   Depreciation on plant assets: Department A, $500; Department B, $900; Maintenance & Repair, $250; Factory Office, $150.

(7)   Factory office costs are allocated on the basis of total man-hours worked in each department: Department A, 400 man-hours; Department B, 600 man-hours; Maintenance & Repair, 200 man-hours.

(8)   Maintenance and repair costs are allocated on the basis of services given: Department A, 70%; Department B, 30%.

(9)   Factory overhead is applied at predetermined rates: Department A, 80% of direct labor costs; Department B, 75% of direct labor costs.

(10)   Completed production, Department A, 2,000 units.

(11)   Completed production, Department B, 1,500 units of Cameo Crispies and 2,000 units of Cameo Creamies. The unit sales price is $12 for Cameo Crispies and $18 for Cameo Creamies.

Additional data: Finished goods inventories at January 1: Cameo Crispies, 400 units @ $8; Cameo Creamies, 600 units @ $14. There was no work in process inventory at the beginning or at the end of the month.

Prepare general journal entries to record the above transactions.

(1)		
(2)		
(3)		
(4)		
(5)		
(6)		

(7)		
(8)		
(9)		
(10)		
(11)		

SOLUTION

(1)	Materials	15,000	
	Accounts Payable		15,000
(2)	Work in Process, Department A	11,000	
	Work in Process, Department B	8,650	
	Factory Overhead, Department A	2,600	
	Factory Overhead, Department B	1,400	
	Maintenance & Repair	600	
	Materials		24,250
(3)	Factory Overhead, Department A	700	
	Factory Overhead, Department B	450	
	Maintenance & Repair	350	
	Factory Office	235	
	Accounts Payable		1,735
(4)	Work in Process, Department A	8,250	
	Work in Process, Department B	6,000	
	Factory Overhead, Department A	600	
	Factory Overhead, Department B	400	
	Maintenance & Repair	950	
	Factory Office	750	
	Wages Payable		16,950
(5)	Factory Overhead, Department A	80	
	Factory Overhead, Department B	60	
	Maintenance & Repair	150	
	Factory Office	65	
	Prepaid Expenses		355
(6)	Factory Overhead, Department A	500	
	Factory Overhead, Department B	900	
	Maintenance & Repair	250	
	Factory Office	150	
	Accumulated Depreciation, Plant Assets		1,800

(7)	Factory Overhead, Department A (400 man-hours)	400	
	Factory Overhead, Department B (600 man-hours)	600	
	Maintenance & Repair (200 man-hours)	200	
	Factory Office		1,200*
	* 235 + 750 + 65 + 150		
(8)	Factory Overhead, Department A (70%)	1,750	
	Factory Overhead, Department B (30%)	750	
	Maintenance & Repair		2,500*
	* 600 + 350 + 950 + 150 + 250 + 200		
(9)	Work in Process, Department A	6,600	
	Work in Process, Department B	4,500	
	Factory Overhead, Department A (80%)		6,600
	Factory Overhead, Department B (75%)		4,500
(10)	Work in Process, Department B	25,850	
	Work in Process, Department A		25,850*
	* 11,000 + 8,250 + 6,600		
(11)	Finished Goods, Cameo Crispies	15,000	
	Finished Goods, Cameo Creamies	30,000	
	Work in Process, Department B		45,000*
	* 8,650 + 6,000 + 4,500 + 25,850		

Allocation of Joint Costs in the Ratio of Sales Values

Joint Product	Units Produced	Unit Sales Price	Sales Value	Ratio	Joint Cost	Unit Cost
Cameo Crispies	1,500	$12	$18,000	1/3	$15,000	$10
Cameo Creamies	2,000	18	36,000	2/3	30,000	15
			$54,000		$45,000	

5.10. The Augusta Dairy had the following data on its books for January 197–:

Inventories, January 1

Raw Materials	$35,000
Work in Process, Materials	12,000
Work in Process, Labor	15,000
Work in Process, Factory Overhead	10,000
Finished Goods	20,000

Transactions During January

Materials Purchased	$90,000
Direct Labor Cost	75,000
Factory Overhead (80% of direct labor cost)	60,000

Inventories, January 31

Raw Materials	$25,000
Work in Process, Materials	20,000
Work in Process, Labor	18,000
Work in Process, Factory Overhead	15,000
Finished Goods	33,000

Prepare "T" accounts showing the flow of cost of goods manufactured and sold. (Use three work in process accounts.)

Finished Goods			
Inv., 1/1	20,000		

Work in Process, Materials			
Inv., 1/1	12,000		

Work in Process, Labor			
Inv., 1/1	15,000		

Work in Process, Factory Overhead			
Inv., 1/1	10,000		

Raw Materials			
Inv., 1/1	35,000		

Cost of Goods Sold

SOLUTION

Finished Goods

Inv., 1/1	20,000	Transf.	206,000	(3)
(2) Transf.	219,000	Inv., 1/31	33,000	
	239,000		239,000	

Work in Process, Materials

Inv., 1/1	12,000	Transf.	92,000	(2)
(1) Transf.	100,000	Inv., 1/31	20,000	
	112,000		112,000	

Work in Process, Labor

Inv., 1/1	15,000	Transf.	72,000	(2)
Incurred	75,000	Inv., 1/31	18,000	
	90,000		90,000	

Work in Process, Factory Overhead

Inv., 1/1	10,000	Transf.	55,000	(2)
Applied	60,000	Inv., 1/31	15,000	
	70,000		70,000	

Raw Materials

Inv., 1/1	35,000	Transf.	100,000	(1)
Purchased	90,000	Inv., 1/31	25,000	
	125,000		125,000	

Cost of Goods Sold

(3) 206,000	

Flow of Costs

(1) Raw Materials to Work in Process

(2) Work in Process to Finished Goods

(3) Finished Goods to Cost of Goods Sold

Chapter 6

Cost Systems

6.1 INTRODUCTION

A *cost system* is a method of accumulating and assigning costs. It is essential that a manufacturing company know quickly the cost of making a product, performing a factory operation, or carrying out any other activity of the business. Decisions of the highest importance depend on the accuracy of the cost data. For example, an understatement in the cost of producing an automobile would result in a lower selling price than warranted and cause losses of perhaps millions of dollars. Trading and service companies, as well, have developed cost systems for their operations.

A good cost system also provides a means of *cost control*. Thus, management can compare cost data with budgets and standards to effectively plan and control all business activities.

In Secs. 6.2 and 6.3 we outline the two principal cost systems. The procedure given in Chapter 5 for the procurement and issue of materials, the compiling of labor costs, and the application of overhead generally applies to both these cost systems. Special procedures for each system will be described as required.

6.2 JOB ORDER COST SYSTEM

Under this system the cost of raw materials, direct labor, and factory overhead are accumulated according to the particular job order or lot number. To arrive at the average unit cost the total cost is divided by the number of completed units.

Generally, the job order cost system is most suitable where the product is made to individual customers' specifications and where the price quoted is closely tied to the cost (for instance, cost plus 15%).

EXAMPLE 1.

The accounting cycle will be completed for the Smith Manufacturing Company, which uses a job order cost system. The company's fiscal year ends December 31. The trial balance at November 30, 197–, is shown below.

Cash	$ 30,000	
Accounts Receivable	31,000	
Finished Goods	25,000	
Work in Process	15,000	
Raw Materials	10,000	
Prepaid Expenses	3,000	
Plant Assets	244,000	
Accumulated Depreciation, Plant Assets		$ 85,000
Accounts Payable		30,000
Wages Payable		16,000
Common Stock		200,000
Retained Earnings		27,000
	$358,000	$358,000

Opening Balances

The inventory details for the above control accounts at November 30 are as follows:

Finished Goods		Work in Process		Raw Materials	
Product M	$12,000	Job #99	$10,000	Material x	$ 5,000
Product N	8,000	Job #100	5,000	Material y	3,000
Product O	5,000			Material z	2,000
	$25,000		$15,000		$10,000

Transactions for the Month

Cost-related transactions for December are summarized below, the general journal entry being given after each transaction. Three jobs are in process — Job #101, Job #102, and Job #103 — and these use Material x, Material y, and Material z, in varying proportions.

(1) Purchases of Materials

Material x	$12,000
Material y	16,000
Material z	3,000
	$31,000

Raw Materials	31,000	
Accounts Payable		31,000

(2) Materials Requisitioned and Placed in Production

Raw materials, $28,000; indirect materials, $2,000

JOB	AMOUNT	MATERIAL	AMOUNT
#101	$ 8,000	x	$10,000
102	14,000	y	15,000
103	6,000	z	3,000
	$28,000		$28,000

Work in Process	28,000	
Factory Overhead	2,000	
Raw Materials		30,000

(3) Payroll for the Period

Direct labor, $50,000; supervision and administration, $15,000

JOB	AMOUNT
#101	$30,000
102	15,000
103	5,000
	$50,000

Work in Process	50,000	
Factory Overhead	15,000	
Wages Payable		65,000

(4) Accounts Payable for Costs Incurred

Factory Overhead	23,000	
Accounts Payable		23,000

(5) Prepaid Expenses Used Up

Factory Overhead	600	
Prepaid Expenses		600

(6) Depreciation for the Period

Factory Overhead	4,000	
Accumulated Depreciation, Plant Assets		4,000

(7) Factory Overhead

Applied at departmental rate of direct labor cost

RATE	JOB	AMOUNT
90%	#101	$27,000
80%	102	12,000
120%	103	6,000
		$45,000

Work in Process	45,000	
Factory Overhead		45,000

(8) Jobs Completed

JOB	AMOUNT	PRODUCT	AMOUNT
# 99	$ 10,000	M	$ 75,000
100	5,000	N	46,000
101	65,000		$121,000
102	41,000		
	$121,000		

Finished Goods	121,000	
Work in Process		121,000

(9) Cost of Goods Sold

PRODUCT	AMOUNT
M	$ 73,000
N	43,000
O	2,000
	$118,000

Cost of Goods Sold	118,000	
Finished Goods		118,000

Ledger Accounts

The opening balances at November 30 and the transactions for December have been posted to the control accounts:

Raw Materials				Work in Process		
Bal. 10,000	28,000 (2)			Bal.	15,000	121,000 (8)
(1) 31,000				(2)	28,000	
41,000				(3)	50,000	
Bal. 13,000				(7)	45,000	
					138,000	
				Bal.	17,000	

Finished Goods

Bal.	25,000		118,000	(9)
(8)	121,000			
	146,000			
Bal.	28,000			

and to the subsidiary ledgers:

MATERIALS LEDGER

Material x

Bal.	5,000		10,000	(2)
(1)	12,000			
	17,000			
Bal.	7,000			

Material y

Bal.	3,000		15,000	(2)
(1)	16,000			
	19,000			
Bal.	4,000			

Material z

Bal.	2,000		3,000	(2)
(1)	3,000			
	5,000			
Bal.	2,000			

COST LEDGER

Job #99

Bal.	10,000		10,000	(8)

Job #100

Bal.	5,000		5,000	(8)

Job #101

(2)	8,000		65,000	(8)
(3)	30,000			
(7)	27,000			
	65,000			

Job #102

(2)	14,000		41,000	(8)
(3)	15,000			
(7)	12,000			
	41,000			

Job. #103

(2)	6,000	
(3)	5,000	
(7)	6,000	
Bal.	17,000	

FINISHED GOODS LEDGER

Product M

Bal.	12,000		73,000	(9)
(8)	75,000			
	87,000			
Bal.	14,000			

Product N

Bal.	8,000		43,000	(9)
(8)	46,000			
	54,000			
Bal.	11,000			

Product O

Bal.	5,000		2,000	(9)
Bal.	3,000			

and to the factory overhead account:

Factory Overhead

(2)	2,000	45,000	(7)
(3)	15,000		
(4)	23,000		
(5)	600		
(6)	4,000		
	44,600	45,000	
	400		
	45,000	Bal. 400	

It is seen that factory overhead was *overapplied* for the month; that is, the estimated overhead ($45,000) exceeded the actual charges ($44,600). The resulting credit balance ($400) will be included in the balance sheet as a liability. Had factory overhead been *underapplied,* there would have been a debit balance which would be shown as a deferred charge on the balance sheet. At the end of the period any amount of underapplied or overapplied overhead would be closed out to Cost of Goods Sold.

Agreement of Subsidiary and Control Accounts

Observe the agreement between the subsidiary ledger balances and the control account balances:

Control Accounts		Subsidiary Ledgers	
Raw Materials	$13,000	Material x	$ 7,000
		Material y	4,000
		Material z	2,000
Work in Process	17,000	Job #103	17,000
Finished Goods	28,000	Product M	14,000
		Product N	11,000
		Product O	3,000

6.3 PROCESS COST SYSTEM

Under this system, the costs are accumulated according to each department or process for a given time period. Thus the average unit departmental cost for a day, week, month, or year is arrived at by dividing the total departmental cost by the number of units (or tons, gallons, etc.) produced in the particular period.

The process cost system is used by manufacturers of goods such as paper and steel, which are produced in large volumes on a continuous basis. Section 6.7 gives a detailed illustration of this system.

6.4 SUPPLEMENTARY COSTING PRACTICES

Either of the following two procedures can be used in conjunction with the job order system or with the process cost system.

STANDARD COSTS

A large number of manufacturers determine representative costs ahead of time and use them to predict actual costs. Special variance accounts are provided to pinpoint the discrepancies between standard and actual. Standard costs, and the related subject of *budgets,* are discussed in Chapter 7.

DIRECT (VARIABLE) COSTING

Under this procedure, only costs which increase in direct proportion to the volume produced become part of the cost of the product. Thus, raw materials costs, direct labor cost, and some items of overhead are included; but items such as rent and administrative salaries, which do not change with the quantity produced, are excluded.

Direct costing brings the cost of goods sold into closer relation with the sales for the period. When full costs — that is, variable plus fixed costs — are used, the average cost per unit goes down as more units are produced. This might suggest higher profits than is the case; actually, a larger portion of the fixed costs is now included in the inventory cost.

6.5 FLOW OF GOODS. EQUIVALENT UNITS

Usually the products for which process costing is employed will have a number of different production operations performed on them. Thus, the goods pass from one department to another and the costs applied to date are maintained in the cost records.

EXAMPLE 2.

The Wamo Manufacturing Company has two departments, a machining department and an assembly department. In the machining department the various parts are cut from steel bars. In the assembly department the parts are secured and bolted to a frame to make up the finished product. Suppose that the parts for 5,000 units were transferred from machining to assembly during the month. The costs for raw materials and for the labor and overhead applied in the machining department amounted to $3.50 per unit.

Work in Process, Assembly Department

5,000 units from Mach. Dept. @ $3.50		17,500	5,000 units to Fin. Goods @ $6.00		30,000
Direct Labor	7,500				
Factory Overhead	5,000	12,500			
		30,000			

The unit cost passed on to Finished Goods is $6.00; it is composed of $3.50 for the machining department and $2.50 = ($7,500 + $5,000)/5,000 for the assembly department. These costs can be compared with the unit costs for other periods and the causes of any differences found.

Example 2 represents a special situation, in that all units received by the assembly department during the month were completed and sent on within that same month. Now, usually, not all the work begun during the period will be finished at the end of the period: there will be an ending inventory of units in various stages of completion. Likewise, there will be an opening inventory of units only partially completed during the previous period. This more general situation is described by the flow equation

UNITS AVAILABLE DURING PERIOD $=$ **UNITS DISPOSED OF DURING PERIOD** (1)

OPENING INVENTORY

+ UNITS PUT INTO PRODUCTION

UNITS TRANSFERRED TO NEXT DEPT.

+ ENDING INVENTORY

When any three terms in the flow equation are known, the missing piece of data can be computed from the equation itself.

EXAMPLE 3.

As in Example 2, 5,000 units are put into production in the assembly department during the month. At the beginning of the month 1,500 units (2/3 completed) were on hand in the assembly department and 1,000 units (3/5 completed) were on hand at the end of the month. How many completed units were transferred to finished goods during the month?

UNITS AVAILABLE $=$ **UNITS DISPOSED OF**

1,500 + 5,000

UNITS TRANSFERRED + 1,000

or,   UNITS TRANSFERRED   =   1,500 + 5,000 − 1,000   =   5,500

To allocate costs when inventories of partially finished goods are involved, we need a common measure for all goods. Therefore, we express both the work in process and the finished goods in terms of completed units known as *equivalent units of production*.

EXAMPLE 4.

    (a) 1,500 units, 2/3 completed, are equivalent to 1,000 completed units.

    (b) 1,000 units, 3/5 completed, are equivalent to 600 completed units.

    (c) An inventory consists of 900 units, 1/3 completed; 600 units, 3/4 completed; and 100 fully completed units. The inventory contains $900 (1/3) + 600 (3/4) + 100 (1) = 850$ equivalent completed units.

EXAMPLE 5.

How many equivalent units were produced during the month by the assembly department in Example 3?

We reason this way: The work done by the department had two and only two effects: (a) it changed the inventory from $1,500 \times 2/3 = 1,000$ equivalent units (opening) to $1,000 \times 3/5 = 600$ equivalent units (ending) and (b) it brought into being $5,500(1) = 5,500$ equivalent units of finished goods. The net increase in equivalent units was thus

$$(600 − 1,000) + 5,500 = 5,100$$

and this must represent the production of the department.

The above reasoning is quite general, and we have analogous to the flow equation (1):

$$\text{EQUIVALENT UNITS OF PRODUCTION} \qquad (2)$$
$$= \text{EQUIVALENT UNITS OF ENDING INVENTORY}$$
$$- \text{EQUIVALENT UNITS OF OPENING INVENTORY}$$
$$+ \text{EQUIVALENT UNITS OF FINISHED GOODS}$$

6.6   FLOW OF COSTS

With all inventories and production reduced to equivalent units, we can calculate unit costs for use in conjunction with FIFO, LIFO, Weighted Average, or some other inventory costing method. It should be emphasized that the number of equivalent units involved is determined solely by the manufacturing process and is quite independent of the choice of costing method.

EXAMPLE 6.   FIFO.

The physical data for the assembly department of the Wamo Manufacturing Company are as in Examples 3 and 5. If FIFO costing is used, the departmental work in process account for the current month appears as follows:

Work in Process, Assembly Department

Opening Inventory (1,500 units,			*Finished Goods (5,500 units)*	25,700
2/3 completed)		4,200	*Ending Inventory (1,000 units,*	
Put Into Production			*3/5 completed)*	3,800
Materials (5,000 units @ $2)		10,000		
Direct Labor	8,500			
Factory Overhead	6,800	15,300		
		29,500		29,500

Let us see how each cost was arrived at.

The number of equivalent units produced in the department has already been calculated in Example 5; it is 5,100. This gives a unit processing cost of $15,300/5,100 = $3. The unit materials cost is $2. Because only assembling is involved, even the uncompleted units will carry the full materials cost. We then have, under FIFO:

Opening Inventory. There were 1,500 units that were 2/3 completed in the previous period and had costs applied of $4,200 at the end of that period.

Put into Production. There were 5,000 new units put into production during the month with a related cost of $25,300. This cost consisted of $10,000 for materials, $8,500 for direct labor, and $6,800 for factory overhead.

Finished Goods. There were 5,500 units of production finished this period and transferred to finished goods, at a total cost of $25,700, as shown below.

	UNITS	SUBTOTAL	AMOUNT
Opening inventory	1,500		
Balance, 2/3 completed		$ 4,200	
Processing cost (500 × $3)		1,500	
			$ 5,700
Started and completed during period	4,000		
Materials cost in period @ $2		$ 8,000	
Processing cost for period @ $3		12,000	
Total (Unit cost: $20,000 ÷ 4,000 = $5)			20,000
Goods finished in period	5,500		$25,700

Ending Inventory. The ending inventory is composed of 1,000 units of materials at $2.00 per unit, or $2,000 (the full materials cost), and 600 equivalent units of processing cost (1,000 units, 3/5 completed) at $3.00 per unit, or $1,800, as shown below.

	UNITS	AMOUNT
Ending inventory	1,000	
Materials cost in period @ $2		$2,000
Processing cost (600 × $3)		1,800
Total	1,000	$3,800

Different costs would be obtained in Example 6 under LIFO or Weighted Average. If LIFO is used, the 5,500 units transferred would be assumed to consist of the 5,000 units put into production during the month and 500 units from the opening inventory.

In the Weighted Average method, the cost of the opening inventory and the cost of goods put into production would be added, and the sum ($29,500) divided by the equivalent units of production (5,100). This would provide the unit cost, which would be applied to *both the goods transferred and the ending inventory.*

6.7 COMPREHENSIVE ILLUSTRATION OF PROCESS COSTS

The Brown Manufacturing Company uses a process cost system for Product X. All materials are placed in production in Department A. A by-product, Product Y, is also obtained in this department. Factory overhead is applied on the basis of direct labor cost, the rate being 90% in Department A and 50% in Department B. There are inventories of work in process *in Department B only.* Maintenance and Power are the two service departments.

The company has a fiscal year ending December 31. Following are the inventory balances on November 30:

Finished Goods, Product X	$ 5,000
Finished Goods, Product Y	400
Work in Process, Department B	9,400
Materials	10,000
	$24,800

The transactions for December are summarized in general journal form below.

(1) Purchases of Materials

Materials	27,500	
Accounts Payable		27,500

(2) Materials Placed in Production

Power Department	500	
Maintenance Department	2,500	
Factory Overhead, Department A	1,500	
Factory Overhead, Department B	1,000	
Work in Process, Department A	20,000	
Materials		25,500

(3) Factory Payroll for the Period

Power Department	950	
Maintenance Department	1,800	
Factory Overhead, Department A	900	
Factory Overhead, Department B	600	
Work in Process, Department A	7,500	
Work in Process, Department B	14,400	
Wages Payable		26,150

(4) Accounts Payable for Costs Incurred

Power Department	100	
Maintenance Department	200	
Factory Overhead, Department A	500	
Factory Overhead, Department B	300	
Accounts Payable		1,100

(5) Prepaid Expenses Used Up

Power Department	150	
Maintenance Department	250	
Factory Overhead, Department A	600	
Factory Overhead, Department B	400	
Prepaid Expenses		1,400

(6) Depreciation for the Period

Power Department	200	
Maintenance Department	400	
Factory Overhead, Department A	700	
Factory Overhead, Department B	1,000	
Accumulated Depreciation, Plant Assets		2,300

(7) Distribution of Power Department Costs to Production Departments Based on Kilowatt-Hours Supplied

Maintenance Department	200	
Factory Overhead, Department A	800	
Factory Overhead, Department B	900	
Power Department		1,900*

* 500 + 950 + 100 + 150 + 200

(8) Distribution of Maintenance Department Costs to Production Departments on the Basis of Maintenance Services Rendered

Factory Overhead, Department A	2,600	
Factory Overhead, Department B	2,750	
Maintenance Department		5,350**

** 2,500 + 1,800 + 200 + 250 + 400 + 200

(9) Factory Overhead Applied

Work in Process, Department A		
(90% of $7,500)	6,750	
Work in Process, Department B		
(50% of $14,400)	7,200	
Factory Overhead, Department A		6,750
Factory Overhead, Department B		7,200

In addition to the entries from the books of original entry, there are entries transferring goods from one department or process to the next, as illustrated below.

(a) Transfer of Production: Department A to Department B

There were 5,000 units of Product X fully processed and transferred to Department B. There were no inventories of Product X in Department A at the beginning or end of the month. There were 3,125 pounds of the by-product, Product Y, produced, which is to be valued at 40¢ a pound. Product Y is considered as finished goods since it will be sold in this form. From the total department cost of $34,250 is to be deducted the by-product cost of $1,250, leaving $33,000 applicable to Product X, as shown below.

Total cost, Department A	$34,250
Less: Product Y	1,250
Cost of Product X transferred	$33,000
Unit cost of Product X transferred	
($33,000 ÷ 5,000)	$6.60

Entry

Work in Process, Department B	33,000	
Finished Goods, Product Y	1,250	
Work in Process, Department A		34,250

(b) Transfer of Production: Department B to Finished Goods

Opening inventory in process in Department B consisted of 1,200 units, 1/3 completed. There were 5,200 units completed during the month, and ending inventory in process was 1,000 units, 3/5 completed.

Equivalent Units of Production

Ending inventory in process (1,000 × 3/5)	600	
Less: Opening inventory in process (1,200 × 1/3)	400	200
Finished goods (5,200 × 1)		5,200
Total equivalent units of production		5,400

Processing Costs

Direct labor **(3)**	$14,400
Factory overhead **(9)** (50%)	7,200
Total processing costs	$21,600
Unit processing cost of product	
transferred to Finished Goods	
($21,600 ÷ 5,400)	$4.00

On the basis of FIFO, costs are allocated to Department B as follows:

Opening Inventory in Process (1,200 units, 1/3 completed)	$ 9,400	
Processing costs in period (800 @ $4.00)	3,200	
Total (Unit cost: $12,600 ÷ 1,200 = $10.50)		$12,600
Started and Completed During Period		
From Department A (4,000 @ $6.60)	$26,400	
Processing costs (4,000 @ $4.00)	16,000	
Total (Unit cost: $42,400 ÷ 4,000 = $10.60)		$42,400
Total transferred to Finished Goods		$55,000
Ending Inventory in Process		
From Department A (1,000 @ $6.60)	$ 6,600	
Processing costs (600 @ $4.00)	2,400	
Total work in process (3/5 completed)		$ 9,000
Total costs charged to Department B		$64,000

Entry	*Finished Goods, Product X*	55,000	
	Work in Process, Department B		55,000

(c) Cost of Goods Sold

The opening inventory of Finished Goods, Product X was 500 units (unit cost: $5,000 ÷ 500 = $10.00) and there were 5,200 units of Product X completed during the month. Of the total of 5,700 units, 4,700 were shipped out. Costing under FIFO is as follows:

Product X (4,700 units)		
500 units @ 10.00	$ 5,000	
1,200 units @ $10.50	12,600	
3,000 units @ $10.60	31,800	
Total cost of Product X sold		$49,400
Product Y (2,625 pounds @ $ .40)		1,050
Total cost of goods sold		$50,450

Entry	*Cost of Goods Sold*	50,450	
	Finished Goods, Product X		49,400
	Finished Goods, Product Y		1,050

The net underapplied factory overhead, $600 ($850 − $250), will be shown as part of deferred charges.

The balances in the inventory accounts at December 31 are:

Finished Goods, Product X	$10,600
Finished Goods, Product Y	600
Work in Process, Department B	9,000
Materials	10,000
	$32,200

FLOW OF COSTS — PROCESS COST ACCOUNTS

Work in Process, Department A

(2)	20,000	34,250	(a)
(3)	7,500		
(9)	6,750		
	34,250		
Bal.	0		

Work in Process, Department B

Bal.	9,400	55,000	(b)
(3)	14,400		
(9)	7,200		
(a)	33,000		
	64,000		
Bal.	9,000		

Finished Goods, Product X

Bal.	5,000	49,400	(c)
(b)	55,000		
	60,000		
Bal.	10,600		

Finished Goods, Product Y

Bal.	400	1,050	(c)
(a)	1,250		
	1,650		
Bal.	600		

Factory Overhead, Department A

(2)	1,500	6,750	(9)
(3)	900		
(4)	500		
(5)	600		
(6)	700		
(7)	800		
(8)	2,600		
	7,600		
Bal.	850		

Factory Overhead, Department B

(2)	1,000	7,200	(a)
(3)	600		
(4)	300		
(5)	400		
(6)	1,000		
(7)	900		
(8)	2,750		
	6,950	Bal. 250	

Maintenance Department

(2)	2,500	5,350	(8)
(3)	1,800		
(4)	200		
(5)	250		
(6)	400		
(7)	200		
	5,350		

Power Department

(2)	500	1,900	(7)
(3)	950		
(4)	100		
(5)	150		
(6)	200		
	1,900		

Summary

(1) The job order cost system is most suitable if the product is _____.

(2) For which of the following would a job order cost system be best: a steel mill, a printing shop, a flour mill? _____.

(3) For the data below, the cost of materials issued to production under the first-in-first-out method is $ _____.

Beginning balance	300 units at $2.00
Purchases	400 units at $2.25
Issued to production	200 units

(4) For the data in (3) above, the cost of materials issued to production under the last-in-first-out method is $ _____.

(5) Under the job order cost system the costs are accumulated according to _____.

(6) Under the job order cost system the unit cost is determined by dividing the _____ _____ by the _____.

(7) The process cost system is most suitable where the product is _____.

(8) Under the process cost system the costs are accumulated according to _____ _____.

(9) The number of equivalent units of production equals the number of _____ for a processing department in which there is no work in process at the beginning or end of the period.

(10) Under the process cost system goods are transferred from production departments to _____.

Answers: (1) custom-made; (2) printing shop; (3) 400; (4) 450; (5) job orders; (6) cost of the job, number of completed units; (7) mass-produced; (8) departments or processes; (9) completed units; (10) finished goods

Solved Problems

6.1. The Nostrand Company has the following entries on its books relating to material x for July 197–.

Balance

July 1:   300 units at $8

Received during July

July 3:   300 units at $8
July 15:   500 units at $9
July 24:   400 units at $10

Issued during July

July 7:   200 units for Job #151
July 17:   300 units for Job #153
July 28:   450 units for Job #156

Compute the cost of each of the issues using (*a*) FIFO, (*b*) LIFO.

(a)

_____
_____
_____
_____
_____
_____

(b)

_____
_____
_____
_____
_____
_____

SOLUTION

(a)	July 7:	200 @ $8		$1,600
	July 17:	300 @ $8		$2,400
	July 28:	100 @ $8	$ 800	
		350 @ $9	3,150	$3,950

(b)	July 7:	200 units @ $10		$2,000
	July 17:	200 units @ $10	$2,000	
		100 units @ $9	900	$2,900
	July 28:	400 units @ $9	$3,600	
		50 units @ $8	400	$4,000

6.2. The Hebb Manufacturing Company has the following estimated costs for the current year:

	Department A	Department B
Estimated direct labor cost	$60,000	$48,000
Estimated factory overhead cost	75,000	....
Estimated machine hours	....	24,000

Factory overhead is applied to jobs on the basis of direct labor dollars in Department A and on machine hours in Department B. Departmental accounts are kept for work in process and factory overhead. Following are the actual costs for March.

	Department A	Department B
Actual direct labor cost	$5,500	....
Actual factory overhead cost	7,000	$3,600
Actual machine hours	....	2,000

(a) Compute the factory overhead rate for each department.

(b) Prepare the general journal entries to apply overhead to March production.

(c) Determine the departmental factory overhead balances and show whether they are underapplied or overapplied as of March 31.

(a)

_____
_____

(b)

_____
_____
_____
_____

(c)

			Balance	
	Actual	Standard	Underapplied	Overapplied
Department A				
Department B				

SOLUTION

(a)

Department A:	$75,000 ÷ $60,000 = 125% of direct labor cost
Department B:	$48,000 ÷ $24,000 = $2 per machine hour

(b)

Work in Process, Department A	6,875	
Factory Overhead, Department A ($5,500 × 125%)		6,875
Work in Process, Department B	4,000	
Factory Overhead, Department B ($2 × 2,000)		4,000

(c)

			Balance	
	Actual	Standard	Underapplied	Overapplied
Department A	7,000	6,875	125	
Department B	3,600	4,000		400

6.3. The Hayden Manufacturing Company has the following entries for the month of May:

Work in Process

Bal., May 1	*19,400*
Direct Materials	*37,300*
Direct Labor	*25,000*
Factory Overhead	*20,000*

The following jobs were completed during May: Job #210, $15,600; Job #215, $28,300; Job #217, $27,400; Job #220, $13,800. (a) Show the general journal entry for the jobs completed. (b) Determine the amount applicable to uncompleted jobs at May 31.

(a)

(b)

SOLUTION

(a)

Finished Goods	85,100	
Work in Process		85,100

(b)

Balance, May 1	$ 19,400
Add: Direct materials	37,300
Direct labor	25,000
Factory overhead	20,000
	$101,700
Less: Jobs finished during May	85,100
Balance of Work in Process, May 31	$ 16,600

6.4. The Klussman Manufacturing Company produces special equipment made to customer specifications. Below is the data for Job #86.

Description: 20 pattern cutters, Style B

Date started: September 1

Date promised: September 15

Materials Used, Department 1	$4,800
Direct Labor Rate, Department 1	$4.20 per hour
Labor Hours Used, Department 1	1,200
Direct Labor Rate, Department 2	$2.00 per hour
Labor Hours Used, Department 2	300
Machine Hours, Department 2	400
Applied Factory Overhead, Department 1	$4.00 per labor hour
Applied Factory Overhead, Department 2	$1.80 per machine hour

Compute (a) the cost for Job #86, (b) the cost per unit.

(a)

	Department 1	Department 2	Total

(b)

SOLUTION

(a)

	Department 1	Department 2	Total
Materials	$ 4,800		$ 4,800
Direct labor			
Department 1 ($4.20 × 1,200)	5,040		5,040
Department 2 ($2.00 × 300)		$ 600	600
Factory overhead			
Department 1 ($4.00 × 1,200)	4,800		4,800
Department 2 ($1.80 × 400)		720	720
Total	$14,640	$1,320	$15,960

(b)   Cost per unit: $15,960 ÷ 20 = $798

6.5. The Plastine Manufacturing Corporation, which produces special plastic compounds, uses a job order cost system. Subsidiary ledger balances on October 31, the end of the first month of the current fiscal year, were as follows.

Finished Goods Subsidiary Ledger

Polyester (500 lbs.), $2,500; Epoxy (6,000 lbs.), $30,000; Urethane (3,000 lbs.), $12,000

Work in Process Subsidiary Ledger

Job #690, $8,600; Job #691, $11,400

Raw Materials Subsidiary Ledger

Petroleum Resin, $25,250; Benzine, $12,050; Lubricating Grease, $5,000

The corporation's trial balance as of October 31 was:

Cash	$148,300	
Accounts Receivable	140,000	
Materials Inventory	42,300	
Work in Process Inventory	20,000	
Finished Goods Inventory	44,500	
Prepaid Insurance	5,000	
Plant and Equipment	170,080	
Accounts Payable		$ 54,260
Accrued Wages Payable		10,600
Accumulated Depreciation, Plant and Equipment		115,210
Capital Stock		250,000
Retained Earnings		120,300
Sales		108,100
Cost of Goods Sold	72,000	
Factory Overhead		410
Marketing and Administrative Expenses	16,700	
	$658,880	$658,880

The following transactions took place during November.

(1) Materials purchased on account: petroleum resin, $17,300; benzine, $8,400; lubricating grease, $3,500

(2) Materials issued during the month

Job #690:	petroleum resin, $11,300; benzine, $6,300	$17,600
Job #691:	petroleum resin, $7,000; benzine, $4,700	11,700
Job #692:	petroleum resin, $4,400; benzine, $2,100	6,500

Supplies issued to factory

Lubricating grease   740

(3) Payroll for the month: Job #690, $12,400; Job #691, $9,900; Job #692, $4,300; Indirect Labor, $3,300

(4) Factory overhead expenses of $20,600 were incurred on account

(5) Insurance of $850 expired on the prepaid insurance account

(6) Marketing and administrative expenses of $17,300 were incurred on account

(7) Factory payroll checks amounting to $34,600 were distributed

(8) Payments of accounts payable totaled $64,300

(9) Depreciation for the month on plant and equipment was $1,500

(10) Factory overhead is charged to production jobs at 100% of direct labor cost

(11) Jobs finished during the month: Job #690, 10,000 lbs. of polyester; Job #691, 8,500 lbs. of epoxy

(12) Sales on account were $120,000, covering 9,000 lbs. of polyester @ $7.67, 5,500 lbs. of epoxy @ $7.50, and 1,620 lbs. of urethane @ $6.00. FIFO is used to compute cost of goods sold

(a) Set up general ledger "T" accounts, and subsidiary "T" accounts for Work in Process, Finished Goods, and Materials. Insert opening dollar balances and include quantities in the finished goods ledger. Prepare general journal entries for the month of November. Post to general ledger "T" accounts and subsidiary ledger "T" accounts, using numbers 1–12 to identify transactions.

(b) Check the general ledger account balances with appropriate balances in the subsidiary ledgers.

(*c*) Prepare a trial balance as of November 30.

(*a*) ## GENERAL LEDGER

Cash	Accounts Payable

Accounts Receivable	
	Accrued Wages Payable

Materials Inventory	
	Capital Stock

Work in Process Inventory	Retained Earnings
	Sales

Finished Goods Inventory	
	Cost of Goods Sold

Prepaid Insurance	Factory Overhead

Plant and Equipment	

Accumulated Deprec., Plant and Equip.	Marketing and Administrative Exp.

FINISHED GOODS LEDGER

Polyester	*Urethane*

| *Epoxy* |

WORK IN PROCESS LEDGER

| *Job #690* | *Job #692* |

| *Job #691* |

MATERIALS LEDGER

| *Petroleum Resin* | *Lubricating Grease* |

| *Benzine* |

(1)		
(2)		
(3)		
(4)		
(5)		
(6)		

(7)		
(8)		
(9)		
(10)		
(11)		
(12)		

(b)

Finished Goods Ledger

Work in Process Ledger

Materials Ledger

(c)

SOLUTION

(a)　　　　　　　　　　　　　　　**GENERAL LEDGER**

Cash		
Bal. 148,300	34,600	(7)
Bal. 49,400	64,300	(8)
	98,900	

Accounts Receivable	
Bal. 140,000	
(12) 120,000	
Bal. 260,000	

Materials Inventory		
Bal. 42,300	36,540	(2)
(1) 29,200		
71,500		
Bal. 34,960		

Work in Process Inventory		
Bal. 20,000	93,900	(11)
(2) 35,800		
(3) 26,600		
(10) 26,600		
109,000		
Bal. 15,100		

Finished Goods Inventory		
Bal. 44,500	79,830	(12)
(11) 93,900		
138,400		
Bal. 58,570		

Prepaid Insurance		
Bal. 5,000	850	(5)
Bal. 4,150		

Plant and Equipment	
Bal. 170,080	

Accumulated Deprec., Plant and Equip.		
	Bal. 115,210	
	1,500	(9)
	Bal. 116,710	

Accounts Payable		
(8) 64,300	Bal. 54,260	
	29,200	(1)
	20,600	(4)
	17,300	(6)
	121,360	
	Bal. 57,060	

Accrued Wages Payable		
(7) 34,600	Bal. 10,600	
	29,900	(3)
	40,500	
	Bal. 5,900	

Capital Stock	
	Bal. 250,000

Retained Earnings	
	Bal. 120,300

Sales		
	Bal. 108,100	
	120,000	(12)
	Bal. 228,100	

Cost of Goods Sold	
Bal. 72,000	
(12) 79,830	
Bal. 151,830	

Factory Overhead		
(2) 740	Bal. 410	
(3) 3,300	26,600	(10)
(4) 20,600	27,010	
(5) 850	Bal. 20	
(9) 1,500		
26,990		

Marketing and Administrative Exp.	
Bal. 16,700	
(6) 17,300	
Bal. 34,000	

FINISHED GOODS LEDGER

Polyester	Urethane
Bal. 500 lbs. 2,500	9,000 lbs. 45,850 **(12)**	Bal. 3,000 lbs. 12,000	1,620 lbs. 6,480 **(12)**
(11) 10,000 lbs. 51,000			

Epoxy
Bal. 6,000 lbs. 30,000	5,500 lbs. 27,500 **(12)**
(11) 8,500 lbs. 42,900	

WORK IN PROCESS LEDGER

Job #690	Job #692
Bal. 8,600	51,000 **(11)**	**(2)** 6,500	
(2) 17,600		**(3)** 4,300	
(3) 12,400		**(10)** 4,300	
(10) 12,400			
51,000	51,000		

Job #691
Bal. 11,400	42,900 **(11)**
(2) 11,700	
(3) 9,900	
(10) 9,900	
42,900	42,900

MATERIALS LEDGER

Petroleum Resin	Lubricating Grease
Bal. 25,250	22,700 **(2)**	Bal. 5,000	740 **(2)**
(1) 17,300		**(1)** 3,500	

Benzine
Bal. 12,050	13,100 **(2)**
(1) 8,400	

(1)	Materials	29,200	
	Accounts Payable		29,200
(2)	Work in Process	35,800	
	Factory Overhead	740	
	Materials Inventory		36,540
(3)	Work in Process	26,600	
	Factory Overhead	3,300	
	Accrued Wages Payable		29,900
(4)	Factory Overhead	20,600	
	Accounts Payable		20,600
(5)	Factory Overhead	850	
	Prepaid Insurance		850
(6)	Marketing and Administrative Expenses	17,300	
	Accounts Payable		17,300

(7)	Accrued Wages Payable		34,600	
	Cash			34,600
(8)	Accounts Payable		64,300	
	Cash			64,300
(9)	Factory Overhead		1,500	
	Accumulated Depreciation, Plant and Equipment			1,500
(10)	Work in Process (100% of Direct Labor)		26,600	
	Factory Overhead Applied			26,600
(11)	Finished Goods		93,900*	
	Work in Process			93,900
	*Job #690: $51,000			
	Job #691: $42,900			
(12)	Accounts Receivable		120,000	
	Sales			120,000
	Cost of Goods Sold		79,830*	
	Finished Goods			79,830
	* Polyester (9,000 lbs.)	$45,850		
	Epoxy (5,500 lbs.)	27,500		
	Urethane (1,620 lbs.)	6,480		
		$79,830		

(b)

Finished Goods Ledger

Polyester	$ 7,650
Epoxy	45,400
Urethane	5,520
	$58,570

Balance in control account is $58,570.

Work In Process Ledger

Job #692	$15,100

Balance in control account is $15,100.

Materials Ledger

Petroleum Resin	$19,850
Benzine	7,350
Lubricating Grease	7,760
	$34,960

Balance in control account is $34,960.

(c)

Cash	$ 49,400	
Accounts Receivable	260,000	
Materials Inventory	34,960	
Work in Process Inventory	15,100	
Finished Goods Inventory	58,570	
Prepaid Insurance	4,150	
Plant and Equipment	170,080	
Accounts Payable		$ 57,060

(continued next page)

Accrued Wages Payable		5,900
Accumulated Depreciation, Plant and Equipment		116,710
Capital Stock		250,000
Retained Earnings		120,300
Sales		228,100
Cost of Goods Sold	151,830	
Factory Overhead		20
Marketing and Administrative Expenses	34,000	
	$778,090	$778,090

6.6. The Hankinson Company manufactures one product which passes through three production departments by a continuous process. For the month of July, $46,500 of direct materials were issued and $85,600 of direct labor cost was incurred in Department A. The factory overhead rate is 75% of direct labor cost. The work in process in Department A was $26,200 at the beginning of the month and $22,400 at the end of the month. Prepare journal entries to show (a) the costs put into production for the month, and (b) the transfer of production costs to Department B.

(a)

(b)

SOLUTION

(a)

Work in Process, Department A	46,500	
Materials		46,500
Work in Process, Department A	85,600	
Wages Payable		85,600
Work in Process, Department A	64,200	
Factory Overhead, Department A		64,200

(b)

Work in Process, Department B	200,100	
Work in Process, Department A		200,100*

* 26,200 (beginning inventory) + 196,300 (production cost) − 22,400 (ending inventory)

6.7. The Farnell Company has the following entries at December 31.

Work in Process, Department A

2,000 units, 75% completed	17,400	To Department B (5,000 units)	64,800
Direct Materials (3,000 units @ $6)	18,000		
Direct Labor	19,600		
Factory Overhead	9,800		
	64,800		64,800

All direct materials are put into production at the beginning of the process. Compute (*a*) equivalent units of production, (*b*) processing cost per equivalent unit of production, (*c*) total and unit cost of product started in prior period and completed in current period, (*d*) total and unit cost of product started and completed in current period.

(*a*)

(*b*)

(*c*)

(*d*)

SOLUTION

(*a*)

Ending inventory in process	0	
Less: Opening inventory in process (2,000 units × 75%)	1,500	− 1,500
Finished goods (5,000 × 1)		5,000
Total equivalent units of production		3,500

(*b*)

Direct labor	$19,600
Factory overhead	9,800
Total processing costs	$29,400
Processing cost per equivalent	
unit of production ($29,400 ÷ 3,500)	$8.40

(*c*)

Costs in prior period (2,000 units, 75% completed)	$17,400
Processing costs in current period (500 @ $8.40)	4,200
Total cost	$21,600
Unit cost ($21,600 ÷ 2,000)	$10.80

(*d*)

Direct materials (3,000 units @ $6.00)	$18,000
Processing costs (3,000 units @ $8.40)	25,200
Total cost	$43,200
Unit cost ($43,200 ÷ 3,000)	$14.40

6.8. The R. Strauss Company has the following expenditures for the Assembly Department for the month of June: Work in Process Inventory, June 1 (2,500 units, 1/2 completed), $15,000; Materials from Machining Department (7,500 units), $60,000; Direct Labor, $18,375; Factory Overhead, $11,025. During June, 6,500 units of finished goods were assembled, and the work in process inventory on July 1 consisted of 3,500 units, 3/5 completed.   Prepare a cost of production report for the Assembly Department for the month of June.

R. Strauss Company

Cost of Production, Assembly Department

month of June, 197—

Quantities

Units Accounted For

Equivalent Units of Production

Costs

Allocation of Costs

SOLUTION

R. Strauss Company
Cost of Production, Assembly Department
month of June, 197—

Quantities		
Work in Process Inventory, June 1		2,500
Received from Machining Department		7,500
Total Units to be Accounted For		10,000

Units Accounted For		
Transferred to Finished Goods		6,500
Work in Process Inventory, July 1		3,500
Total Units Accounted For		10,000

Equivalent Units of Production		
Ending Inventory in Process (3,500 × 3/5)	2,100	
Less: Opening Inventory in Process (2,500 × 1/2)	1,250	850
Finished Goods (6,500 × 1)		6,500
Total Equivalent Units of Production		7,350

Costs		
Work in Process Inventory, June 1		$ 15,000
Materials from Machining Department (7,500 units @ $8)		60,000
Processing Costs		
Direct Labor	18,375	
Factory Overhead	11,025	
Total Processing Costs		
(unit cost: $29,400 ÷ 7,350 = $4)		29,400
Total Cost to be Accounted For		$104,400

Allocation of Costs		
Transferred to Finished Goods		
2,500 units ($15,000 + 2,500 × 1/2 × $4)	$20,000	
4,000 units @ $8 + $4 = $12	48,000	
Total Cost of Completed Units		$ 68,000
Work in Process Inventory, July 1		
Direct Materials (3,500 units @ $8)	$28,000	
Processing Costs (3,500 × 3/5 × $4)	8,400	36,400
Total Cost Accounted For		$104,400

6.9. Karl Gurken has recently patented a new machine for skinning cucumbers, which he calls Model SK-74. In the manufacture of this device all materials are introduced at the beginning of the process, and after passing through Department A and Department B, Model SK-74 is complete. On January 31, a report from Department B showed the following information:

Work in Process Inventory, Jan. 1 (1,200 units, 2/3 completed)	$19,560
Finished Goods Inventory, Jan. 1 (1,000 units @ $18)	18,000
Direct Materials in January (1,600 units @ $12.50)	20,000
Direct Labor in January	6,290
Factory Overhead in January	5,950

Work in Process Inventory, Jan. 31 (800 units, 5/8 completed)

Finished Goods Inventory, Jan. 31 (350 units)

The report went on further to show that a total of 2,000 units were transferred from work in process to finished goods. Sales of 2,650 units were reported.

(a) For Department B, calculate: (1) the equivalent units of production for January, (2) the processing cost per unit for January, (3) the total cost of production of completed units of Model SK-74, (4) Work in Process Inventory at January 31, (5) Cost of Goods Sold, (6) Finished Goods Inventory at January 31. (Use FIFO costing.)

(b) Prepare a cost of production report.

(a)   (1)

(2)

(3)

(4)

(5)

(6)

Model SK-74
Cost of Production, Department B
month ended January 31, 197—

Units

Costs

SOLUTION

(a)

(1)	Ending inventory in process (800 × 5/8)		500		
	Less: Opening inventory in process (1,200 × 2/3)		800	− 300	
	Finished goods (2,000 × 1)			2,000	
	Total equivalent units of production			1,700	

(2)	Direct labor	$ 6,290
	Factory overhead	5,950
		$12,240 ÷ 1,700 units = $7.20 per unit

(3)	1,200 units		
	2/3 completed on Jan. 1	$19,560	
	Cost to complete in Jan. (1,200 × 1/3 × $7.20)	2,880	
	Total (unit cost: $22,440 ÷ 1,200 = $18.70)		$22,440
	800 units		
	Materials in January (800 × $12.50)	$10,000	
	Cost to complete in Jan. (800 × $7.20)	5,760	
	Total (unit cost: $15,760 ÷ 800 = $19.70)		15,760
	Total cost of completed units		$38,200

(4)	800 units		
	Materials in January (800 × $12.50)	$10,000	
	Cost to partially complete in		
	January (5/8 × 800 × $7.20)	3,600	
	Work in Process Inventory, Jan. 31		$13,600

(5)	1,000 units @ $18.00	=	$18,000
	1,200 units @ $18.70	=	22,440
	450 units @ $19.70	=	8,865
	2,650 units sold		$49,305

(6)   Finished Goods Inventory, Jan. 31 (350 units @ $19.70) $6,895

(b)

Model SK-74
Cost of Production, Department B
month ended January 31, 197—

Units

Work in Process Inventory, Jan. 1	1,200
Transferred into Department	1,600
Units to be Accounted For	2,800
Transferred to Finished Goods	2,000
Work in Process Inventory, Jan. 31	800
Units Accounted For	2,800

Costs

Work in Process Inventory, Jan. 1		$19,560
Materials into Department		20,000
Direct Labor		6,290
Factory Overhead		5,950
Total Cost to be Accounted For		$51,800
Transferred to Finished Goods		
1,200 units @ $18.70	$22,440	
800 units @ $19.70	15,760	$38,200
Work in Process Inventory, Jan. 31		
800 units materials @ $12.50	$10,000	
800 units, 5/8 completed, @ $7.20	3,600	13,600
Total Cost Accounted For		$51,800

6.10. The Martin Manufacturing Company uses a process cost system for Product N, which requires four processes. The Work in Process, Department 4 shows the following entries for May:

Balance, May 1 (1,600 units, 1/4 completed)	$ 4,060
From Department 3 (4,300 units)	7,525
Direct Labor	12,250
Factory Overhead	3,185

Processing for the month of May consisted in completing the 1,600 units in process on May 1, completing the processing on 3,500 additional units, and leaving 800 units that are 1/4 completed. During June the charges to Work in Process, Department 4 were:

From Department 3 (5,500 units)	$ 8,250
Direct Labor	11,760
Factory Overhead	2,940

By June 30, all beginning Work in Process units were completed and of the 5,500 new units, 1,500 were left only 1/5 completed.

(a) Prepare a work in process account for Department 4, beginning with the May 1 balance and working through to the beginning balances for July.

(*b*) Show supporting computations for both months; namely, the determination of the equivalent units, the processing costs per unit, costs of goods completed and available for transfer to finished goods, and the Work in Process Inventory.

(*a*)

Work in Process, Department 4

May	*May*

Work in Process, Department 4

June	*June*

(*b*) **Equivalent Production for May**

Unit Processing Cost for May

Cost of Goods Finished in May

Work in Process, May 31

Equivalent Production for June

Unit Processing Cost for June

Cost of Goods Finished in June

Work in Process, June 30

SOLUTION

Work in Process, Department 4

May			May		
Bal. (1,600 units, 1/4 completed)	4,060		1,600 units completed	7,840	
4,300 units from Dept. 3	7,525		3,500 units completed	17,150	
Direct Labor	12,250		800 units, 1/4 completed	2,030	
Factory Overhead	3,185				
	27,020			27,020	

Work in Process, Department 4

June			June		
Bal. (800 units, 1/4 completed)	2,030		800 units completed	3,830	
5,500 units introduced to system	8,250		4,000 units completed	18,000	
Direct Labor	11,760		Bal. (1,500 units, 1/5 completed)	3,150	
Factory Overhead	2,940				
	24,980			24,980	
July 1					
Bal. (1,500 units, 1/5 completed)	3,150				

Equivalent Production for May

To complete May 1 inventory (1,600 × 3/4)	1,200
Started and completed during May	3,500
To partially complete units remaining on May 31 (800 × 1/4)	200
Equivalent units of production	4,900

Unit Processing Cost for May

$$(\$12{,}250 + \$3{,}185) \div 4{,}900 \;=\; \$3.15$$

Cost of Goods Finished in May

1,600 units		
1/4 completed at May 1	$ 4,060	
Cost to complete in May (1,600 × 3/4 × $3.15)	3,780	
Total (unit cost: $7,840 ÷ 1,600 = $4.90)		$ 7,840
3,500 units		
Past costs (3,500 × $1.75)	$ 6,125	
Cost applied in May (3,500 × $3.15)	11,025	
Total (unit cost: $17,150 ÷ 3,500 = $5.02)		17,150
Cost of goods finished in May		$24,990

Work in Process, May 31

800 units		
Past costs (800 × $1.75)	$ 1,400	
Cost to partially complete in May (800 × 1/4 × $3.15)	630	$ 2,030

Equivalent Production for June

To complete June 1 inventory (800 × 3/4)	600
Started and completed during June	4,000
To partially complete units remaining on June 30	
(1,500 × 1/5)	300
Equivalent units of production	4,900

Unit Processing Cost for June

$$(\$11{,}760 + \$2{,}940) \div 4{,}900 \;=\; \$3.00$$

Cost of Goods Finished in June

800 units		
1/4 completed at June 1	$ 2,030	
Cost to complete in June (800 × 3/4 × $3.00)	1,800	
Total (unit cost: $3,830 ÷ 800 = $4.79)		$ 3,830
4,000 units		
Past costs (4,000 × $1.50)	$ 6,000	
Cost applied in June (4,000 × $3.00)	12,000	
Total (unit cost: $18,000 ÷ 4,000 = $4.50)		18,000
Cost of goods finished in June		$21,830

Work in Process, June 30

1,500 units		
Past costs (1,500 × $1.50)	$ 2,250	
Cost to partially complete in June (1,500 × 1/5 × $3.00)	900	$ 3,150

Chapter 7

Budgets and Standard Costs

7.1 NATURE OF BUDGETING

A *budget* is a quantitative projection of business operations. It helps management (1) to set specific objectives and (2) to assure that actual operations conform to the established plan.

The budget preparation varies somewhat among companies, but there are a number of budget statements and forms that have become standardized and in general use. These may be grouped under *master budgets, income and expense budgets* (*operating budgets*), and *balance sheet budgets* (*financial budgets*).

7.2 THE MASTER BUDGET

The master budget is the overall, coordinated plan for all the budgets and is usually the responsibility of a special budget officer or budget department. The various income and expense budgets and balance sheet budgets are subsidiary parts of the master budget, as indicated below:

MASTER BUDGET

BUDGETED INCOME STATEMENT	BUDGETED BALANCE SHEET
Sales Budget	Cash Budget
Cost of Goods Sold Budget	Capital Expenditures Budget
Production Budget	
Materials Purchases Budget	
Direct Labor Budget	
Factory Overhead Budget	
Operating Expenses Budget	
Selling Expenses Budget	
General Expenses Budget	

The various components of the master budget are discussed under Secs. 7.3 and 7.4.

Generally, the sequence of procedures in preparing the master budget is: (1) develop objectives and long-range goals; (2) project sales for the period; (3) estimate operating costs (that is, cost of goods sold and operating expenses); (4) estimate the asset, liability, and equity accounts after giving effect to the projected income and expense budgets; (5) prepare an overall budget, including a projected income statement and a projected balance sheet with supporting component budgets.

7.3 BUDGETED INCOME STATEMENT

The budgeted income statement summarizes the various component projections of income and expense, usually for the coming fiscal year. However, for control purposes the budget is commonly divided into quarters, or even months or weeks, depending on the need. Many companies use a *moving budget,* or *continuous budget,* that shows four quarters or twelve months ahead at all times.

EXAMPLE 1.

Bollett Company
Budgeted Income Statement
year ending December 31, 19–

Sales		$879,200
Cost of Goods Sold		602,700
Gross Profit		$276,500
Operating Expenses		
Selling Expenses	$65,000	
General Expenses	57,500	122,500
Net Income Before Taxes		$154,000
Provision for Income Taxes		74,000
Net Income		$ 80,000

SALES BUDGET

The first budget to be prepared is usually the sales budget, since most other budgets will depend on the results of this projection.   The sales budget begins with the estimated quantity of each product to be sold, broken down further by area and by salesman.   The estimates of quantity are based on past experience adjusted for expected changes in general business conditions, industry trends, etc.   The quantities are extended by the unit price to arrive at the sales amount.

EXAMPLE 2.

The sales figure in Example 1 is arrived at as follows.

Bollett Company
Sales Budget
year ending December 31, 19–

	Quantity	Amount
Product A (unit price, $9)		
Area 1	30,200	$271,800
Area 2	20,600	185,400
Area 3	15,500	139,500
Total		$596,700
Product B (unit price, $5)		
Area 1	25,500	$127,500
Area 2	18,600	93,000
Area 3	12,400	62,000
Total		$282,500
Total Sales		$879,200

The actual sales for each area can be shown in relation to the budgeted sales.   Any significant variances between budget and actual can be investigated and any needed corrective action taken.

COST OF GOODS SOLD BUDGET

The various supporting budgets, such as those for production, materials purchases, direct labor, and factory overhead, are used in developing the cost of goods sold budget.

EXAMPLE 3.

Bollett Company
Cost of Goods Sold Budget
year ending December 31, 19–

Finished Goods Inventory, January 1			$ 85,600
Work in Process Inventory, January 1		$ 6,500	
Direct Materials Used			
Inventory, January 1	$ 25,900		
Materials Purchases	133,600		
Available for Use	$159,500		
Less: Budgeted Inventory, December 31	18,000		
Direct Materials Used	$141,500		
Direct Labor	233,200		
Factory Overhead	215,400		
Manufacturing Cost		590,100	
Total Work in Process During Period		$596,600	
Less: Work in Process, December 31		8,200	
Cost of Goods Manufactured			588,400
Finished Goods Available for Sale			$674,000
Less: Finished Goods Inventory, December 31			71,300
Cost of Goods Sold			$602,700

Production budget.   To meet the requirements of the sales and inventory projections it is necessary to determine the number of units of each product to be produced. This is done by adding the desired closing inventory to the projected sales quantity and subtracting from that sum the opening inventory quantity (see Example 4).

EXAMPLE 4.

From Example 2 the budgeted sales of products A and B are 66,300 units and 56,500 units, respectively.

Bollett Company
Production Budget
year ending December 31, 19–

	Units of A	Units of B
Sales	66,300	56,500
Desired Ending Inventory	10,200	8,000
	76,500	64,500
Less: Opening Inventory	9,500	8,000
Production Units Required	67,000	56,500

Materials purchases budget.   The amount of raw materials to be purchased depends on the production budget and the desired inventory amounts. The required production plus the desired ending inventory, less the opening inventory, equals the purchases required.

EXAMPLE 5.

Bollett Company's two products have the following compositions:

Product (1 unit)	Units of Material		
	x	y	z
A	1	2	0
B	1	1	1

From the production budget (Example 4), 67,000 units of A and 56,500 units of B are to be produced.

Bollett Company
Materials Purchases Budget
year ending December 31, 19–

	Units of x	Units of y	Units of z
Production			
Product A (67,000 units)	67,000	134,000	....
Product B (56,500 units)	56,500	56,500	56,500
	123,500	190,500	56,500
Desired Ending Inventory	15,000	25,000	7,000
	138,500	215,500	63,500
Less: Opening Inventory	23,000	35,000	10,000
Units to be Purchased	115,500	180,500	53,500
Unit Price	× $ .30	× $ .40	× $ .50
Materials Purchases	$34,650	$72,200	$26,750

It is seen that the total materials purchases for the three ingredients is $133,600. This amount is reflected in the cost of goods sold budget (Example 3).

Direct labor budget. The direct labor cost is calculated as the number of hours required to accomplish the budgeted production times the hourly labor rate.

EXAMPLE 6.

Assume that products A and B of the Bollett Company are produced in two departments, according to the following schedule:

Product (1 unit)	Hours in Department	
	#1	#2
A	.2	.3
B	.1	.2

Bollett Company
Direct Labor Budget
year ending December 31, 19–

	Department #1	Department #2
Hours Required		
Product A (67,000 units)	13,400	20,100
Product B (56,500 units)	5,650	11,300
Total	19,050	31,400
Hourly Rate	× $4	× $5
Direct Labor Cost	$76,200	$157,000

The total direct labor cost amounting to $233,200 is carried to the cost of goods sold budget (Example 3).

Factory overhead budget.   The factory overhead budget summarizes the projected cost for the many different components of factory overhead.   Separate supporting schedules may be made for each department or cost center, according to the area of each foreman's responsibility.

EXAMPLE 7.

Bollett Company
Factory Overhead Budget
year ending December 31, 19–

Indirect Factory Labor	$ 82,000
Supervision	45,000
Supplies	15,000
Power, Heat, and Light	20,000
Depreciation of Plant and Equipment	25,000
Maintenance	14,000
Property Taxes	10,200
Insurance	4,200
Total Factory Overhead	$215,400

The total appears in the cost of goods sold budget (Example 3).

OPERATING EXPENSES BUDGET

These are the ordinary expenses involved in selling the products or in managing the business; they are chargeable against current income.   Operating expenses would be supported by detailed schedules according to departmental responsibility.   For example, there might be a separate schedule of advertising showing details of the various media used.

Operating expenses are usually separated into *selling expenses* and *general expenses*.

Selling expenses budget.   A budget of selling expenses usually shows individual amounts for the items listed in Example 8.

EXAMPLE 8.

Bollett Company
Selling Expenses Budget
year ending December 31, 19–

Salaries and Commissions	$21,000
Travel and Entertainment	16,000
Advertising	14,000
Supplies	5,000
Shipping and Delivery	3,000
Rent	2,000
Utilities	1,500
Depreciation	1,000
Insurance	500
Telephone	800
Miscellaneous	200
Total Selling Expenses	$65,000

The cost of market research may also be included or it may be separated into a marketing category under the responsibility of a market research manager. Often, for managerial control, selling expenses are classed as fixed or variable (Sec. 6.4) and standards are established for each class.

General expenses budget.   The general expenses budget (sometimes called the *general and administrative expenses budget*) is similar to the selling expenses budget, but its items are less closely linked to specific activities.

EXAMPLE 9.

Bollett Company
General Expenses Budget
year ending December 31, 19–

Officers' Salaries	$32,000
General Office Salaries	15,000
Legal Services	4,000
Pensions	3,000
Payroll Taxes	2,000
Depreciation	600
Telephone	400
Insurance	300
Miscellaneous	200
Total General Expenses	$57,500

7.4   BUDGETED BALANCE SHEET

The results of the various income and expense budgets are reflected in the budgeted balance sheet that is prepared at the end of the budget period. For this statement it is useful to adopt the financial position form, in which current liabilities are subtracted from current assets to arrive at net working capital. The change in net working capital can be shown, and the Statement of Change in Financial Position can conveniently tie in to the figure shown on the balance sheet (see Chapter 9). Some advantages of the budgeted balance sheet are that (1) it discloses possible unfavorable trends far in advance, so that steps can be taken for improvement; (2) it acts as a check on the accuracy of the various operating budgets; and (3) it provides the data for computing the return on investment.

EXAMPLE 10.

Bollett Company
Budgeted Balance Sheet
December 31, 19–

	Actual, Prior Year	Projected, Current Year	Increase or (Decrease)
CURRENT ASSETS			
Cash	$ 40,100	$ 50,600	$ 10,500
Receivables	60,300	78,500	18,200
Inventories	118,000	97,500	(20,500)
Total Current Assets	$218,400	$226,600	$ 8,200

(continued next page)

LESS: CURRENT LIABILITIES

Accounts Payable	$ 40,300	$ 67,500	$ 27,200
Accrued Expenses	8,900	5,500	(3,400)
Income Taxes Payable	14,100	18,400	4,300
Other Current Liabilities	4,000	7,500	3,500
	$ 67,300	$ 98,900	$ 31,600
Net Working Capital	$151,100	$127,700	$(23,400)
Plant and Equipment (net)	531,800	610,500	78,700
Other Assets	28,100	52,800	24,700
Total	$711,000	$791,000	$ 80,000
Less: Long-Term Liabilities	150,000	150,000	....
Total Net Assets	$561,000	$641,000	$ 80,000

CASH BUDGET

The expected receipts and disbursements of cash are shown by the cash budget. The components of this budget, such as collections from sales, expected outlays for manufacturing costs, operating expenses, and other expenses, must be carefully coordinated with other budgets. Also, long-term financing, dividend policies, and other financing that affects cash will have to be considered.

EXAMPLE 11.

Bollett Company
Cash Budget
quarter ending March 31, 19–

	January	February	March
ESTIMATED CASH RECEIPTS			
Cash Sales	$ 19,700	$ 25,500	$ 24,000
Collections of Receivables	52,800	75,000	58,300
Other Sources	2,500	3,000	8,200
Total Cash Receipts	$ 75,000	$103,500	$ 90,500
ESTIMATED CASH DISBURSEMENTS			
Manufacturing Costs	$ 50,500	$ 50,000	$ 65,500
Selling Expenses	5,500	4,500	5,500
General Expenses	5,000	5,000	5,000
Capital Expenditures	29,000	21,000	19,000
Other Disbursements	10,000	6,000	8,000
Total Cash Disbursements	$100,000	$ 86,500	$103,000
Net Increase or (Decrease)	$ (25,000)	$ 17,000	$ (12,500)
Balance at Beginning of Month	110,000	85,000	102,000
Balance at End of Month	85,000	$102,000	$ 89,500
Minimum Cash Balance	60,000	60,000	60,000
Excess or (Deficiency)	$ 25,000	$ 42,000	$ 29,500

CAPITAL EXPENDITURES BUDGET

The amount required for capital expenditures may vary considerably from year to year. This change is due partly to the difference in amounts needed to replace machinery and equipment that has become worn out or obsolete. Also, new products or other expansion may require new machinery and equipment.

Since capital expenditures usually require large outlays and may require long-term financing, it is essential that close control be maintained, generally by means of the capital expenditures budget. Capital expenditures are projected for five or ten years, or longer.

EXAMPLE 12.

Bollett Company
Capital Expenditures Budget
five years ending December 31, 19–

	1973	1974	1975	1976	1977
Machinery					
Department #1	$ 40,000	$15,000	$ 65,000	$45,000	$10,000
Department #2	30,000	25,000	10,000	19,000	15,000
Office Equipment	22,000	15,000	25,000	18,000	20,000
Delivery Equipment	11,000	6,000	7,000	8,000	15,000
Total	$103,000	$61,000	$107,000	$90,000	$60,000

7.5 FLEXIBLE BUDGETS

Where the volume of operations is fairly stable the fixed-budget approach illustrated in Examples 1 through 12 would be suitable. That is the approach of most companies. However, where substantial changes in volume occur, it is better to use a *flexible budget*, which gives separate treatment to fixed and variable costs (see Sec. 6.4) over a series of volume levels.

EXAMPLE 13.

Bollett Company
Flexible Budget
Monthly Operations

Units of Production	10,000	11,000	12,000
Variable Costs			
Indirect Wages	$ 40,000	$ 44,000	$ 48,000
Indirect Materials	30,000	33,000	36,000
Electric Power	15,000	16,500	18,000
Total Variable Costs	$ 85,000	$ 93,500	$102,000
Per Unit	$8.50	$8.50	$8.50
Fixed Costs			
Supervision	$ 30,000	$ 30,000	$ 30,000
Depreciation, Plant	18,000	18,000	18,000
Property Taxes	10,000	10,000	10,000
Insurance	8,000	8,000	8,000
Electric Power	11,000	11,000	11,000
Total Fixed Costs	$ 77,000	$ 77,000	$ 77,000
Per Unit	$7.70	$7.00	$6.40
Total Factory Overhead	$162,000	$170,500	$179,000
Per Unit	$16.20	$15.50	$14.90

Observe that the total cost per unit decreases from $16.20 for 10,000 units to $14.90 for 12,000 units.

Electric power is shown under both Fixed Costs and Variable Costs; it is an example of a *semivariable (semifixed)* cost. For such items, there is a fixed charge for consumption up to a certain level, and a unit charge thereafter.

The relationship of fixed to variable costs is important in determining pricing and manufacturing policies. For instance, if total overhead costs are covered, the only additional costs in making longer runs of a single item would be the variable costs. Thus, it may be profitable to take special orders from chain stores and others at a lower price.

7.6 PERFORMANCE REPORTS

To be most effective, performance reports must be made available periodically to measure progress in meeting the budget goals. A part of the performance report should be comments explaining any significant variances from the budget. Steps to be taken to prevent the recurrence of unfavorable variances should be outlined. Below is shown one form of performance report.

EXAMPLE 14.

Bollett Company
Budget Report
Factory Overhead, Department #1

	Budget	Actual	Over	Under
Indirect Factory Labor	$ 4,000	$ 4,200	$200	
Supervision	2,300	2,300		
Supplies	1,200	1,100		$100
Power, Heat, and Light	1,600	1,550		50
Depreciation of Plant and Equipment	1,400	1,400		
Property Taxes	1,100	1,200	100	
Insurance	900	950	50	
Maintenance	400	500	100	
	$12,900	$13,200	$450	$150

7.7 STANDARD COSTS

Many companies compare the current month, quarter, or year with the same period of the previous year. But that approach presupposes that the previous year is typical, which may or may not be the case. A much better approach, especially for costing products, is the use of *standard costs*. Through these predetermined costs management can find out how much a product should cost and how much it actually costs. Then, by means of variance analysis (Sec. 7.8), management can pinpoint the *cause* of the difference between expected and actual costs.

Standard costs for a manufactured product are established after a study of the factory operations and of the expected costs for materials, labor, and factory overhead. If any of these factors change, the standard should be changed accordingly. It is desirable to make an annual review to ensure that the standards are up to date for the coming year.

Standard costs are used with either the job order or process cost system. When many factory operations are carried on in a single department, specific cost centers, and not the department, should be assigned the standards.

7.8 ANALYSIS OF VARIANCES

When the actual cost of a product or department differs from the established standard cost the difference is called a *variance*. When actual cost is less than standard, the variance is *favorable*; otherwise it is *unfavorable*. Under the principle of "exceptions only," small variances are ignored, and thus most items will not have to be reviewed.

Direct materials variances. Standards are set up both for the quantity required to make one unit of product and for the price of material for one unit of product. It is possible to have a favorable quantity variance and an unfavorable price variance (or vice versa) at the same time, as can be seen in the following example.

EXAMPLE 15.

During the month of November, 20,000 units of Product A were produced. There were 19,600 pounds of materials used at a cost of $1.03 per pound. The standards for that volume were 20,000 pounds of materials and a price of $1.00 per pound.

Bollett Company
Materials Variance
month of November 197–

Quantity Variance		
Actual Quantity	19,600	
Standard Quantity	20,000	
Difference	400	
Standard Price	× $1.00	
Variance (favorable)		$400
Price Variance		
Actual Price	$1.03	
Standard Price	1.00	
Difference	.03	
Actual Quantity	× 19,600	
Variance (unfavorable)		588
Total Materials Variance (unfavorable)		$188*

* Check: $(19,600)(1.03) - (20,000)(1.00) = 20,188 - 20,000 = 188$

Direct labor variances. Standards are set up both for the number of labor hours required to make a unit of product and for the labor rate, or price per unit of product.

EXAMPLE 16.

To produce the 20,000 units of Product A described in Example 15 there were 4,200 hours of labor used at a cost of $2.50 each. The standards for that quantity were 4,000 hours and a rate of $2.65 an hour.

Bollett Company
Labor Variance
month of November 197–

Usage Variance		
Actual Hours	4,200	
Standard Hours	4,000	
Difference	200	
Standard Rate	× $2.65	
Variance (unfavorable)		$530

(continued next page)

Rate Variance

Actual Rate	$2.50
Standard Rate	2.65
Difference	.15
Actual Hours	× 4,200
Variance (favorable)	630
Total Labor Variance (favorable)	$100*

* **Check:**　　(4,000)(2.65) − (4,200)(2.50)　=　10,600 − 10,500　=　100

Factory overhead variances. An overhead variance will usually result from (1) operating above or below the normal capacity (*volume variance*) or (2) incurring a total cost different from the amount budgeted for the level of operations (*controllable variance*).

EXAMPLE 17.

For the 20,000 units of Product A produced during November, the standard and actual data were as follows: *Standard*: 12,000 hours (90% capacity) and a total factory overhead of $31,850. *Actual*: variable factory overhead, $23,200; fixed factory overhead, $10,000.

Bollett Company
Factory Overhead Variance
month of November, 197–

Volume Variance

Normal Capacity	13,300	
Standard for Volume Produced (90%)	12,000	
Productive Capacity Not Used	1,300	
Standard Fixed Overhead Rate	× $ .50	
Variance (unfavorable)		$ 650

Controllable Variance

Actual Factory Overhead	$33,200	
Standard Factory Overhead	31,850	
Variance (unfavorable)		1,350
Total Factory Overhead Variance (unfavorable)		$2,000

Summary

(1)　A budget is a _____ .

(2)　All budgets are coordinated in the _____ .

(3)　The amount of raw materials to be purchased depends on the _____ and the desired _____ .

(4)　The cash budget shows the expected _____ and _____ _____ for the period.

(5)　Alternative levels of operations are allowed for in a _____ budget.

(6)　Standard costs determine how much a product _____ cost and how much it _____ cost.

(7)   A variance is the difference between an _____ cost and a _____ cost.

(8)   The two variances for direct materials are _____ and _____ .

(9)   The two variances for direct labor are _____ and _____ .

(10)   The two variances for factory overhead are _____ and _____ .

Answers: (1) quantitative projection of operations;   (2) master budget;   (3) production budget, inventory amounts;   (4) cash receipts, cash disbursements;   (5) flexible;   (6) should, does;   (7) actual, standard;   (8) quantity, price;   (9) usage, rate;   (10) volume, controllable

Solved Problems

7.1.   The Kuezek Company is interested in developing a flexible budget for monthly operating expenses.   Following is the information needed for each type of expense.

Salesmen's salaries	$30,000
Salesmen's commissions	8% of sales
Advertising expense	$15,000 for $300,000 sales
	$16,000 for $350,000 sales
	$17,000 for $400,000 sales
Miscellaneous selling expenses	1% of sales
Office salaries	$10,000
Office supplies	1/2 of 1% of sales
Miscellaneous general expenses	1% of sales

Prepare a flexible operating expenses budget based on sales of $300,000, $350,000, and $400,000.

Kuezek Company
Flexible Operating Expenses Budget
Monthly Volume, 197—

Total Sales	$300,000	$350,000	$400,000

SOLUTION

	Kuezek Company		
	Flexible Operating Expenses Budget		
	Monthly Volume, 197—		
Total Sales	$300,000	$350,000	$400,000
Selling Expenses			
Salesmen's Salaries	$ 30,000	$ 30,000	$ 30,000
Salesmen's Commissions	24,000	28,000	32,000
Advertising Expense	15,000	16,000	17,000
Miscellaneous Selling Expenses	3,000	3,500	4,000
	$ 72,000	$ 77,500	$ 83,000
General Expenses			
Office Salaries	10,000	10,000	10,000
Office Supplies	1,500	1,750	2,000
Miscellaneous General Expenses	3,000	3,500	4,000
	14,500	15,250	16,000
Total Operating Expenses	$ 86,500	$ 92,750	$ 99,000

7.2.   The actual operating expenses for the Kuezek Company for October were as follows:

Salesmen's salaries	$32,000
Salesmen's commissions	25,500
Advertising expense	19,000
Miscellaneous selling expenses	4,000
Office salaries	10,500
Office supplies	1,650
Miscellaneous general expenses	3,300

Sales for the month were $350,000.   Prepare a budget report for operating expenses, using the standard data developed in Problem 7.1.

	Kuezek Company		
	Budget Report, Operating Expenses		
	October 197—		
	Actual	**Budget**	**Over**	**Under**

SOLUTION

Kuezek Company				
Budget Report, Operating Expenses				
October 197—				
	Actual	**Budget**	**Over**	**Under**
Salesmen's Salaries	$32,000	$30,000	$2,000	
Salesmen's Commissions	25,500	28,000		$2,500
Advertising Expense	19,000	16,000	3,000	
Miscellaneous Selling				
Expenses	4,000	3,500	500	
Office Salaries	10,500	10,000	500	
Office Supplies	1,650	1,750		100
Miscellaneous General				
Expenses	3,300	3,500		200
	$95,950	$92,750	$6,000	$2,800

7.3. The Payne Corporation records show the following data relating to direct materials cost for September:

Units of finished product manufactured	8,700
Standard direct materials per unit of product	5 lbs.
Quantity of direct materials used	45,000 lbs.
Unit cost of direct materials	$4 per lb.
Direct materials quantity variance (unfavorable)	$2,400
Direct materials price variance (favorable)	$5,000

There is no work in process either at the beginning or the end of the month. Determine the standard direct materials cost per unit of finished product.

SOLUTION

Standard units for direct materials	
used (45,000 lbs. ÷ 5 lbs. per unit)	9,000 units
Actual units completed	8,700 units
Excess materials used	300 units
Quantity variance (unfavorable)	$2,400
Standard direct materials cost per unit	
Quantity variance divided by excess	
materials used ($2,400 ÷ 300 units)	$8

7.4. The Benson Company has the following standard and actual costs for the current month.   There were 4,000 units produced.

	Actual	**Standard**
Direct materials	14,000 units @ $2.10	15,000 units @ $2.00
Direct labor	8,000 hours @ $2.75	7,500 hours @ $3.00
Factory overhead		
Variable	$13,500	$1.50 per hour
Fixed	$ 7,500	$ .75 per hour*

* Rate based on normal capacity of 10,000 labor hours

(*a*) For direct materials, compute the quantity variance, price variance, and total materials cost variance.   (*b*) For direct labor, compute the time variance, rate variance, and total direct labor cost variance.   (*c*) For factory overhead, compute the volume variance, controllable variance, and total factory overhead cost variance.

(*a*)   **Quantity variance**   Units

_____

_____

_____

         Price variance   Per unit

_____

_____

_____

_____

_____

(*b*)   **Time variance**   Hours

_____

_____

_____

         Rate variance   Per hour

_____

_____

_____

_____

_____

(*c*)   **Volume variance**   Hours

_____

_____

_____

         Controllable variance

_____

_____

_____

_____

_____

_____

SOLUTION

(a)

Quantity variance	Units	
Standard quantity	15,000	
Actual quantity	14,000	
Variance (favorable)	1,000 × standard	
	price, $2.00	$2,000

Price variance	Per unit	
Actual price	$2.10	
Standard price	2.00	
Variance (unfavorable)	.10 × actual quantity,	
	14,000	1,400
Total direct materials cost variance (favorable)		$ 600

(b)

Time variance	Hours	
Actual time	8,000	
Standard time	7,500	
Variance (unfavorable)	500 × standard rate,	
	$3.00	$1,500

Rate variance	Per hour	
Standard rate	$3.00	
Actual rate	2.75	
Variance (favorable)	$ .25 × actual time,	
	8,000 hours	2,000
Total direct labor cost variance (favorable)		$ 500

(c)

Volume variance	Hours	
Normal capacity at 100%	10,000	
Standard for volume produced	7,500	
Capacity not used (unfavorable)	2,500 × standard rate,	
	$ .75	$1,875

Controllable variance		
Actual factory overhead cost	$21,000	
Budgeted for standard production		
Variable (7,500 × $1.50) $11,250		
Fixed (10,000 × $ .75) 7,500	18,750	
Variance (unfavorable)		2,250
Total factory overhead cost variance (unfavorable)		$4,125

7.5. The Reilly Corporation had the following factory overhead costs for January, in which 9,500 direct labor hours were used: indirect wages, $9,930; indirect materials, $4,570; utilities, $3,540; supervision, $8,520; depreciation, $4,150; insurance, $1,750; property taxes, $1,180. The monthly factory overhead budget, based on normal capacity of 10,000 direct labor hours, has been established as follows: indirect wages, $10,300; indirect materials, $4,700; utilities, $3,800; supervision, $8,520; depreciation, $4,150; insurance, $1,750; property taxes, $1,180. Present a factory overhead report for January based on 9,500 direct labor hours.

Reilly Corporation

Factory Overhead Variance Report

month ended January 31, 197—

	Actual	Budget	Favorable	Unfavorable

SOLUTION

Reilly Corporation

Factory Overhead Variance Report

month ended January 31, 197—

Normal Capacity	10,000	
Actual Production	9,500	
Below Standard (500 ÷ 10,000 = 5%)	500	

	Actual	Budget	Favorable	Unfavorable
Variable Costs				
Indirect Wages	$ 9,930	$ 9,785		$145
Indirect Materials	4,570	4,465		105
Utilities	3,540	3,610	$70	
Total Variable Costs	$18,040	$17,860	$70	$250
Fixed Costs				
Supervision	$ 8,520	$ 8,520		
Depreciation	4,150	4,150		
Insurance	1,750	1,750		
Property Taxes	1,180	1,180		
Total Fixed Costs	$15,600	$15,600		
Total Factory Overhead	$33,640	$33,460		
Total Controllable Variances			$70	$250
Net Controllable Variance (unfavorable)				$180
Volume Variance (unfavorable)				
Idle Hours at Standard Rate for				
Fixed Overhead (500 × $1.56)				780
Total Factory Overhead Variance (unfavorable)				$960

7.6. The B & G Clothing Manufacturing Company prepares monthly estimates of sales, production, and other operating data. Sales and production data for April are shown below.

Estimated sales for April

    Shirts: 35,500 @ $7

    Slacks: 22,000 @ $12

Estimated inventories on April 1

    Direct Materials

        Cloth: 3,500 yards

        Thread: 25 spools

        Buttons: 10,000

        Zippers: 1,100

    Finished Products

        Shirts: 1,500

        Slacks: 1,000

Expected inventories at April 30

    Direct Materials

        Cloth: 4,000 yards

        Thread: 35 spools

        Buttons: 18,000

        Zippers: 1,000

    Finished Products

        Shirts: 2,000

        Slacks: 1,500

Direct materials required for production

    To manufacture shirts

        Cloth: $1\frac{1}{2}$ yards per shirt

        Thread: 1 spool per 100 shirts

        Buttons: 8 buttons per shirt

    To manufacture slacks

        Cloth: $2\frac{1}{2}$ yards per pair of slacks

        Thread: 1 spool per 75 pairs

        Buttons: 2 buttons per pair

        Zippers: 1 zipper per pair

Expected purchase price for direct materials

    Cloth: $1.50 per yard

    Thread: .20 per spool

    Buttons: .01 each

    Zippers: .10 each

Direct labor required

    Shirts

        Cutting Department: 5 shirts per hour @ $5/hour

        Sewing Department: 4 shirts per hour @ $6/hour

        Inspection Department: 30 shirts per hour @ $4/hour

    Slacks

        Cutting Department: 3 pair per hour @ $5/hour

        Sewing Department: 2 pair per hour @ $6/hour

        Inspection Department: 20 pair per hour @ $4/hour

Prepare the following for April: (a) sales budget, (b) production budget, (c) direct materials purchases budget, (d) direct labor cost budget.

(a)

B & G Clothing Manufacturing Company

Sales Budget

month ending April 30, 19—

Product	Unit Sales Volume	Unit Selling Price	Total Sales

(b)

B & G Clothing Manufacturing Company

Production Budget

month ending April 30, 19—

	Shirts	Slacks

(c)

B & G Clothing Manufacturing Company

Direct Materials Purchases Budget

month ending April 30, 19—

	Cloth (yards)	Thread (spools)	Buttons (each)	Zippers (each)

(d)

B & G Clothing Manufacturing Company

Direct Labor Cost Budget

month ending April 30, 19—

	Cutting Department	Sewing Department	Inspection Department

SOLUTION

(a)

B & G Clothing Manufacturing Company
Sales Budget
month ending April 30, 19—

Product	Unit Sales Volume	Unit Selling Price	Total Sales
Shirts	35,500	$ 7.00	$248,500
Slacks	22,000	$12.00	264,000
Total			$512,500

(b)

B & G Clothing Manufacturing Company
Production Budget
month ending April 30, 19—

	Shirts	Slacks
Sales	35,500 units	22,000 units
Expected Inventory, April 30, 19—	2,000	1,500
Total	37,500	23,500
Less: Estimated Inventory, April 1, 19—	1,500	1,000
Total Production	36,000 units	22,500 units

(c)

B & G Clothing Manufacturing Company
Direct Materials Purchases Budget
month ending April 30, 19—

	Cloth (yards)	Thread (spools)	Buttons (each)	Zippers (each)
Required for Production				
Shirts	54,000	360	432,000	0
Slacks	56,250	300	45,000	22,500
Expected Inventory, April 30, 19—	4,000	35	18,000	1,000
Total	114,250	695	495,000	23,500
Less: Estimated Inventory, April 1, 19—	3,500	25	10,000	1,100
Total Units to be Purchased	110,750	670	485,000	22,400
Unit Price	× $1.50	× $ .20	× $ .01	× $ .10
Total Direct Materials Purchases	$166,125	$134	$4,850	$2,240

(d)

B & G Clothing Manufacturing Company
Direct Labor Cost Budget
month ending April 30, 19—

	Cutting Department	Sewing Department	Inspection Department
Hours Required for Production			
Shirts	7,200	9,000	1,200
Slacks	7,500	11,250	1,125
Total	14,700	20,250	2,325
Hourly Rate	× $5	× $6	× $4
Total Direct Labor Cost	$73,500	$121,500	$9,300

7.7. The following tentative trial balance was prepared by the Morton Manufacturing Company as of December 31, 1976, the end of the current fiscal year.

Cash	$ 29,000	
Accounts Receivable	92,600	
Finished Goods	67,300	
Work in Process	31,500	
Materials	15,100	
Prepaid Expenses	3,500	
Plant and Equipment	549,200	
Accumulated Depreciation,		
Plant and Equipment		$193,000
Accounts Payable		53,700
Income Tax Payable		23,500
Common Stock, $11 par		308,000
Retained Earnings		210,000
	$788,200	$788,200

Factory output and sales for 1977 are expected to be 95,000 units of product to be sold at $11 per unit. The quantity and cost of inventories (LIFO method) at December 31, 1977, are expected to remain unchanged from the beginning of the year. Budget estimates of manufacturing costs and operating expenses for 1977 are as follows.

	Fixed (total for year)	Variable (per unit sold)
Cost of Goods Manufactured and Sold		
Direct Materials	...	$1.60
Direct Labor	...	2.60
Factory Overhead		
Depreciation of Plant and		
Equipment	$38,000	...
Other Factory Overhead	94,000	.80
Selling Expenses		
Sales Commissions	14,600	.60
Advertising	21,000	...
Miscellaneous Selling Expenses	6,900	.30
General Expenses		
Office and Officers' Salaries	74,900	.15
Supplies	950	.10
Miscellaneous General Expenses	7,950	.15

Accounts Receivable, Prepaid Expenses, and Accounts Payable are expected to have balances close to those at the beginning of the year. Federal income taxes of $84,700 are expected for 1977, of which $44,200 will be payable during the year. Dividends of 60¢ a share per quarter are expected to be declared and paid in March, June, September, and January. Plant and equipment purchases are expected to be $52,800 in December. (a) Prepare a budgeted income statement for 1977. (b) Prepare a budgeted balance sheet as of December 31, 1977.

(a)

Morton Manufacturing Company
Budgeted Income Statement
year ended December 31, 1977

Sales

(continued next page)

Cost of Goods Sold

Gross Profit on Sales
Operating Expenses

Total Operating Expenses
Income Before Income Tax
Income Tax
Net Income

(b)

Morton Manufacturing Company
Budgeted Balance Sheet
December 31, 1977

ASSETS
Current Assets

Total Current Assets
Plant Assets

Total Assets
LIABILITIES
Current Liabilities

Total Current Liabilities
STOCKHOLDERS' EQUITY
Common Stock
Retained Earnings
Total Stockholders' Equity
Total Liabilities and Stockholders' Equity

SOLUTION

(a)

Morton Manufacturing Company

Budgeted Income Statement

year ended December 31, 1977

Sales			$1,045,000
Cost of Goods Sold			
Direct Materials		$152,000	
Direct Labor		247,000	
Factory Overhead		208,000	
Cost of Goods Sold			607,000
Gross Profit on Sales			$ 438,000
Operating Expenses			
Selling Expenses			
Sales Commissions	$71,600		
Advertising	21,000		
Miscellaneous Selling			
Expenses	35,400		
Total Selling Expenses		$128,000	
General Expenses			
Office and Officers'			
Salaries	$89,150		
Supplies	10,450		
Miscellaneous General			
Expenses	22,200		
Total General Expenses		121,800	
Total Operating Expenses			249,800
Income Before Income Tax			$ 188,200
Income Tax			84,700
Net Income			$ 103,500

(b)

Morton Manufacturing Company

Budgeted Balance Sheet

December 31, 1977

ASSETS

Current Assets			
Cash		$ 67,500*	
Accounts Receivable		92,600	
Inventories			
Finished Goods	$67,300		
Work in Process	31,500		
Materials	15,100	113,900	
Prepaid Expenses		3,500	
Total Current Assets			$277,500
Plant Assets			
Plant and Equipment		$602,000	
Less: Accumulated Depreciation		231,000	371,000
Total Assets			$648,500

(continued next page)

LIABILITIES

Current Liabilities		
Accounts Payable	$ 53,700	
Income Tax Payable	40,500	
Total Current Liabilities		$ 94,200

STOCKHOLDERS' EQUITY

Common Stock	$308,000	
Retained Earnings	246,300**	
Total Stockholders' Equity		554,300
Total Liabilities and Stockholders' Equity		$648,500

* Cash balance, January 1, 1977			$ 29,000
Plus: Cash from operations			
Net income		$103,500	
Plus: Depreciation plant and equipment	$38,000		
Income tax payable, Dec. 31, 1977	40,500	78,500	
		$182,000	
Less: Income tax payable, Jan. 1, 1977		23,500	158,500
			$187,500
Less: Dividends paid in 1977		$ 67,200	
Plant and equipment acquired in 1977		52,800	120,000
Cash balance, December 31, 1977			$ 67,500
** Retained earnings balance, January 1, 1977			$210,000
Plus: Net income for 1977			103,500
			$313,500
Less: Dividends declared during 1977			67,200
Retained earnings balance, December 31, 1977			$246,300

7.8. The Newman Company has prepared the factory overhead budget for the Finishing Department for August as follows.

Direct Labor Hours		
Normal Productive Capacity		20,000
Hours Budgeted		16,000
Variable Costs		
Indirect Factory Wages	$7,500	
Indirect Materials	4,000	
Utilities	3,500	
Total Variable Costs		$15,000
Fixed Costs		
Supervisors' Salaries	$8,000	
Indirect Factory Wages	6,400	
Depreciation on Plant and Equipment	3,500	
Utilities	3,000	
Insurance	1,200	
Property Taxes	900	
Total Fixed Costs		$23,000
Total Factory Overhead Cost		$38,000

For the month of September actual factory overhead costs were:

Variable Costs	
Indirect Factory Wages	$ 7,000
Indirect Materials	3,000
Utilities	3,300
Fixed Costs	
Supervisors' Salaries	8,000
Indirect Factory Wages	6,400
Depreciation	3,500
Utilities	3,000
Insurance	1,200
Property Taxes	900
Total Overhead Cost	$36,300

(a) On the basis of the August budget, prepare a flexible budget for the month of September, with direct labor hours of 15,000, 18,000, 20,000, and 22,000. Determine also the standard factory overhead rate per direct labor hour.

(b) Prepare a standard factory overhead cost variance report for September. Direct labor hours in September for the Finishing Department was 18,000.

(a)

The Newman Company
Factory Overhead Cost Budget, Finishing Department
month ending September 30, 197—

Percent of Normal Capacity	75%	90%	100%	110%
Budgeted Factory Overhead				
Variable Costs				
Total Variable Costs				
Fixed Costs				
Total Fixed Costs				
Total Factory Overhead Cost				

(b)

The Newman Company
Factory Overhead Cost Variance Report, Finishing Department
month ending September 30, 197—

Normal Capacity for the Month	
Actual Production for the Month	

(continued next page)

	Budget	Actual	Favorable	Unfavorable
Variable Costs				
Total Variable Costs				
Fixed Costs				
Total Fixed Costs				
Total Factory Overhead Costs				
Total Controllable Variance				
Net Controllable Variance				
Volume Variance				
Total Factory Overhead Cost Variance				

SOLUTION

(a)

The Newman Company
Factory Overhead Cost Budget, Finishing Department
month ending September 30, 197—

	75%	90%	100%	110%
Percent of Normal Capacity	75%	90%	100%	110%
Direct Labor Hours	15,000	18,000	20,000	22,000
Budgeted Factory Overhead				
Variable Costs				
Indirect Factory Wages	$ 5,625	$ 6,750	$ 7,500	$ 8,250
Indirect Materials	3,000	3,600	4,000	4,400
Utilities	2,625	3,150	3,500	3,850
Total Variable Costs	$11,250	$13,500	$15,000	$16,500
Fixed Costs				
Supervisors' Salaries	$ 8,000	$ 8,000	$ 8,000	$ 8,000
Indirect Factory Wages	6,400	6,400	6,400	6,400
Depreciation	3,500	3,500	3,500	3,500
Utilities	3,000	3,000	3,000	3,000
Insurance	1,200	1,200	1,200	1,200
Property Taxes	900	900	900	900
Total Fixed Costs	$23,000	$23,000	$23,000	$23,000
Total Factory Overhead Cost	$34,250	$36,500	$38,000	$39,500

Standard overhead rate per direct labor hour is $38,000 ÷ 20,000 = $1.90.

(b)

The Newman Company
Factory Overhead Cost Variance Report, Finishing Department
month ending September 30, 197—

Normal Capacity for the Month	20,000 hours
Actual Production for the Month	18,000 hours

(continued next page)

CHAP. 7]   BUDGETS AND STANDARD COSTS   179

	Budget	Actual	Favorable	Unfavorable
Variable Costs				
Indirect Factory Wages	$ 6,750	$ 7,000		$ 250
Indirect Materials	3,600	3,000	$600	
Utilities	3,150	3,300		150
Total Variable Costs	$13,500	$13,300		
Fixed Costs				
Supervisors' Salaries	8,000	8,000		
Indirect Factory Wages	6,400	6,400		
Depreciation	3,500	3,500		
Utilities	3,000	3,000		
Insurance	1,200	1,200		
Property Taxes	900	900		
Total Fixed Costs	$23,000	$23,000		
Total Factory Overhead Costs	$36,500	$36,300		
Total Controllable Variance			$600	$ 400
Net Controllable Variance (favorable)			$200	
Volume Variance (unfavorable)				
Idle Hours at Standard Rate for Fixed Overhead				
(2,000 × $23,000/20,000)				$2,300
Total Factory Overhead Cost Variance (unfavorable)				$2,100

7.9. From the information below, prepare a monthly cash budget for the next quarter (October–December) for the Golden Company.

	October	November	December
Sales	$750,000	$800,000	$900,000
Manufacturing costs	450,000	480,000	540,000
Operating expenses	225,000	240,000	270,000
Capital expenditures	....	60,000	....

Golden Company expects 25% of its sales to be in cash, and of the accounts receivable, 70% will be collected within the next month. Depreciation, insurance, and property taxes comprise $25,000 of monthly manufacturing costs and $10,000 of the operating expenses. Insurance and property taxes are paid in February, June, and September. The rest of the manufacturing costs and operating expenses will be paid off, one-half in the month in which incurred and the rest in the following month. The current assets on October 1 are made up of

- Cash, $70,000
- Marketable securities, $50,000
- Accounts receivable, $600,000 ($450,000 from September, $150,000 from August)

and current liabilities include

- $60,000, 6%, 90-day note payable due October 18
- Accounts payable for $200,000 for September manufacturing expenses
- Accrued liabilities of $100,000 for September operating expenses

Dividends of $1,000 should be received in November. An income tax payment of $50,000 will be made in November.

Golden Company
Cash Budget
three months ending December 31, 197—

	October	November	December
Estimated Cash Receipts from:			
Total Cash Receipts			
Estimated Cash Disbursements for:			
Total Cash Disbursements			
Cash Increase or (Decrease)			
Cash Balance at Beginning of Month			
Cash Balance at End of Month			

SOLUTION

Golden Company
Cash Budget
three months ending December 31, 197—

	October	November	December
Estimated Cash Receipts from:			
Cash Sales	$187,500	$200,000	$225,000
Collections of Accounts Receivable*	465,000	528,750	588,750
Dividends Received	....	1,000	....
Total Cash Receipts	$652,500	$729,750	$813,750
Estimated Cash Disbursements for:			
Manufacturing Costs**	$425,000	$465,000	$510,000
Operating Expenses***	212,500	232,500	255,000
Capital Expenditures	....	60,000	....
Other Purposes			
Notes Payable (including interest)	60,900	....	....
Income Tax	....	50,000	....
Total Cash Disbursements	$698,400	$807,500	$765,000
Cash Increase or (Decrease)	(45,900)	(77,750)	48,750
Cash Balance at Beginning of Month	70,000	24,100	(53,650)
Cash Balance at End of Month	$ 24,100	$(53,650)	$ (4,900)

*Computation:	October	November	December
August sales	$150,000	....	....
September sales	315,000	$135,000	....
October sales	....	393,750	$168,750
November sales	....	....	420,000
	$465,000	$528,750	$588,750

** Computation:	October	November	December
Payment of accounts payable, beginning of month balance	$200,000	$225,000	$240,000
Payment of current month's costs	225,000	240,000	270,000
	$425,000	$465,000	$510,000

*** Computation:	October	November	December
Payment of accrued expenses, beginning of month balance	$100,000	$112,500	$120,000
Payment of current month's costs	112,500	120,000	135,000
	$212,500	$232,500	$255,000

7.10. The Kelsch Company uses a standard cost system and maintains perpetual inventories for materials, work in process, and finished goods.

	Standard	Standard Cost per Unit
Direct materials	3 lbs. @ $2 per lb.	$ 6.00
Direct labor	3 hrs. @ $4 per hr.	12.00
Factory overhead	$3 per direct labor hour	9.00
		$27.00

There was no beginning or ending work in process inventory for January. The transactions for production completed during January are as follows:

(1) Materials bought on account, $33,000.

(2) $29,250 of direct materials was used; this is 15,000 lbs. @ $1.95.

(3) Direct labor was $59,450; this is 14,500 hours @ $4.10.

(4) Factory overhead for the month was: indirect labor, $15,000; depreciation, $9,000; utilities, $8,000; miscellaneous costs, $3,000. Utilities, indirect labor, and miscellaneous costs were paid during January. Of the total factory overhead costs of $35,000, fixed costs were $12,000 and variable costs were $23,000.

(5) Goods finished during January, 4,200 units.

(a) Prepare general journal entries to record the transactions, assuming that the work in process account is debited for actual production costs and credited with standard costs for completed goods.

(b) Set up a "T" account for work in process and post to the account, using the specified numbers.

(c) Show the variances for direct materials cost, direct labor cost, and factory overhead cost. Normal capacity for the plant is 15,000 direct labor hours.

(d) Compare the sum of the standard cost variances with the total of the work in process.

(a)

(1)		
(2)		
(3)		
(4)		
(5)		

(b)

Work in Process

(c)

Direct Materials Cost Variance

Quantity variance

Price variance

Total direct materials cost variance

Direct Labor Cost Variance

Time variance

Rate variance

Total direct labor cost variance

Factory Overhead Cost Variance

Volume variance

(continued next page)

Controllable variance

Total factory overhead cost variance

(d)

SOLUTION

(a)

(1)	Materials	33,000	
	Accounts Payable		33,000
(2)	Work in Process	29,250	
	Materials		29,250
(3)	Work in Process	59,450	
	Cash		59,450
(4)	Work in Process	35,000	
	Cash		26,000
	Accumulated Depreciation		9,000
(5)	Finished Goods	113,400	
	Work in Process		113,400

(b)

Work in Process

(2)	29,250	113,400	(5)
(3)	59,450		
(4)	35,000		

(c)

Direct Materials Cost Variance

Quantity variance		
Actual quantity	15,000 lbs.	
Standard quantity	12,600 lbs.*	
Variance (unfavorable)	2,400 lbs. × standard price, $2	$4,800
Price variance		
Standard price	$2.00 per lb.	
Actual price	1.95 per lb.	
Variance (favorable)	$ .05 per lb. × actual quantity, 15,000 lbs.	750
Total direct materials cost variance (unfavorable)		$4,050

* 4,200 finished units × 3 lbs. per unit

Direct Labor Cost Variance

Time variance		
Actual time	14,500 hrs.	
Standard time	12,600 hrs.	
Variance (unfavorable)	1,900 hrs. × standard rate, $4/hr.	$7,600
Rate variance		
Actual rate	$4.10	
Standard rate	4.00	
Variance (unfavorable)	$ .10 × actual time, 14,500 hrs.	1,450
Total direct labor cost variance (unfavorable)		$9,050

Factory Overhead Cost Variance		
Volume variance		
Normal productive capacity of 100%	15,000 hrs.	
Standard for product produced	12,600 hrs.	
Productive capacity not used	2,400 hrs.	
Standard fixed factory overhead rate	× .80*	
Variance (unfavorable)		$1,920
Controllable variance		
Budgeted factory overhead	$39,720**	
Actual factory overhead costs incurred	35,000	
Variance (favorable)		4,720
Total factory overhead cost variance (favorable)		$2,800

* Fixed factory overhead		$12,000
Normal production capacity in direct labor hours		÷ 15,000
Standard fixed factory overhead rate per direct labor hour		$ .80
** Variable factory overhead costs (12,600 standard hours × $2.20 standard variable rate)†		$27,720
Fixed factory overhead costs		12,000
Budgeted factory overhead for standard product produced		$39,720
† Standard factory overhead rate		$3.00
Less: Standard fixed factory overhead		.80
Standard variable factory overhead rate		$2.20

(d)	Direct materials cost variance (unfavorable)	$ 4,050
	Direct labor cost variance (unfavorable)	9,050
	Factory overhead cost variance (favorable)	(2,800)
	Balance, work in process	$10,300

Examination II
Chapters 5-7

Part I. *Circle* T *for true,* F *for false.*

1. T F   The three types of inventory in a manufacturing company are: direct materials, indirect materials, and factory overhead.

2. T F   Direct labor includes the wages of factory employees who are associated with the product, such as supervisors and timekeepers.

3. T F   Product costs are part of the inventory cost, while period costs are not.

4. T F   Under the job order cost system the costs are accumulated by departments or cost centers.

5. T F   Under the process cost system the average unit cost is obtained by dividing the departmental cost by the number of units produced during the period.

6. T F   "Equivalent units" means that the same number of units should be on hand at the end of the period as at the beginning of the period.

7. T F   The direct labor budget represents the number of hours to complete the budgeted production times the direct labor rate.

8. T F   Fixed costs include indirect labor and indirect materials.

9. T F   Standard costs may be used with either the job order system or the process cost system.

10. T F   When the budgeted cost exceeds the actual cost the variance is unfavorable.

Part II. *Circle the letter identifying the best answer.*

1. Merchandising companies sell products:
    a. they manufacture
    b. in the same form as purchased
    c. based on costs
    d. in raw material form

2. Manufacturing companies sell products:
    a. they produce
    b. based on selling price
    c. based on material cost
    d. at a percentage over cost

3. An additional account required by a manufacturing company is:
    a. Current Assets
    b. Plant and Equipment
    c. Accounts Payable
    d. Finished Goods

4. Under a perpetual inventory system it is:

    a. necessary to take a physical inventory

    b. best to use standard costs

    c. hard to take a physical inventory

    d. not necessary to take a physical inventory

5. Under the job order cost system:

    a. subsidiary ledgers are not maintained

    b. the costs are applied to specific jobs

    c. the costs are in good order

    d. the jobs are costed at standard

6. Equivalent units are used with:

    a. actual costs

    b. standard costs

    c. process costs

    d. prime costs

7. Overhead costs are overapplied if:

    a. standard overhead costs exceed actual costs

    b. actual overhead costs exceed standard costs

    c. controllable overhead costs exceed fixed costs

    d. fixed overhead costs exceed actual costs

8. A budget performance report

    a. reports the complete budget

    b. compares actual costs to standard

    c. compares fixed costs to controllable costs

    d. is a continuous budget of costs

9. If the standard cost for a certain material used is 2,000 pounds at $10 and the actual cost is 2,100 pounds at $9, the quantity variance is:

    a. $100

    b. $90

    c. $1,000

    d. $900

10. The price variance for the data in Question 9 is:

    a. $1,000

    b. $2,100

    c. $1,100

    d. $3,200

Part III. *Insert the answer in the amount column below.*

Compute	Amount	Question Data
1. Purchases		Raw material used, $36,000; raw material inventory decreased by $8,500 during period.
2. Overhead rate		Three direct labor employees work 40 hours a week for 50 weeks a year. Factory overhead cost of $60,000 is distributed on the basis of direct labor hours.
3. Cost of goods manufactured		Raw materials: beginning inventory, $35,000; ending inventory, $30,000; purchases, $50,000. Direct labor, $40,000. Factory overhead, $32,000. Work in process: beginning, $95,000; ending, $90,000. Finished goods: beginning inventory, $18,000; ending inventory, $24,000.
4. Cost of goods sold		Same as in Question 3.
5. (a) Work in process by jobs (b) Overapplied overhead in total		(see data below)
6. Equivalent units of production		Opening inventory: 1,000 units, 2/5 completed. Completed during period: 5,000 units. Closing inventory: 1,200 units, 2/3 completed.
7. Processing cost per equivalent unit		The costs in the work in process account for the equivalent units in Question 6 were: Materials, $4,000; Direct Labor, $6,000; Factory Overhead, $4,800.
8. Production budget		Expected quantities for November were: opening inventory, 5,000; desired closing inventory, 6,000; expected sales volume (section 1), 6,000; expected sales volume (section 2), 4,000.
9. (a) Quantity variance (b) Price variance		The direct materials standard for the period was 15,000 pounds at $1.00; the actual was 15,500 pounds at $1.25.
10. (a) Time variance (b) Rate variance		The labor standard for the period was 10,000 hours at $3.00; the actual was 9,600 hours at $3.20.

Data for Question 5:

	Total	#1	#2	#3	#4
Raw material used	$ 6,500	$2,000	$2,500	$1,500	$ 500
Direct labor	10,000	3,000	4,000	2,000	1,000
Factory overhead incurred	7,500				
Factory overhead applied (80%)					

Jobs #1 and #2 were completed.

Answers to Examination II

Part I

1. F,   2. F,   3. T,   4. F,   5. T,   6. F,   7. T,   8. F,   9. T,   10. F

Part II

1. b,   2. a,   3. b,   4. d,   5. b,   6. c,   7. a,   8. b

9. c: $100 \times \$10 = \$1,000$ (unfavorable)

10. b: $2,100 \times \$1 = \underline{2,100}$ (favorable)

$\$1,100 (= 2,000 \times \$10 - 2,100 \times \$9)$

Part III

1. $\$36,000 - \$8,500 = \$27,500$

2. $\$60,000 \div 6,000$ hours $= \$10$ per hour

3. $\$95,000 + \$35,000 + \$50,000 + \$40,000 + \$32,000 - \$30,000 - \$90,000 = \$132,000$

4. $\$18,000 + \$132,000 - \$24,000 = \$126,000$

5.   (a)   Job #3: $\$1,500 + \$2,000 + \$1,600 = \$5,100$
         Job #4: $\$500 + \$1,000 + \$800 = \$2,300$

     (b) $\$8,000 - \$7,500 = \$500$

6. $1,200 \times 2/3 - 1,000 \times 2/5 + 5,000 \times 1 = 5,400$

7. $(\$6,000 + \$4,800) \div 5,400 = \$2$ per equivalent unit

8. $\$6,000 + \$4,000 + \$6,000 - \$5,000 = \$11,000$

9.   (a) $(15,500 - 15,000) \times \$1.00 = \$500$ (unfavorable)

     (b) $(\$1.25 - \$1.00) \times 15,500 = \$3,875$ (unfavorable)

10.   (a) $(10,000 - 9,600) \times \$3.00 = \$1,200$ (favorable)

      (b) $(\$3.20 - \$3.00) \times 9,600 = \$1,920$ (unfavorable)

Chapter 8

Financial Statement Analysis

8.1 INTRODUCTION

The periodic financial statements give owners, employees, creditors, investors, government agencies, and others a picture of management's performance. Thus, the solvency of the enterprise is presented in the balance sheet, and its profitability in the income statement.

To obtain further details of the performance results it is necessary to subject the published data to various analytical measurements. The measurements fall into three main types, which are presented in Sections 8.2, 8.3, and 8.4.

8.2 AMOUNT AND PERCENTAGE CHANGES (HORIZONTAL ANALYSIS)

In most cases published annual reports to stockholders show financial statements for prior years, sometimes extending back over a ten-year period. The year-to-year changes in each item can then be computed and intercompared. In such a *horizontal analysis* the changes may be specified as absolute amounts or as percentages.

EXAMPLE 1.

The Ryefield Company
Comparative Balance Sheet
years ended December 31, 1973, 1972, and 1971

	1973	1972	1971	Increase or (Decrease) 1973-72	Increase or (Decrease) 1972-71	Percent of Increase or (Decrease) 1973-72	Percent of Increase or (Decrease) 1972-71
ASSETS							
Current Assets	$130,000	$120,000	$100,000	$10,000	$20,000	8.3%	20.0%
Plant Assets	69,000	60,000	65,000	9,000	(5,000)	15.0%	(13.0%)
Total Assets	$199,000	$180,000	$165,000	$19,000	$15,000	10.6%	9.1%
LIABILITIES							
Current Liabilities	$ 50,000	$ 60,000	$ 55,000	$(10,000)	$ 5,000	(16.7%)	9.1%
Long-Term Liabilities	85,000	70,000	70,000	15,000	....	21.4%	....
Total Liabilities	$135,000	$130,000	$125,000	$ 5,000	$ 5,000	3.8%	4.0%
STOCKHOLDERS' EQUITY							
Preferred Stock, 5%, $100 par	$ 10,000	$ 10,000	$ 10,000	....	....	....	....
Common Stock, $5 par	30,000	30,000	30,000	....	....	....	....
Retained Earnings	24,000	10,000	....	14,000	10,000	140.0%	....
Total Stockholders' Equity	$ 64,000	$ 50,000	$ 40,000	$14,000	$10,000	28.0%	25.0%
Total Liabilities and Stockholders' Equity	$199,000	$180,000	$165,000	$19,000	$15,000	10.6%	9.1%

The above horizontal analysis of the balance sheets of the Ryefield Company covers a three-year period. The total assets increased from 9.1% to 10.6% while liabilities decreased from 4.0% to 3.8%, resulting in an increase in stockholders' equity from 25.0% to 28.0%.

EXAMPLE 2.

The following horizontal analysis of the Ryefield Company's income statements covers a two-year period.

The Ryefield Company
Comparative Income Statement
years ended December 31, 1973 and 1972

	1973	1972	Increase or (Decrease) Amount	Percent
Sales	$158,000	$100,000	$58,000	58.0%
Sales Returns and Allowances	8,000	10,000	(2,000)	(20.0%)
Net Sales	$150,000	90,000	60,000	66.7%
Cost of Goods Sold	96,000	49,000	47,000	95.9%
Gross Profit	$ 54,000	$ 41,000	$13,000	31.7%
Selling Expenses	$ 15,000	$ 10,000	$ 5,000	50.0%
General Expenses	10,000	8,000	2,000	25.0%
Total Operating Expenses	$ 25,000	$ 18,000	$ 7,000	38.9%
Net Operating Income	$ 29,000	$ 23,000	$ 6,000	26.0%
Other Expenses	5,000	7,000	(2,000)	28.6%
Income Before Income Tax	$ 24,000	$ 16,000	$ 8,000	50.0%
Income Tax	10,000	6,000	4,000	66.7%
Net Income	$ 14,000	$ 10,000	$ 4,000	40.0%

It is seen that while the net sales increased by a substantial amount, 66.7%, the cost of sales increased by even more, 95.9%. This would indicate a decrease in percentage of gross profit in relation to sales – a feature shown more clearly in the component analysis (vertical analysis) in Example 4.

8.3 COMPONENT PERCENTAGES (VERTICAL ANALYSIS)

In this type of analysis each item is expressed as a percentage of a significant total (e.g., an asset item would be expressed as a percentage of total assets). Percentages for various years can then be compared, as in horizontal analysis.

EXAMPLE 3.

For the balance sheets of the Ryefield Company (see Example 1) we have the following vertical analysis:

The Ryefield Company
Comparative Balance Sheet
years ended December 31, 1973, 1972, and 1971

	Amount			Percent of Group Total		
ASSETS	1973	1972	1971	1973	1972	1971
Current Assets	$130,000	$120,000	$100,000	65.3%	66.7%	60.6%
Plant Assets	69,000	60,000	65,000	34.7%	33.3%	39.4%
Total Assets	$199,000	$180,000	$165,000	100.0%	100.0%	100.0%

(continued next page)

	Amount			Percent of Group Total		
	1973	**1972**	**1971**	**1973**	**1972**	**1971**
LIABILITIES						
Current Liabilities	$ 50,000	$ 60,000	$ 55,000	25.1%	33.3%	33.3%
Long-Term						
Liabilities	85,000	70,000	70,000	42.7%	38.9%	42.5%
Total Liabilities	$135,000	$130,000	$125,000	67.8%	72.2%	75.8%
STOCKHOLDERS' EQUITY						
Preferred Stock	$ 10,000	$ 10,000	10,000	5.0%	5.6%	6.0%
Common Stock	30,000	30,000	30,000	15.1%	16.6%	18.2%
Retained Earnings	24,000	10,000	....	12.1%	5.6%	....
Total Stockholders'						
Equity	$ 64,000	$ 50,000	$ 40,000	32.2%	27.8%	24.2%
Total Liabilities						
and Stockholders'						
Equity	$199,000	$180,000	$165,000	100.0%	100.0%	100.0%

The current assets showed an improvement from 60.6% in 1971 to 65.3% in 1973, indicating an improvement in working capital. Current liabilities showed a decrease from 33.3% in 1971 to 25.1% in 1973, which further helped working capital. The specific improvement in working capital will be shown in Example 5.

EXAMPLE 4.

For the income statements of Example 2 we have the following vertical analysis:

The Ryefield Company
Comparative Income Statement
years ended December 31, 1973 and 1972

	Amount		Percent	
	1973	**1972**	**1973**	**1972**
Sales	$158,000	$100,000	105.3%	111.1%
Sales Returns and Allowances	8,000	10,000	5.3%	11.1%
Net Sales	$150,000	$ 90,000	100.0%	100.0%
Cost of Goods Sold	96,000	49,000	64.0%	54.4%
Gross Profit	$ 54,000	$ 41,000	36.0%	45.6%
Selling Expenses	$ 15,000	$ 10,000	10.0%	11.1%
General Expenses	10,000	8,000	6.7%	8.9%
Total Operating Expenses	$ 25,000	$ 18,000	16.7%	20.0%
Net Operating Income	$ 29,000	$ 23,000	19.3%	25.6%
Other Expenses	5,000	7,000	3.3%	7.8%
Income Before Income Tax	$ 24,000	$ 16,000	16.0%	17.8%
Income Tax	10,000	6,000	6.7%	6.7%
Net Income	$ 14,000	$ 10,000	9.3%	11.1%

As was pointed out in Example 2, there was a substantial increase in sales, which was favorable, but there was an even greater increase in cost of goods sold, which would indicate a decrease in gross profit. This is clearly borne out in the above vertical analysis. A serious problem is indicated for The Ryefield Company, since there is normally a tendency for the cost of goods sold percentage to *decrease* when there is a very large increase in sales. Further investigation would be required to pinpoint the cause. There may have been an increase in purchase prices which was not yet reflected in sales prices. If manufacturing was involved, the increase may be due to increases in labor rates or labor use, materials cost, etc.

The percentages developed for one company by vertical analysis can be compared to those of another company or to the industry percentages that are published by trade associations and financial services. The comparison is displayed on a *common-size statement*, so called because all dollar amounts are omitted.

8.4 ANALYSIS BY RATIOS

In both horizontal and vertical analysis we compare one figure to another figure of the same category. In many cases it is more revealing to relate, by forming their ratio, two figures belonging to different categories.

RATIOS FOR WORKING CAPITAL

A company's *working capital* is the excess of its current assets over its current liabilities.

Current ratio.   This is the ratio of current assets to current liabilities. Since it tells *how many times over* the company could pay its current debts, it is a better index of solvency than the dollar amount of working capital.

EXAMPLE 5.

The Ryefield Company
Current Ratio
1973 and 1972

	1973	1972
Current Assets	$130,000	$120,000
Less: Current Liabilities	50,000	60,000
Working Capital	$ 80,000	$ 60,000
Current Ratio	2.6	2.0

The improvement in the current ratio from 2.0 to 2.6 might influence a banker to make a short-term loan to the company. The current ratio is sometimes called the *banker's ratio.*

Quick or acid-test ratio.   When inventories and prepaid expenses are excluded from current assets, the current ratio becomes the *quick ratio,* a measure of the company's ability to pay its debts quickly. Inventories are left out because they are subject to decline in market value and because much time may be needed to convert them into cash.

EXAMPLE 6.

The Ryefield Company (Example 5) had inventories of $75,000 in 1973 and $60,000 in 1972.

The Ryefield Company
Quick Assets
1973 and 1972

	1973	1972
Quick Assets	$65,000	$60,000
Current Liabilities	50,000	60,000
Quick Ratio	1.3	1.0

RATIOS FOR ACCOUNTS RECEIVABLE

The control of the amount of accounts receivable at any given moment is an important part of the overall control of working capital. Through effective control of accounts receivable, inventories, and other components of working capital many companies today have been able to finance a volume of sales two or three times that of a decade ago without a comparable increase in working capital.

Turnover of accounts receivable. This ratio is formed by dividing the net sales for the year by the average balance of accounts receivable for the year. Thus, the ratio reflects the number of times the accounts receivable amount has *turned over* during the year. To compute the average balance of accounts receivable one can take half the sum of the beginning and year-end balances. (A better average can be obtained from the monthly balances, but usually these are known only to management.) If a breakdown between charge and cash sales is available, only the charge sales should be included in net sales.

EXAMPLE 7.

The Cornfeld Company
Turnover of Accounts Receivable
1973 and 1972

	1973	1972
Net Sales for the Year	$1,250,000	$1,000,000
Accounts Receivable (net)		
Beginning of the Year	72,000	88,000
End of the Year	93,600	72,000
Total	$ 165,600	$ 160,000
Average	$ 82,800	$ 80,000
Turnover of Accounts Receivable	15.1	12.5

The larger the turnover the better; therefore, the trend from 1972 to 1973 was favorable.

Number of days' sales in receivables. Another measure of accounts receivable activities is computed by dividing the accounts receivable at the end of the year by the average daily sales on account. The latter figure is obtained by dividing net sales on account by 365. For this ratio, small values are desirable, as they indicate small amounts of working capital tied up in receivables.

EXAMPLE 8.

From Example 7 the average daily sales on account are $1,000,000/365 = $2,740 for 1972 and $1,250,000/365 = $3,425 for 1973.

The Cornfeld Company
Number of Days' Sales in Receivables
1973 and 1972

	1973	1972
Accounts Receivable at End of Year	$93,600	$72,000
Average Daily Sales on Account	3,425	2,740
Number of Days' Sales in Receivables	27.3	26.3

Here the trend is unfavorable, since the number of days' sales in receivables *increased* from 26.3 to 27.3.

RATIOS FOR INVENTORY

The firm's investment in inventory also has a direct effect on its working capital. If there is excess inventory, it means that funds are tied up in inventory that could be used more profitably elsewhere. Also, additional costs are being incurred for storage, insurance, and property taxes, not to mention the danger of a price decline and obsolescence of goods. The two principal ratios for inventory are exactly analogous to those for accounts receivable.

Turnover of inventory. This is the ratio of the cost of goods sold to the average inventory. The average inventory in most published statements is obtained by taking half the sum of the beginning and ending inventories.

EXAMPLE 9.

The Oates Company
Turnover of Inventory
1973 and 1972

	1973	1972
Cost of Goods Sold	$750,000	$550,000
Merchandise Inventory		
Beginning of the Year	84,200	53,300
End of the Year	130,100	84,200
Total	$214,300	$137,500
Average	$107,150	$ 68,750
Turnover of Inventory	7.0	8.0

In this case there was an unfavorable trend in inventory turnover from 8.0 in 1972 to 7.0 in 1973. While cost of goods sold increased by 36.4%, average inventory increased by 55.9%. The various classifications of inventory should be compared for the two years to find the classification in which the large change occurred. A new product requiring the carrying of additional items in inventory often accounts for part of an increase. *

Number of days' sales in inventory. The relationship between inventory and cost of goods sold can also be expressed as the number of days' sales in inventory. In this ratio the inventory at the end of the year is divided by the average daily cost of goods sold. The latter figure is determined by dividing the cost of goods sold by 365. The number of days' sales in inventory provides a rough measure of the length of time required to buy, sell, and then replace the inventory.

EXAMPLE 10.

For the Oates Company (Example 9) the average daily cost of goods sold is $550,000/365 = $1,507 for 1972 and $750,000/365 = $2,055 for 1973.

The Oates Company
Number of Days' Sales in Inventory
1973 and 1972

	1973	1972
Inventory at End of Year	130,100	84,200
Average Daily Cost of Goods Sold	2,055	1,507
Number of Days' Sales in Inventory	63.3	55.9

This ratio would, of course, reflect the same unfavorable trend as in Example 9. Here the number of days' sales in inventory increased from 55.9 days to 63.3 days.

RATIO OF EQUITY TO LIABILITIES

It is important to know the sources of funds for an enterprise. If funds obtained from creditors are large in proportion to stockholders' equity, there will likely be a substantial fixed obligation each period in the form of interest. The equity-to-liabilities ratio indicates the margin of safety for creditors and the ability of the enterprise to weather business hardship.

EXAMPLE 11.

From the data in Example 3:

The Ryefield Company
Ratio of Stockholders' Equity to Liabilities
1973 and 1972

	1973	1972
Total Stockholders' Equity	$ 64,000	$ 50,000
Total Liabilities	135,000	130,000
Ratio of Stockholders' Equity to Liabilities	.47	.38

The slight improvement in the ratio is due primarily to the increase in owners' equity.

RATIO OF PLANT ASSETS TO LONG-TERM LIABILITIES

This ratio gauges the safety of those holding notes or bonds of the firm. Further, it gives an indication of the extent of possible additional long-term borrowings.

EXAMPLE 12.

From the data in Example 3:

The Ryefield Company
Ratio of Plant Assets to Long-Term Liabilities
1973 and 1972

	1973	1972
Plant Assets (net)	$69,000	$60,000
Long-Term Liabilities	85,000	70,000
Ratio of Plant Assets to Long-Term Liabilities	.81	.86

RATIO OF NET SALES TO ASSETS

This ratio is a good means of comparing companies in regard to their utilization of assets. For example, two companies may have approximately the same amount of assets but the sales of one may be two or three times those of the other. Long-term investments are excluded from total assets as they are unrelated to sales. As the denominator of the ratio one uses an average of the total assets based on as much data as possible. Thus, one may take the average of the beginning and year-end amounts, which are usually shown in published reports. For internal company purposes the average may be based on monthly totals.

EXAMPLE 13.

From the data in Examples 3 and 4:

The Ryefield Company
Ratio of Net Sales to Assets
1973 and 1972

	1973	1972
Net Sales	$150,000	$ 90,000
Total Assets		
Beginning of Year	180,000	165,000
End of Year	199,000	180,000
Total	$379,000	$345,000
Average	$189,500	$172,500
Ratio of Net Sales to Assets	.79	.52

RATE EARNED ON TOTAL ASSETS

This is the ratio of net income (suitably defined) to average total assets. It indicates the productivity of the total assets without distinguishing between stockholders' equity and liabilities. Therefore the rate is independent of whether the company uses equity funding, debt funding, or a combination of the two. (See Sec. 4.4.) Since interest expense is related to a particular method of financing, the amount in the current year is added back to true net income to give the "net income" that is divided by total assets.

EXAMPLE 14.

The Ryefield Company
Rate Earned on Total Assets
1973 and 1972

	1973	1972
Net Income	$ 14,000	$ 10,000
Add: Interest Expense	4,200	4,200
Total	$ 18,200	$ 14,200
Total Assets		
Beginning of Year	$180,000	$165,000
End of Year	199,000	180,000
Total	$379,000	$345,000
Average	$189,500	$172,500
Rate Earned on Total Assets	10.1%	8.2%

EARNINGS PER SHARE ON COMMON STOCK

Earnings per share on common stock is the financial ratio that is quoted most often. Where there are both preferred stock and common stock, the net income must be reduced by preferred stock dividends to arrive at the amount applicable to common stock. Where there is only one class of stock, the full net income is divided by the number of shares outstanding to give the earnings per share on common stock. Any changes in outstanding shares, such as those from stock dividends or stock splits, should be disclosed when reporting earnings per share on common stock. If extraordinary items are included in net income, the per share earnings should be shown in three amounts: (1) net income per share before extraordinary items, (2) extraordinary gain (or loss) per share, and (3) net income per share. The earnings per share is used by the investor to evaluate the performance of a company and to estimate its future possibilities. Also, the dividends that might be expected by the investor are generally tied to earnings.

EXAMPLE 15.

The Ryefield Company
Earnings per Share
1973 and 1972

	1973	1972
Net Income	$14,000	$10,000
Less: Preferred Dividends	500	500
Available for Common Stock	$13,500	$ 9,500
Shares of Common Stock Outstanding	6,000	6,000
Earnings per Share on Common Stock	$2.25	$1.58

Summary

(1) The analysis of changes in each item in comparative financial statements is called _____ analysis.

(2) The analysis of changes of each item expressed as a percentage of a significant total is called _____ analysis.

(3) The vertical analysis of the percentages of one company compared with percentages published by trade associations is presented in _____.

(4) The excess of current assets over current liabilities is referred to as _____.

(5) The ratio obtained by dividing current assets by current liabilities is called the _____ ratio.

(6) The _____ ratio indicates the ability of a company to pay its debts quickly.

(7) Accounts receivable turnover is computed by dividing _____ by the average balance of _____.

(8) Merchandise inventory turnover is computed by dividing the _____ _____ by the _____.

(9) The rate earned on stockholders' equity is computed by dividing _____ by _____.

(10) The earnings per common share, where there is only one class of stock, is computed by dividing _____ by the _____.

Answers: (1) horizontal; (2) vertical; (3) common-size statements; (4) working capital; (5) current; (6) acid-test; (7) net sales on account, accounts receivable; (8) cost of goods sold, average inventory; (9) net income, total stockholders' equity; (10) net income, number of shares outstanding

Solved Problems

8.1. The Epp Company had the following income and expense data:

	Year 2	Year 1
Net sales	$350,000	$200,000
Cost of goods sold	245,000	130,000
Expenses	70,000	40,000

(a) Prepare a comparative income statement for Year 1 and Year 2 showing each item in relation to sales.   (b) Comment on the significant changes shown by the statement.

(a)

The Epp Company
Comparative Income Statement
years ended December 31, Year 2 and Year 1

	Dollars		Percentages	
	Year 2	Year 1	Year 2	Year 1

SOLUTION

(a)

The Epp Company
Comparative Income Statement
years ended December 31, Year 2 and Year 1

	Dollars		Percentages	
	Year 2	Year 1	Year 2	Year 1
Net Sales	$350,000	$200,000	100%	100%
Cost of Goods Sold	245,000	130,000	70	65
Gross Profit	$105,000	$ 70,000	30%	35%
Expenses	70,000	40,000	20	20
Net Income	$ 35,000	$ 30,000	10%	15%

(b) The cost of goods sold showed a substantial increase, from 65% to 70%, giving an increase of cost of $17,500 (5% × $350,000). The percentage of expenses to sales remained the same. Net income was $5,000 more in Year 2, but the percentage to sales decreased from 15% to 10%. If the percentage of net income for Year 2 had been the same as for Year 1, the amount of net income would have been $52,500 instead of $35,000.

8.2. The Reilly Company had the following financial position data:

	Year 2	Year 1
Cash	$ 95,000	$50,000
Marketable securities	50,000	35,000
Receivables (net)	90,000	60,000
Inventories	100,000	85,000
Prepaid expenses	15,000	20,000
Notes payable	55,000	30,000
Accounts payable	70,000	40,000
Accrued liabilities	50,000	30,000

Compute (a) working capital, (b) current ratio, (c) acid-test ratio.

(a)   **Year 2   Year 1**

(b)

(c)

SOLUTION

(a)   **Year 2   Year 1**

		Year 2	Year 1
	Current assets	$350,000	$250,000
	Less: Current liabilities	175,000	100,000
	Working capital	$175,000	$150,000

(b)   Current assets ÷ Current
      liabilities

$$\frac{\$350,000}{\$175,000} = 2.0 \text{ to } 1$$

$$\frac{\$250,000}{\$100,000} = 2.5 \text{ to } 1$$

(c)   Quick assets ÷ Current
      liabilities

$$\frac{\$235,000}{\$175,000} = 1.3 \text{ to } 1$$

$$\frac{\$145,000}{\$100,000} = 1.45 \text{ to } 1$$

8.3. Hebbco and Davco are considering a merger and have prepared the following financial data:

	Hebbco	Davco
Sales, all on account	$2,000,000	$1,500,000
Total assets	1,000,000	500,000
Total liabilities	200,000	100,000
Gross profit, based on sales	40%	33%
Operating expenses, based on sales	30%	20%
Net income, based on sales	8%	9%

Compute for each company: (a) net income as a percentage of sales, (b) net income as a percentage of total assets, (c) net income as a percentage of stockholders' equity.

(a)

	Hebbco	Davco

(b)   **Hebbco:**
      Davco:

(c)

	Hebbco	Davco

Hebbco:
Davco:

SOLUTION

(a)

		Hebbco		Davco
Sales		$2,000,000		$1,500,000
Cost of goods sold		1,200,000		1,000,000
Gross profit	(40%)	$ 800,000	(33%)	$ 500,000
Operating expenses	(30%)	600,000	(20%)	300,000
Operating income		$ 200,000		$ 200,000
Income tax		40,000		65,000
Net income	(8%)	$ 160,000	(9%)	$ 135,000

(b)   **Hebbco:** $160,000 ÷ $1,000,000 = 16%
      Davco: $135,000 ÷ $500,000 = 27%

(c)

	Hebbco	Davco
Total assets	$1,000,000	$500,000
Less: Total liabilities	200,000	100,000
Stockholders' equity	$ 800,000	$400,000

Hebbco: $160,000 ÷ $300,000 = 20%
Davco: $135,000 ÷ $400,000 = 34%

8.4.   The Giordano Company has the following data:

	Year 2	Year 1
Accounts receivable, end of year	$ 380,000	$ 370,000
Monthly average of accounts receivable (net)	410,000	390,000
Net sales on account	3,000,000	2,500,000

Terms of sale: 1/10, n/60

(a) Compute for each year (i) the number of days' sales in receivables, and (ii) the accounts receivable turnover.

(b) Analyze the results obtained in (a).

(a)   **Year 2**   **Year 1**

(i)

(ii)

SOLUTION

(a)   **Year 2**   **Year 1**

(i) $\dfrac{\$3,000,000}{365} = \$8,219$ $\dfrac{\$2,500,000}{365} = \$6,849$

       $\dfrac{\$380,000}{\$8,219} = 46 \text{ days}$ $\dfrac{\$370,000}{\$6,849} = 54 \text{ days}$

(ii) $\dfrac{\$3,000,000}{\$410,000} = 7.3 \text{ times}$ $\dfrac{\$2,500,000}{\$390,000} = 6.4 \text{ times}$

(b) The number of days' sales in receivables dropped from 54 to 46. However, this is still not satisfactory in view of the credit terms, since many customers pay their bills during the discount period. The accounts receivable turnover increased from 6.4 to 7.3, a substantial favorable change. Even with the above improvements the credit and collection policies should be reviewed for possible further improvements.

8.5. The Whyte Company's income statements show the following data:

	Year 2	Year 1
Sales	$1,500,000	$1,200,000
Beginning inventory	250,000	225,000
Purchases	750,000	550,000
Ending inventory	200,000	175,000

(a) Compute for each year (i) the inventory turnover, and (ii) the number of days' sales in inventory.

(b) Analyze the results obtained in (a).

(a)

	Year 2	Year 1
(i)		
(ii)		

SOLUTION

(a)

	Year 2	Year 1
(i)	$800,000 ÷ $225,000 = 3.6	$600,000 ÷ $200,000 = 3.0
(ii)	$800,000 ÷ 365 = $2,192	$600,000 ÷ 365 = $1,644
	$200,000 ÷ $2,192 = 91.2 days	$175,000 ÷ $1,644 = 106.4 days

(b) The inventory turnover and the number of days' sales in inventory showed favorable trends for the current year. Further comparisons should be made with the data of other firms in the same industry.

8.6. The Folk Company balance sheet showed the following data:

Total current liabilities	$275,000
Bonds payable, 7% (issued in 1965, due in 1985)	300,000
Preferred stock, 7%, $100 par	200,000
Common stock, $20 par	400,000
Premium on common stock	250,000
Retained earnings	175,000

The income before income tax was $150,000 and income taxes were $60,000 for the current year. Compute (a) rate earned on total assets, (b) rate earned on common stock, (c) number of times bond interest charges were earned, (d) earnings per share on common stock.

(a) _____

(b) _____

(c) _____

(d) _____

SOLUTION

(a) NET INCOME, $90,000 ($150,000 − $60,000) + INTEREST EXPENSE, $21,000 = $111,000 ÷ TOTAL ASSETS, $1,6000,000 (equal to liabilities and capital) = 7.0%

(b) NET INCOME, $90,000 − PREFERRED DIVIDENDS, $14,000 = $76,000 ÷ COMMON STOCKHOLDERS' EQUITY, $825,000 = 9.2%

(c) INCOME BEFORE INCOME TAX, $150,000 + INTEREST EXPENSE, $21,000 = $171,000 ÷ INTEREST CHARGES, $21,000 = 8.1 times

(d) NET INCOME, $90,000 − PREFERRED DIVIDENDS, $14,000 = $76,000 ÷ NUMBER OF SHARES OF COMMON STOCK, 20,000 = $3.80

8.7. The following data have been taken from the current balance sheet of the Rolston Manufacturing Company:

Cash	$ 83,000
Marketable securities (at cost)	40,000
Accounts receivable	95,000
Allowance for uncollectible accounts	3,000
Inventories	199,000
Prepaid expenses	16,000
Accounts payable	80,000
Notes payable (short-term)	16,000
Income taxes payable	11,000
Accrued liabilities	18,000
Current portion of long-term debt	10,000

(a) Compute the working capital, current ratio, and acid-test ratio.

(b) State the *immediate* effect (increase, decrease, no change) that each of the following transactions has on the working capital, the current ratio, and the acid-test ratio. Use the letters I, D, and N to indicate your answers. Consider each transaction separately, but indicate a transaction's *simultaneous* effect on all three of the above.

(1) Wrote off an account receivable against the allowance for uncollectible accounts, $10,000
(2) Purchased raw materials on account, $50,000
(3) Collected cash in payment of an account receivable, $15,000
(4) Paid for fire insurance in advance, $12,000
(5) Paid a short-term note payable, $30,000
(6) Declared and distributed a 10% stock dividend, $40,000
(7) Sold marketable securities costing $20,000 for $15,000
(8) Borrowed $10,000 from the bank on a short-term note
(9) Disposed of equipment with a book value of $12,000 for $5,000 cash
(10) Declared and paid a cash dividend, $6,000
(11) Issued additional common stock for $20,000
(12) Purchased raw materials for cash, $15,000

(a)

(b)

	Effect on		
	Work. Cap.	Curr. Ratio	Acid-Test Ratio
(1)			
(2)			
(3)			
(4)			
(5)			
(6)			
(7)			
(8)			
(9)			
(10)			
(11)			
(12)			

SOLUTION

(a)

Current assets	$430,000
Less: Current liabilities	135,000
Working capital	$295,000

Current ratio = Current assets ÷ Current liabilities
= $430,000 ÷ $135,000
= 3.2 : 1

Acid-test ratio = Quick assets ÷ Current liabilities
= $215,000 ÷ $135,000
= 1.6 : 1

(b)

	Effect on			Stated in M Dollars				Ratios	
	Work. Cap.	Curr. Ratio	Acid-Test Ratio	Quick Assets	Curr. Assets −	Curr. Liabil. =	Work. Cap.	Curr. Ratio	Acid-Test Ratio
Bal.				215	430	135	295	3.2	1.6
(1)	N	N	N	−10 +10	−10 +10		0		
Bal.				215	430	135	295	3.2	1.6
(2)	N	D	D		+50	+50	0		
Bal.				215	480	185	295	2.6	1.2
(3)	N	N	N	+15 −15	+15 −15				
Bal.				215	430	135	295	3.2	1.6
(4)	N	N	D		−3 +3				
Bal.				−12 203	430	135	295	3.2	1.5
(5)	N	I	I	−30	−30	−30			
Bal.				185	400	105	295	3.8	1.8
(6)	N	N	N	0	0	0			
Bal.				215	430	135	295	3.2	1.6
(7)	D	D	D	+15 −20	+15 −20		−5		
Bal.				210	425	135	290	3.15	1.56
(8)	N	D	D	+10	+10	+10			
Bal.				225	440	145	295	3.0	1.55
(9)	I	I	I	+5	+5		+5		
Bal.				220	435	135	300	3.22	1.63
(10)	D	D	D	−6	−6		−6		
Bal.				209	424	135	289	3.1	1.55
(11)	I	I	I	+20	+20		+20		
Bal.				235	450	135	315	3.3	1.7
(12)	N	N	D	−15	+15 −15				
Bal.				200	430	135	295	3.2	1.5

8.8.   Revenue and expense data for the current calendar year for Timpano Toy Company and for the toy manufacturing industry are presented below.

	Timpano Toy Company	Toy Industry Averages
Sales	$4,590,000	101.5%
Sales returns and allowances	90,000	1.5%

(continued next page)

Cost of goods sold	2,655,000	61.2%
Selling expenses	450,000	9.5%
General expenses	427,500	8.8%
Other income	49,500	.5%
Other expenses	54,000	1.0%
Income tax	495,000	10.5%

(a) Prepare a common-size income statement comparing operations for Timpano Toy Company with the toy industry. (b) Comment on the relationships revealed in the common-size income statement.

(a)

Timpano Toy Company and Industry Averages

Common-Size Income Statement

year ended December 31, 197—

	Timpano	Industry

SOLUTION

(a)

Timpano Toy Company and Industry Averages

Common-Size Income Statement

year ended December 31, 197—

	Timpano	Industry
Sales	102.0%	101.5%
Sales Returns and Allowances	2.0	1.5
Net Sales	100.0%	100.0%
Cost of Goods Sold	59.0	61.2
Gross Profit	41.0%	38.8%
Selling Expenses	10.0%	9.5%
General Expenses	9.5	8.8
Total Operating Expense	19.5%	18.3%
Net Operating Income	21.5%	20.5%
Other Income	1.1	.5
	22.6%	21.0%
Other Expenses	1.2	1.0
Income Before Income Tax	21.4%	20.0%
Income Tax	11.0	10.5
Net Income	10.4%	9.5%

(b) The net income of Timpano Toy Company is .9% over the industry average, mainly because Timpano's cost of goods sold is 2.2% below the industry average. This condition is the result of efficiency in the purchasing department and minimal amounts of lost and spoiled goods. The total operating expense percentage of Timpano Toy Company is 1.2% above the industry average. This warrants a close look at general and selling expenses to determine where expenses can be cut. The percentage of sales returns and allowances for Timpano Toy Company is .5% higher than the industry average — a situation that also warrants attention.

8.9. The Catanese Company is in the midst of a promotional campaign to boost sales. In Year 2 an additional $70,000 was spent for advertising. Presented below are revenue and expense data for the company.

	Year 2	Year 1
Sales	$816,000	$656,500
Sales returns and allowances	16,000	6,500
Cost of goods sold	400,000	312,000
Selling expenses	200,000	130,000
General expenses	120,000	78,000
Other income	6,400	6,500
Income tax	32,000	67,600

(a) Prepare a comparative income statement for Year 2 and Year 1 for the Catanese Company. (b) Comment on the relationships revealed in the comparative income statement.

(a)

	Dollars		Percentages	
	Year 2	Year 1	Year 2	Year 1

SOLUTION

(a)

	Dollars		Percentages	
	Year 2	Year 1	Year 2	Year 1
Sales	$816,000	$656,500	102.0%	101.0%
Sales Returns and Allowances	16,000	6,500	2.0	1.0
Net Sales	$800,000	$650,000	100.0%	100.0%
Cost of Goods Sold	400,000	312,000	50.0%	48.0
Gross Profit	$400,000	$338,000	50.0%	52.0%

(continued next page)

	Dollars		Percentages	
	Year 2	**Year 1**	**Year 2**	**Year 1**
Selling Expenses	$200,000	$130,000	25.0%	20.0%
General Expenses	120,000	78,000	15.0	12.0
Total Operating Expense	$320,000	$208,000	40.0%	32.0%
Net Operating Income	$ 80,000	$130,000	10.0%	20.0%
Other Income	6,400	6,500	.8	1.0
Income Before Tax	$ 86,400	$136,500	10.8%	21.0%
Income Tax	32,000	67,600	4.0	10.4
Net Income	$ 54,400	$ 68,900	6.8%	10.6%

(b) Among the significant relationships revealed by the comparative income statement are:

(1) The ratio of cost of goods sold increased and thus the gross profit ratio decreased from 52% to 50%; the Catanese Company suffered a $16,000 (2% × $800,000) decrease in potential gross profit.

(2) The rate of selling expenses rose from 20% to 25%. This can be explained by the increase in advertising expense.

(3) The 3% general expense increase may be explained by a strike in the Hicksville plant.

(4) The sales returns and allowances doubled. This may be a result of poorer product quality or a too-aggressive sales policy.

8.10. The financial statements of B. R. Blaine & Co. are presented below.

B. R. Blaine & Co.
Balance Sheet
December 31, 197–

ASSETS

Current Assets

Cash	$ 102,600	
Marketable Securities	57,000	
Accounts Receivable (net)	303,000	
Merchandise Inventory	476,000	
Prepaid Expenses	11,400	
Total Current Assets		$ 950,000
Long-Term Investments		
Investment in Affiliated Company		190,000
Plant Assets		
Equipment (net)	617,500	
Buildings (net)	1,163,750	
Land	118,750	
Total Plant Assets		1,900,000
Total Assets		$3,040,000

LIABILITIES

Current Liabilities		
Accounts Payable		$ 469,000
Long-Term Liabilities		
Mortgage Note Payable, due 1990	$ 170,000	
Bonds Payable, 5%, due 1995	570,000	
Total Long-Term Liabilities		740,000
Total Liabilities		$1,209,000

(continued next page)

STOCKHOLDERS' EQUITY

Preferred Stock, 6%, cumulative,		
nonparticipating, $100 par	$ 475,000	
Common Stock, $25 par	475,000	
Retained Earnings	881,000	
Total Stockholders' Equity		1,831,000
Total Liabilities and Stockholders'		
Equity		$3,040,000

The following data is from the balance sheet at December 31 of the preceding year:

Accounts Receivable (net)	$ 211,000
Long-Term Investments	166,250
Total Assets	2,940,000
Total Stockholders' Equity	1,755,000

B. R. Blaine & Co.
Income Statement
year ended December 31, 197–

Sales	$2,935,500	
Less: Sales Returns and Allowances	85,500	
Net Sales		$2,850,000
Cost of Merchandise Sold		
Merchandise Inventory,		
January 1, 197–	360,000	
Purchases (net)	2,111,000	
Merchandise Available for Sale	2,471,000	
Merchandise Inventory,		
December 31, 197–	476,000	
Cost of Merchandise Sold		1,995,000
Gross Profit on Sales		$ 855,000
Operating Expenses		
Selling Expenses	$ 427,500	
General Expenses	133,000	
Total Operating Expenses		560,500
Net Operating Income		$ 294,500
Other Income		8,550
		$ 303,050
Other Expense (Interest)		38,000
Income Before Income Tax		$ 265,050
Income Tax		126,350
Net Income		$ 138,700

B. R. Blaine & Co.
Retained Earnings Statement
year ended December 31, 197–

Retained Earnings, January 1, 197–		$805,000
Add: Net Income for Year		138,700
Total		$943,700
Deduct: Dividends		
On Preferred Stock	$28,500	
On Common Stock	34,200	62,700
Retained Earnings, December 31, 197–		$881,000

The number of preferred and common shares and their dollar value are the same for both years. Determine for 197–: (a) working capital, (b) current ratio, (c) acid-test ratio, (d) accounts receivable turnover, (e) number of days' sales in receivables, (f) merchandise inventory turnover, (g) number of days' sales in merchandise inventory, (h) ratio of plant assets to long-term liabilities, (i) ratio of stockholders' equity to liabilities, (j) rate earned on total assets, (k) rate earned on stockholders' equity, (l) earnings per share on common stock.

(a) _____
(b) _____
(c) _____
(d) _____
(e) _____
(f) _____
(g) _____
(h) _____
(i) _____
(j) _____
(k) _____
(l) _____

SOLUTION

(a) $950,000 − $469,000 = $481,000

(b) $950,000 ÷ $469,000 = 2.0

(c) $462,600 ÷ $469,000 = 1.0

(d) $2,850,000 ÷ $\frac{1}{2}$($303,000 + $211,000) = 11.1

(e) $2,850,000 ÷ 365 = $7,808; $303,000 ÷ $7,808 = 38.9 days

(f) $1,995,000 ÷ $\frac{1}{2}$($476,000 + $360,000) = 4.8

(g) $1,995,000 ÷ 365 = $5,466; $476,000 ÷ $5,466 = 87.1 days

(h) $1,900,000 ÷ $740,000 = 2.6

(i) $1,831,000 ÷ $1,209,000 = 1.5

(j) $176,700 ÷ $\frac{1}{2}$($3,040,000 + $2,940,000) = 5.9%

(k) $138,700 ÷ $\frac{1}{2}$($1,831,000 + $1,755,000) = 7.7%

(l)   ($138,700 − $28,500) ÷ 19,000 = $5.80 per share

Chapter 9

Changes in Financial Position

9.1 INTRODUCTION

By a company's *funds* we mean either its *working capital*, its cash, or sometimes its cash and marketable securities. Working capital is the excess of total current assets over total current liabilities. On any basis the amount of funds is subject to continual change, and management and stockholders want to know:

(1) where funds are coming from (*sources of funds*)

(2) where funds are going (*applications of funds*)

Only partial data are obtainable from the income statement, balance sheet, and retained earnings statement. Hence the need for a detailed accounting of the flow of funds, which is presented in the Statement of Change in Financial Position.

9.2 CHANGES IN WORKING CAPITAL

Example 1 below shows a typical comparative schedule by which the change in working capital is calculated from the changes in individual current asset and current liability items.

EXAMPLE 1.

The Chamberlain Company
Comparative Working Capital Schedule
December 31, 1974 and 1973

Current Assets	1974	1973	Increase or (Decrease)
Cash	$ 75,000	$ 60,000	$15,000
Marketable Securities	35,000	31,000	4,000
Receivables	125,000	128,000	(3,000)
Inventories	650,000	638,000	12,000
Prepaid Expenses	15,000	13,000	2,000
Total	$900,000	$870,000	$30,000
Current Liabilities			
Notes Payable	$ 75,000	$ 60,000	$15,000
Accounts Payable	430,000	450,000	(20,000)
Accrued Liabilities	75,000	70,000	5,000
Income Tax Payable	50,000	40,000	10,000
Total	$630,000	$620,000	$10,000
Working Capital	$270,000	$250,000	$20,000

Since working capital is the difference of current assets and current liabilities, it will be unaffected by any transaction that changes current assets and current liabilities equally (e.g. decreasing a current liability through cash payment).

SOURCES OF WORKING CAPITAL

Increases in working capital are associated with the following sources.

Funds from operations (net income).   The operations of the company produce funds from sales in the form of cash and accounts receivable, while funds flow out for goods and expenses.   Thus, working capital is increased by an excess of sales over costs and expenses.

Funds from sale of noncurrent assets (decrease in noncurrent assets).   When plant, property or equipment, long-term investments, or other noncurrent assets are sold, working capital increases.

Funds from long-term obligations (increase in noncurrent liabilities).   When long-term obligations are issued, such as long-term notes, mortgages or bonds, the proceeds increase working capital.

Funds from sale of stock (increase in stockholders' equity).   Assets and stockholders' equity are increased by profitable operation (see above). In addition, equity is increased by sales of capital stock.   The amount of working capital provided by such sales will not necessarily be reflected entirely in the capital stock account, for stock may be sold above or below par and the difference shown in paid-in capital accounts.   Certain entries in stockholders' equity accounts do not affect working capital, such as transfer of retained earnings to paid-in capital accounts on issue of a stock dividend.   Also, transfers between retained earnings and appropriation accounts do not affect working capital.

APPLICATIONS OF WORKING CAPITAL

Decreases in working capital result from:

Increases in noncurrent assets due to the purchase of equipment, buildings, or long-term securities, or the acquisition of various other noncurrent assets.   The net change in the asset account is generally not the amount to be reported in the funds statement; additional information must be obtained from the pertinent accounts.   For instance, a net change of $20,000 in the total equipment balance may represent $30,000 in acquisitions and $10,000 in retirements of assets. Also, the amount of property, plant and equipment, or other noncurrent assets, may sometimes be shown on the funds statement as the net amount after the accumulated depreciation.   Each component — the acquisition, the retirement, and the related depreciation — is to be shown separately on the funds statement.

Decreases in noncurrent liabilities.   Any amount applied to reducing bonds or long-term notes reduces working capital.   If there are any related balances of unamortized premium or discount, or any gain or loss involved in the transaction, such items would have to be considered and proper disposition recorded.

Decreases in stockholders' equity.   Cash dividends represent the most common application of funds to stockholders' equity.   Other applications to stockholders' equity are the purchase of treasury stock and the redemption of preferred stock.   The issuance of stock dividends does not affect financial position, since funds are not distributed.

JOINT SOURCES AND APPLICATIONS

Certain transactions that have no effect on funds should nevertheless be reported (APB Opinion No. 19). Generally these transactions would be shown on the funds statement as if they were two separate transactions: a source of funds and an application of funds. Among these transactions are: issuance of capital stock for land [shown as an increase in land (application) and an increase in stockholders' equity (source)], conversion of bonds (application) for capital stock (source) [or common stock (source) for preferred stock (application)], and receipt of a gift (source) of property and plant from a municipality (application).

9.3 STATEMENT OF CHANGE IN FINANCIAL POSITION

Balance sheets issued in formal reports to stockholders generally follow the accounting equation form: ASSETS = LIABILITIES + STOCKHOLDERS' EQUITY. However, in their internal reporting and presentation of statements many companies use a form in which the working capital is shown as an integral part:

(CURRENT ASSETS − CURRENT LIABILITIES)
    + (NONCURRENT ASSETS − NONCURRENT LIABILITIES)
   = STOCKHOLDERS' EQUITY

This form eliminates the need for a separate working capital schedule (see Example 1).

EXAMPLE 2.

The Barton Company
Comparative Balance Sheet
December 31, 1974 and 1973

	1974	1973	Increase or (Decrease)
Current Assets			
Cash	$ 20,000	$ 35,000	$(15,000)
Trade Receivables	75,000	55,000	20,000
Inventories	150,000	133,000	17,000
Prepaid Expenses	15,000	12,000	3,000
Total	$260,000	$235,000	$ 25,000
Less: Current Liabilities			
Accounts Payable	$ 50,000	$ 46,000	$ 4,000
Dividends Payable	15,000	15,000	. . . .
Income Tax Payable	5,000	4,000	1,000
Total	$ 70,000	$ 65,000	$ 5,000
Working Capital	$190,000	$170,000	$ 20,000
Noncurrent Assets			
Investments (long-term)	60,000	44,000	16,000
Land	15,000	. . . .	15,000
Property, Plant, and Equipment	200,000	186,000	14,000
Accumulated Depreciation	(38,000)	(35,000)	(3,000)
Total Working Capital and Noncurrent Assets	$427,000	$365,000	$ 62,000
Less: Noncurrent Liabilities			
Notes Payable	$ 45,000	$ 35,000	$ 10,000
Bonds Payable	100,000	150,000	(50,000)
Total	$145,000	$185,000	$(40,000)
Net Assets	$282,000	$180,000	$102,000

(continued next page)

Stockholders' Equity

Common Stock	$220,000	$150,000	$ 70,000
Retained Earnings	62,000	30,000	32,000
Total	$282,000	$180,000	$102,000

In the above comparative balance sheet it can be readily seen that there was an increase of $20,000 in working capital and at the same time a decrease of $15,000 in cash.

We now illustrate the preparation of the Statement of Change of Financial Position, using the balance sheet data of Example 2.

EXAMPLE 3.   Working Capital Form.

Only noncurrent accounts have to be analyzed, as the current accounts were already used in arriving at the figures for Working Capital in Example 2.

Investments.   The balance sheet shows that there was an increase $16,000 in this account. An examination of the investment account shows there was a purchase of $40,000 and a sale of $24,000. The description in the account states that the investment was sold for $35,000 cash. The gain of $11,000 is shown on the income statement as an extraordinary item, less the related income tax of $3,000. The sale would be shown on the financial position statement as a source of working capital of $8,000. The purchase of $40,000 will be shown as an application of working capital.

Land.   The balance in the land account increased by $15,000. However the description in the land account shows that the property was acquired by issuing common stock, so that no funds were expended. Nevertheless, this is a significant transaction and should be handled as if the stock had been issued for cash, then the cash used to purchase the land. Therefore, under "Source of Working Capital" would be shown the issue of common stock at par for land, $15,000, and under "Application of Working Capital" the purchase of land by issue of common stock at par, $15,000.

Property, plant, and equipment.   The balance in this account increased by $14,000 during the year. This is the net difference between two separate transactions, the purchase cost of $25,000 and the retirement of fully depreciated assets costing $11,000. The depreciation for the year was $14,000. There was no salvage value on disposal and thus no effect on working capital from this source. Under "Application of Working Capital" would be shown the purchase of $25,000; under "Source of Working Capital" the $14,000 depreciation taken in the current year, which is a noncash expense, would be added back to Net Income.

Notes payable.   This balance increased $10,000 during the year. This item would be shown under "Source of Working Capital" as Issuance of Notes Payable, $10,000.

Bonds payable.   This balance decreased $50,000 during the year. In examining the bonds payable account we note that one-third of the bonds payable became due during the year. The transaction would be shown under "Application of Working Capital" as Retirement of Bonds Payable, $50,000.

Common stock.   As described under Land, there was an exchange of $15,000 common stock at par for a parcel of land. The remaining $55,000 of common stock was issued for cash. The data would be shown under "Source of Working Capital" as two separate items: Issuance of Common Stock at Par for Land, $15,000, and Issuance of Common Stock at Par for Cash, $55,000.

Retained earnings.   This account showed a net increase of $32,000 for the year. Examination of the retained earnings account discloses that net income, including extraordinary gain of $8,000 ($11,000 less applicable income tax of $3,000), was $52,000. The cash dividends for the year were $20,000, resulting in a net change of $32,000. The sale of investments and the related gain will be reported as a separate item. Therefore, to avoid duplication of the amount $8,000, the net amount of gain after taxes will be deducted from net income, giving the income from normal operations as $44,000. The depreciation of $14,000 taken during the year was, of course, deducted in arriving at the net income amount. However, depreciation is a noncash item; that is, no cash was expended this year, as the asset was purchased previously. Therefore, to arrive at the cash brought in by operations, the $14,000 would be added back. The cash dividends would be shown under "Application of Working Capital" as Declaration of Cash Dividends, $20,000.

The Barton Company
Statement of Change in Financial Position
year ended December 31, 1974

Source of Working Capital

Operations for the Year		
Income Exclusive of		
Extraordinary Item	$44,000	
Add: Noncash Item —		
Depreciation	14,000	$58,000
Sale of Investments		32,000
Issuance of Common Stock		
at Par for Land		15,000
Issuance of Common Stock		
at Par for Cash		55,000
Issuance of Notes Payable		10,000	$170,000

Application of Working Capital

Purchase of Investments	$40,000	
Purchase of Land by Issuance		
of Common Stock at Par	15,000	
Purchase of Property, Plant, and		
Equipment	25,000	
Retirement of Bonds Payable	50,000	
Declaration of Cash Dividends	20,000	150,000
Increase in Working Capital		$ 20,000

EXAMPLE 4.   Cash Form.

In preparing the Statement of Change in Financial Position based on the cash form it is necessary to examine all accounts other than Cash. Since we have already discussed the various noncurrent accounts in Example 3, it will only be necessary to consider the various current accounts from Example 2.

Trade receivables. This account balance increased by $20,000 during the current year. Thus the amount shown as Sales on the income statement included $20,000 that did not provide cash during the year. Therefore, in the financial position statement, $20,000 is to be deducted from income.

Inventories. This account increased $17,000 during the current year. Thus the cost of merchandise purchased exceeded the cost of merchandise sold by $17,000. The $17,000 must be deducted from income to arrive at the amount provided by operations.

Prepaid expenses. This balance increased by $3,000 during the year. This did not represent a cash outlay during the year, so $3,000 must be deducted from income to arrive at the cash provided by operations.

Accounts payable. There was an increase of $4,000 in Accounts Payable during the year. Since costs included $4,000 for which there had been no cash outlay during the year, this amount must be added to income to determine the amount of cash provided by operations.

Income tax payable. The current year's balance exceeded the previous year's balance by $1,000. The income tax expense exceeded the payment by $1,000, which must be added to income to arrive at the amount of cash provided by operations.

The Barton Company
Statement of Change in Financial Position
year ended December 31, 1974

Source of Cash

Operations for the Year				
Income Exclusive of				
Extraordinary Item	$44,000			
Add: Noncash Item				
Depreciation	14,000	$58,000		
Increase in				
Accounts Payable	4,000			
Increase in Income				
Tax Payable	1,000	5,000		
		$63,000		
Deduct:				
Increase in Trade				
Receivables	$20,000			
Increase in				
Inventories	17,000			
Increase in Prepaid				
Expenses	3,000	40,000	$23,000	
Sale of Investments			32,000	
Issuance of Common Stock at Par for Land			15,000	
Issuance of Common Stock at Par for Cash			55,000	
Issuance of Notes Payable			10,000	$135,000

Application of Cash

Purchase of Investments			$40,000	
Purchase of Land by Issuance of				
Common Stock at Par			15,000	
Purchase of Property, Plant and				
Equipment			25,000	
Retirement of Bonds Payable			50,000	
Declaration of Cash Dividends			20,000	150,000
Decrease in Cash				$ 15,000

Summary

(1) The term *funds*, in reference to changes in financial position, may mean _____ _____ , _____ , or _____ .

(2) Revenue from operations is a _____ of funds.

(3) Purchase of equipment is an _____ of funds.

(4) If a fully depreciated machine is abandoned with no salvage value, working capital is _____ .

(5) The purchase of office equipment _____ working capital.

(6) The purchase of merchandise for cash _____ working capital.

(7) The purchase of merchandise on account _____ working capital.

(8) The sale of equipment at a gain represents a _____ of funds and it _____ working capital.

(9) The declaration of a cash dividend _____ working capital, while the later payment of the dividend _____ working capital.

(10) If commissions on sales were $200,000 for the year, and receivables were $40,000 at the beginning of the year and $10,000 at the end of the year, the amount of cash received during the year was _____ .

Answers: (1) working capital, cash, cash and marketable securities; (2) source; (3) application; (4) not affected; (5) decreases; (6) has no effect on; (7) has no effect on; (8) source, increases; (9) decreases, has no effect on; (10) $230,000

Solved Problems

9.1. Indicate the effect of the following transactions on working capital by placing a checkmark if there is no effect, or by indicating the amount of increase or decrease.

	No Effect	Amount	
		Increase	Decrease
(a) Purchased $5,000 of merchandise on account			
(b) Sold $4,000 worth of merchandise for $6,500			
(c) Recorded depreciation of $7,000			
(d) Paid cash for operating expenses of $9,000			
(e) Purchased plant equipment of $12,000 on account			
(f) Paid $15,000 on accounts payable			
(g) Received $2,000 on account from customers			
(h) Declared and paid a cash dividend of $4,000			
(i) Issued $10,000 in capital stock at par, for cash			
(j) Borrowed $20,000 on a 60-day note			

SOLUTION

	No Effect	Amount	
		Increase	Decrease
(a)	✓		
(b)		$ 2,500	
(c)	✓		
(d)			$ 9,000
(e)			$12,000
(f)	✓		
(g)	✓		
(h)			$ 4,000
(i)		$10,000	
(j)	✓		

9.2. The Allen Company had the following financial data at December 31 of the years indicated. The net income for year 2 was $46,000 and depreciation was $6,600.

	Year 2	Year 1
Cash	$ 42,600	$ 37,500
Accounts Receivable (net)	34,300	38,700
Notes Receivable	15,000	7,000
Inventories	120,000	136,000
Prepaid Expenses	3,000	2,500
Accounts Payable	26,300	29,700
Notes Payable	20,000	15,000
Dividends Payable	5,000	3,500
Taxes Payable	7,500	10,000
Plant Property	65,000	55,000
Accumulated Depreciation, Plant Property	13,600	7,000
Mortgage Payable	15,000	60,000
Common Stock	125,000	125,000
Retained Earnings	67,500	26,500

Prepare (a) the "source of working capital" section of the Statement of Change in Financial Position and (b) a schedule of changes in components of working capital (see Examples 1 and 2).

(a)

(b)   **Increase (Decrease) in Current Assets**

(continued next page)

Increase (Decrease) in Current Liabilities		

SOLUTION

(a)

Operations During the Year		
Net Income	$46,000	
Add: Noncash Deduction –		
Depreciation	6,600	
Total Source of Working Capital		$52,600

(b)

Increase (Decrease) in Current Assets		
Cash	$ 5,100	
Accounts Receivable	(4,400)	
Notes Receivable	8,000	
Inventories	(16,000)	
Prepaid Expenses	500	$(6,800)
Increase (Decrease) in Current Liabilities		
Accounts Payable	$(3,400)	
Notes Payable	5,000	
Dividends Payable	1,500	
Taxes Payable	(2,500)	600
Decrease in Working Capital		$ 7,400

Summary

Source of Working Capital	$52,600
Application of Working Capital	60,000
Decrease in Working Capital	$ 7,400

9.3. Prepare the "application of working capital" section of the Statement of Change in Financial Position, based on the data in Problem 9.2.

SOLUTION

Plant Property	$10,000
Mortgage Payable	45,000
Dividends Payable	5,000
Total Application of Working Capital	$60,000

9.4. The equipment account for the Mitchell Company shows an increase of $25,000 for the year. An analysis of the account shows that equipment costing $40,000 was acquired and that equipment costing $15,000, with accumulated depreciation of $10,000, was sold for $5,000. Show the effect on the Statement of Change in Financial Position.

_____
_____
_____
_____
_____
_____
_____

SOLUTION

The increase of $25,000 in equipment is actually the net of (1) a $40,000 purchase and (2) a $15,000 sale. There is a source of funds (3) of $5,000 from the sale, and an application of funds of (1) $40,000 due to the purchase. The charge to Accumulated Depreciation (4) of $10,000 does not affect working capital.

	Debit or (Credit)	Working Capital Effect		
		No Effect	Increase	Decrease
Purchase of equipment (1)	$40,000			(1) $40,000
Sale of equipment (2)	(15,000)	(4) ($10,000)	(3) $5,000	
	$25,000			

9.5. The Miller Company reported a net income of $50,000, exclusive of extraordinary items, for the current year. Depreciation for the year was $15,000. Prepare the "cash provided by operations" section of the Statement of Change in Financial Position (cash form), using the following data:

	Year 2	Year 1
Accounts Receivable	$40,000	$30,000
Inventories	65,000	50,000
Prepaid Expenses	9,000	8,000
Accounts Payable	20,000	17,000
Taxes Payable	10,000	12,000

_____
_____
_____
_____
_____
_____
_____
_____
_____
_____
_____
_____
_____

SOLUTION

Net Income		$50,000
Add: Deductions		
Depreciation	$15,000	
Increase in Accounts Payable	3,000	18,000
		68,000
Deduct: Additions		
Increase in Accounts Receivable	$10,000	
Increase in Inventories	15,000	
Increase in Prepaid Expenses	1,000	
Decrease in Taxes Payable	2,000	28,000
Total Cash Provided		$40,000

9.6. The Thompson Company had the following comparative balance sheet:

Thompson Company
Comparative Balance Sheet
December 31, 19X1 and 19X0

	19X1	19X0	Increase or (Decrease)
Current Assets			
Cash	$ 47,000	$ 31,000	$ 16,000
Accounts Receivable (net)	58,000	70,000	(12,000)
Inventories	85,000	75,000	10,000
Prepaid Expenses	5,000	3,000	2,000
	$195,000	$179,000	$ 16,000
Less: Current Liabilities			
Accounts Payable	$ 13,000	$ 35,500	$(22,500)
Salaries Payable	3,000	2,000	1,000
Income Tax Payable	4,000	2,500	1,500
	20,000	40,000	(20,000)
Working Capital	$175,000	$139,000	$ 36,000
Land	25,000	25,000	. . . .
Buildings (net)	75,000	65,000	10,000
Equipment (net)	30,000	25,000	5,000
	$305,000	$254,000	$ 51,000
Less: Mortgage Notes Payable	30,000	30,000	. . . .
Net Assets	$275,000	$224,000	$ 51,000
Stockholders' Equity			
Capital Stock	$225,000	$200,000	$ 25,000
Retained Earnings	50,000	24,000	26,000
	$275,000	$224,000	$ 51,000

The net income for 19X1 was $60,000 and cash dividends were $34,000. Additions to the buildings for the current year were $16,000 and annual depreciation on the buildings was $6,000. Additions to equipment were $12,000 and depreciation on the equipment was $7,000. Prepare a Statement of Change in Financial Position, expressed as working capital.

Thompson Company
Statement of Change in Financial Position
year ended December 31, 19X1

Source of Working Capital

Application of Working Capital

SOLUTION

Thompson Company			
Statement of Change in Financial Position			
year ended December 31, 19X1			
Source of Working Capital			
Operations During the Year			
Net Income	$60,000		
Add: Noncash Deduction —			
Depreciation	13,000*	$73,000	
Issuance of Capital Stock		25,000	
Total Source of Working Capital			$98,000
Application of Working Capital			
Additions to Building		$16,000	
Purchase of Equipment		12,000	
Declaration of Cash Dividend		34,000	62,000
Increase in Working Capital			$36,000

* Buildings, $6,000; Equipment, $7,000

9.7. From the data in Problem 9.6, prepare a Statement of Change in Financial Position, expressed as cash.

Thompson Company
Statement of Change in Financial Position
year ended December 31, 19X1
Source of Cash
Application of Cash

SOLUTION

Thompson Company			
Statement of Change in Financial Position			
year ended December 31, 19X1			

Source of Cash

Operations During the Year			
Net Income	$60,000		
Add: Noncash Deduction —			
Depreciation	13,000	$73,000	
Add: Decrease in			
Receivables	$12,000		
Increase in Salaries			
Payable	1,000		
Increase in Income			
Tax Payable	1,500	14,500	
		87,500	
Deduct:			
Increase in Inventories	$10,000		
Increase in Prepaid			
Expenses	2,000		
Decrease in Accounts			
Payable	22,500	34,500	
		$53,000	
Issuance of Capital Stock		25,000	$78,000

Application of Cash

Additions to Building		$16,000	
Purchase of Equipment		12,000	
Declaration of Cash Dividends		34,000	62,000
Increase in Cash			$16,000

9.8. The comparative balance sheet of the JDB Corporation at December 31, 1974 and 1973, is shown below:

ASSETS	1974	1973
Cash	$ 39,561	$ 31,420
Marketable Securities	39,200	26,100
Accounts Receivable	87,555	56,000
Notes Receivable	10,000	....
Inventories	35,176	27,415
Prepaid Expenses	2,857	2,442
Buildings	225,000	150,000
Accumulated Depreciation, Buildings	(50,000)	(50,000)
Machinery and Equipment	87,000	87,000
Accumulated Depreciation, Machinery and Equipment	(32,000)	(19,000)
Land	30,000	30,000
Patents	56,000	62,000
Total Assets	$530,349	$403,377

(continued next page)

LIABILITIES AND STOCKHOLDERS' EQUITY	1974	1973
Accounts Payable	$ 32,237	$ 22,577
Salaries Payable	15,000	13,500
Mortgage Notes Payable	90,000	....
Bonds Payable	25,000	85,000
Common Stock, $10 par	215,000	155,000
Preferred Stock, $100 par	60,000	60,000
Premium on Common Stock	15,000	15,000
Retained Earnings	78,112	52,300
Total Liabilities and Stockholders' Equity	$530,349	$403,377

The income statement and analysis of applicable balance sheet accounts disclosed the following information.

(1)   Net income for the year, $57,324.
(2)   Cash dividends declared for the year, $31,512.
(3)   Depreciation expenses for the year: Buildings, $15,000; Machinery and Equipment, $13,000.
(4)   A building costing $15,000 and fully depreciated was abandoned.
(5)   Patent amortization for the year, $6,000.
(6)   A mortgage note, due in 1978, was issued for a building costing $90,000.
(7)   6,000 shares of stock were issued in exchange for $60,000 of bonds payable.

Prepare a Statement of Change in Financial Position, expressed as working capital, including a schedule of changes in working capital.

JDB Corporation
Statement of Change in Financial Position
year ended December 31, 1974

Source of Working Capital

Application of Working Capital

Schedule of Changes in Working Capital

	1974	1973	Increase or (Decrease)

SOLUTION

JDB Corporation
Statement of Change in Financial Position
year ended December 31, 1974

Source of Working Capital

Operations			
Net Income	$57,324		
Add: Expenses Not			
Requiring Funds			
Depreciation of			
Buildings	15,000		
Depreciation of			
Machinery and			
Equipment	13,000		
Patent Amortization	6,000	$91,324	
Issuance of Common Stock		60,000	
Issuance of Mortgage Note		90,000	$241,324

Application of Working Capital

Purchase of Building		$90,000	
Retirement of Bonds		60,000	
Cash Dividends		31,512	181,512
Increase in Working Capital			$ 59,812

Schedule of Changes in Working Capital

	1974	1973	Increase or (Decrease)
Cash	$ 39,561	$ 31,420	$ 8,141
Marketable Securities	39,200	26,100	13,100
Accounts Receivable	87,555	56,000	31,555
Notes Receivable	10,000	. . . .	10,000
Inventories	35,176	27,415	7,761
Prepaid Expenses	2,857	2,442	415
Accounts Payable	(32,237)	(22,577)	(9,660)
Salaries Payable	(15,000)	(13,500)	(1,500)
Total Working Capital	$167,112	$107,300	
Increase in Working Capital			$59,812

9.9. The Bass Corporation had the following comparative balance sheet at June 30 for the specified years.

	1974	1973
ASSETS		
Cash	$ 22,000	$ 29,110
Accounts Receivable (net)	125,130	149,990
Merchandise Inventory	124,075	137,230
Prepaid Expenses	3,655	4,300
Machinery and Equipment	149,152	61,440
Accumulated Depreciation,		
Machinery and Equipment	(100,848)	(88,560)
Land	30,000	30,000
Buildings	204,770	179,084
Accumulated Depreciation,		
Buildings	(80,916)	(70,916)
	$477,018	$431,678
LIABILITIES AND STOCKHOLDERS' EQUITY		
Accounts Payable	$ 85,200	$ 73,250
Bonds Payable (long-term)	20,000	35,000
Mortgage Notes Payable (long-term)	40,000	52,000
Common Stock, $10 par	200,000	180,000
Premium on Common Stock	5,000	. . . .
Retained Earnings	126,818	91,428
	$477,018	$431,678

Data obtained from the income statement and from an analysis of applicable balance sheet accounts follow:

(1) Net income for the year, $60,527.

(2) Depreciation expense for the year, $36,602.

(3) Cash dividends declared during the year, $25,137.

(4) Payment on mortgage note, $12,000.

(5) Payment on outstanding bonds, $15,000.

(6) New machinery and equipment purchased during the year for the production of a new product, $87,712. No old equipment was retired.

(7) Additions to building for production of new product were $40,000. Fully depreciated building appurtenances of $14,314 were retired.

(8) During the year, 2,000 shares of stock were issued at $12.50 per share.

Prepare a Statement of Change in Financial Position, expressed as working capital, and a schedule of changes in working capital.

Bass Corporation

Statement of Change in Financial Position

year ended June 30, 1974

Source of Working Capital

(continued next page)

Application of Working Capital

Schedule of Changes in Working Capital

	June 30		Increase or
	1974	**1973**	**(Decrease)**

SOLUTION

Bass Corporation
Statement of Change in Financial Position
year ended June 30, 1974

Source of Working Capital

Operations			
Net Income	$60,527		
Add: Noncash Item —			
Depreciation of Plant			
Assets	36,602	$97,129	
Issuance of Common Stock		25,000	$122,129

Application of Working Capital

Additions to Building		$40,000	
Purchase of Machinery and			
Equipment		87,712	
Payment on Mortgage Note		12,000	
Payment on Bonds, due 1974		15,000	
Declaration of Cash Dividend		25,137	179,849
Decrease in Working Capital			$ 57,720

Schedule of Changes in Working Capital

	June 30		Increase or
	1974	**1973**	**(Decrease)**
Cash	$ 22,000	$ 29,110	$ (7,110)
Accounts Receivable (net)	125,130	149,990	(24,860)
Merchandise Inventory	124,075	137,230	(13,155)
Prepaid Expenses	3,655	4,300	(645)
Accounts Payable	(85,200)	(73,250)	(11,950)
Total Working Capital	$189,660	$247,380	
Decrease in Working Capital			$ 57,720

9.10. Presented below are the comparative balance sheet and pertinent ledger accounts for the Kelschman Company at December 31, 1974 and 1973.

	1974	1973
ASSETS		
Cash	$ 84,900	$ 57,300
Accounts Receivable (net)	75,000	60,000
Inventories	167,380	193,470
Prepaid Expenses	4,220	3,530
Building	343,500	275,000
Accumulated Depreciation, Building	(93,000)	(83,000)
Equipment	500,000	340,000
Accumulated Depreciation, Equipment	(120,000)	(100,000)
Land	100,000	180,000
Discount on Bonds Payable	9,000	....
	$1,071,000	$926,300
LIABILITIES AND STOCKHOLDERS' EQUITY		
Accounts Payable	$ 25,400	$249,300
Income Taxes Payable	15,600	17,000
Bonds Payable	300,000	....
Common Stock	540,000	500,000
Premium on Common Stock	93,000	90,000
Appropriation for Contingencies	20,000	10,000
Retained Earnings	77,000	60,000
	$1,071,000	$926,300

Building

Jan. 1	Bal.	275,000			
Apr. 28	Purchased for Cash	68,500			

Equipment

Jan. 1	Bal.	340,000	May 7	Equipment Discarded (no value)	15,000
June 23	Purchased for Cash	50,000			
July 24	Purchased for Cash	55,000			
Sept. 9	Purchased for Cash	70,000			

Land

Jan. 1 Bal.	180,000	June 30	Sold Land for $90,000 Cash	80,000

Bonds Payable

		July 1	Issued 10-year Bonds	300,000

Accumulated Depreciation, Building

		Jan. 1	Bal.	83,000
		Dec. 31	Depreciation for Year	10,000

Accumulated Depreciation, Equipment

| May 7 Discarded | 15,000 | Jan. 1 Bal. | 100,000 |
| | | Dec. 31 Depreciation for Year | 35,000 |

Discount on Bonds Payable

| July 1 Bonds Issued | 10,000 | Dec. 31 Amortization | 1,000 |

Common Stock

| | | Jan. 1 Bal. | 500,000 |
| | | Nov. 20 Stock Dividend | 40,000 |

Premium on Common Stock

| | | Jan. 1 Bal. | 90,000 |
| | | Nov. 20 Stock Dividend | 3,000 |

Appropriation for Contingencies

| | | Jan. 1 Bal. | 10,000 |
| | | Dec. 31 Appropriation | 10,000 |

Retained Earnings

June 30 Cash Dividend	23,000	Jan. 1 Bal.	60,000
Nov. 20 Stock Dividend	43,000	Dec. 31 Net Income	93,000
Dec. 31 Appropriated	10,000		

Prepare a Statement of Change in Financial Position, expressed as working capital, including a schedule of changes in working capital. (Exclude from operating income the gain on the sale of land.)

Kelschman Company

Statement of Change in Financial Position

year ended December 31, 1974

Source of Working Capital

Application of Working Capital

Schedule of Changes in Working Capital

	December 31		Increase or
	1974	**1973**	**(Decrease)**

SOLUTION

Kelschman Company
Statement of Change in Financial Position
year ended December 31, 1974

Source of Working Capital

Operations			
Net Income, exclusive of $10,000			
gain on sale of land	$83,000		
Add: Deductions Not			
Requiring Funds			
Depreciation on Plant and			
Equipment	45,000		
Amortization of Discount on			
Bonds Payable	1,000	$129,000	
Issuance of Bonds		290,000	
Sale of Land		90,000	$509,000

Application of Working Capital

Purchase of Building		68,500	
Purchase of Equipment		175,000	
Declaration of Cash Dividends		23,000	266,500
Increase in Working Capital			$242,500

Schedule of Changes in Working Capital

	December 31		Increase or
	1974	**1973**	**(Decrease)**
Cash	$ 84,900	$ 57,300	$ 27,600
Accounts Receivable (net)	75,000	60,000	15,000
Inventories	167,380	193,470	(26,090)
Prepaid Expenses	4,220	3,530	690
Accounts Payable	(25,400)	(249,300)	223,900
Income Tax Payable	(15,600)	(17,000)	1,400
Total Working Capital	$290,500	$ 48,000	
Increase in Working Capital			$242,500

Chapter 10

Income Taxes

10.1 INTRODUCTION

For the businessman who must choose an inventory method, a depreciation method, or a method of determining uncollectible accounts, tax considerations are of the greatest importance. A background of accounting knowledge is a prerequisite to the understanding of the impact of income taxes on business decisions.

Of the four main types of taxes designed to produce revenue in the United States (income taxes, sales taxes, excise taxes, and property taxes), the federal income tax exceeds all others in the amount of revenue generated. The statutes underlying this tax are combined in the Internal Revenue Code (IRC), which is administered and enforced by the Internal Revenue Service (IRS), a division of the Treasury Department. Although the primary function of the federal income tax is to raise revenue, it has other goals as well:

- to redistribute national income on an equitable basis
- to create a more stable economic environment
- to influence the rate of economic growth so as to encourage full employment

In general, taxes fall into three categories, depending on the relation of the tax rate (expressed as a percentage of the base) and the base (the amount subject to the tax). If the rate is independent of the base, the tax is *proportional*; if the rate decreases as the base increases, the tax is *regressive*; if the rate increases as the base increases, the tax is *progressive*.

EXAMPLE 1.

A state imposes a sales tax of 6%. This is a proportional tax, since the rate does not depend on the amount of purchase.

EXAMPLE 2.

A state imposes a $10,000 license fee on all firms doing business in the state. This represents a regressive tax; for instance, a $100,000 business would pay $10,000/$100,000 = 10%, while a $150,000 business would pay $10,000/$150,000 = 6.7%.

EXAMPLE 3.

Consider the federal income tax schedule shown in Fig. 10-1, page 233. It is seen that the tax is progressive in nature: the higher the income, the greater the rate at which it is taxed. The basic intention is to distribute the tax burden according to the ability to pay.

10.2 TAXATION OF BUSINESSES

In the following table we compare the income taxation of the sole proprietorship, the partnership, and the corporation. (Estates and trusts are two other major taxpayers; their treatment is highly specialized and will not be discussed here.)

Form of Business Organization	Tax Treatment for the Business	Tax Treatment for the Owners
Sole Proprietorship	The sole proprietorship as a business entity does not pay income tax nor does it have to file a return. Rather, the information is incorporated into the return of the individual.	The owner of the sole proprietorship pays taxes on his entire taxable income each year, whether or not the earnings of the business are withdrawn by the individual. Taxation is progressive, ranging from 14% to 70%.
Partnership	The partnership as a business entity does not pay income taxes. However, it must file an information return (Form 1065) which reveals the taxable income of the partnership and the method of sharing net income.	Each partner pays taxes on his share of the taxable income of the partnership even if he does not withdraw funds from the business. Tax rates are as for the sole proprietorship.
Corporation	The corporation as a business entity *does pay* an income tax. There is a 22% normal tax on all taxable income and a 26% surtax on taxable income in excess of $25,000.	The corporation declares dividends from its earnings and distributes them to stockholders, who must include the amount in individual tax returns.

Note 1.   Corporations making well over $25,000 essentially pay income tax at the flat rate of $22 + 26 = 48\%$ (proportional tax). Hence, the saving of one dollar in income tax is almost equivalent to the earning of two dollars of additional income before taxes. That is why tax planning is so important.

Note 2.   It is seen that corporate income that flows to the stockholders is taxed twice. The corporation, at its option, could retain its earnings and not declare a dividend. However, if this were done by a closely held corporation in order to avoid the double taxation of income, the retained earnings would be subject to a penalty.

The differences in tax treatment are vital elements in deciding which organizational form a business — particularly a small business — ought to take. There is, however, a provision in the tax law whereby the closely held corporation may choose to be taxed as a partnership or the partnership may choose to be taxed as a corporation. This is permitted so that income taxes will not be the *only* basis for the choice of organization.

EXAMPLE 4.

B. Cohen forms a printing service business and estimates the following annual operating figures: gross income from business, $300,000; business expenses (except for his salary), $160,000; his withdrawal of salary for the year, $40,000; total itemized deductions and exemptions, $20,000. Should he run the business as a sole proprietorship (in which case his salary is not deductible as a business expense) or should he incorporate (in which case his salary is deductible from corporate income)?

TAXATION AS SOLE PROPRIETORSHIP

Income from business	$300,000	
Less: Business expenses	160,000	$140,000
Less: Itemized deductions and exemptions		20,000
Taxable income		$120,000
Income tax liability (from tax table, Fig. 10-1)		$ 57,580

TAXATION AS CORPORATION

Corporate Tax Computation

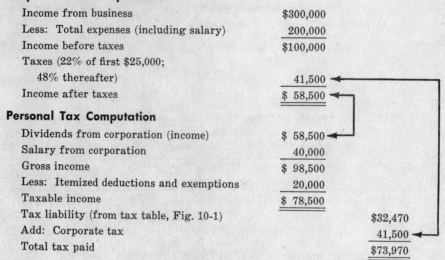

Income from business	$300,000
Less: Total expenses (including salary)	200,000
Income before taxes	$100,000
Taxes (22% of first $25,000; 48% thereafter)	41,500
Income after taxes	$ 58,500

Personal Tax Computation

Dividends from corporation (income)	$ 58,500	
Salary from corporation	40,000	
Gross income	$ 98,500	
Less: Itemized deductions and exemptions	20,000	
Taxable income	$ 78,500	
Tax liability (from tax table, Fig. 10-1)		$32,470
Add: Corporate tax		41,500
Total tax paid		$73,970

Thus, tax savings of $73,970 − $57,580 = $16,390 result if the sole proprietorship is chosen.

Under a different assumption the choice might be different. Suppose that Cohen decided to leave the corporate income ($58,500) in the business and to withdraw only his $40,000 salary. The tax that he would pay as a business and as an individual would be computed as:

Dividends from corporation	0
Salary from corporation	$40,000
Gross income	$40,000
Less: Itemized deductions and exemptions	20,000
Taxable income	$20,000
Tax liability	$ 4,380
Add: Corporate tax	41,500
Total tax paid	$45,880

Now incorporation is the better choice, with tax savings of $57,580 − $45,880 = $11,700.

10.3 INCOME TAX FORMULA FOR INDIVIDUALS

The income tax for individuals can be computed in three steps.

(1) GROSS INCOME (Sec. 10.4) − DEDUCTIONS FROM GROSS INCOME (Sec. 10.5)
= ADJUSTED GROSS INCOME

(2) ADJUSTED GROSS INCOME
− DEDUCTIONS FROM ADJUSTED GROSS INCOME (Sec. 10.6)
− EXEMPTIONS (Sec. 10.7)
= TAXABLE INCOME

The amount of the individual's tax liability is found by applying the tax table to his taxable income. Then:

(3) TAX LIABILITY − TAX CREDITS (Sec. 10.8)
= BALANCE DUE GOVERNMENT OR REFUND DUE INDIVIDUAL

10.4 GROSS INCOME

For tax purposes gross income is defined as all income from whatever source derived (salaries, dividends, interest, rents, fees, bonuses, commissions, tips, etc.), unless expressly excluded by law. Among the exclusions are workmen's compensation and social security benefits, gifts, scholarships, life insurance proceeds, inheritances, and municipal bonds (bonds of a city, state, or local government).

10.5 DEDUCTIONS FROM GROSS INCOME

All ordinary expenses needed to carry on a business or profession are deductible from gross income. A physician's fees, for example, are listed under gross income but all necessary expenses of carrying on his practice (rent, depreciation, maintenance, salaries of employees, etc.) will be deducted from gross income to arrive at adjusted gross income. Also, one-half of excess long-term capital gain (see Sec. 10.9) may be deducted from gross income.

10.6 DEDUCTIONS FROM ADJUSTED GROSS INCOME

These consist of personal expenses, and the taxpayer is permitted either to itemize the deductions or to use the standard deduction.

ITEMIZED DEDUCTIONS

(1) *Medical and dental expenses.* These expenses of the taxpayer and his family are deductible to the extent that they exceed 3% of the adjusted gross income. Amounts expended for medicines and drugs are includable only to the extent that they exceed 1% of adjusted gross income. A taxpayer may also deduct one-half of his annual medical insurance costs or $150, whichever is smaller, without regard to the 3% exclusion. The remaining amount of such premium will be combined with his other medical expenses. (See Example 5 below.)

(2) *Taxes.* Most state and local taxes are deductible. These include state and local income taxes, real estate taxes, personal property taxes, general sales tax, and gasoline taxes. Federal taxes do not usually qualify as a deduction.

(3) *Interest.* Interest charges on personal debts are deductible. The most common deduction of this type is interest on a mortgage. Other examples are interest charges for purchases, credit card charges, and carrying charges.

Married Taxpayers Filing Joint Returns and Certain Widows and Widowers

If the amount on Form 1040, line 48, is:		Enter on Form 1040, line 16:	
Not over $1,000		14% of the amount on line 48.	

Over—	But not over—		of excess over—
$1,000	$2,000	$140+15%	$1,000
$2,000	$3,000	$290+16%	$2,000
$3,000	$4,000	$450+17%	$3,000
$4,000	$8,000	$620+19%	$4,000
$8,000	$12,000	$1,380+22%	$8,000
$12,000	$16,000	$2,260+25%	$12,000
$16,000	$20,000	$3,260+28%	$16,000
$20,000	$24,000	$4,380+32%	$20,000
$24,000	$28,000	$5,660+36%	$24,000
$28,000	$32,000	$7,100+39%	$28,000
$32,000	$36,000	$8,660+42%	$32,000
$36,000	$40,000	$10,340+45%	$36,000
$40,000	$44,000	$12,140+48%	$40,000
$44,000	$52,000	$14,060+50%	$44,000
$52,000	$64,000	$18,060+53%	$52,000
$64,000	$76,000	$24,420+55%	$64,000
$76,000	$88,000	$31,020+58%	$76,000
$88,000	$100,000	$37,980+60%	$88,000
$100,000	$120,000	$45,180+62%	$100,000
$120,000	$140,000	$57,580+64%	$120,000
$140,000	$160,000	$70,380+66%	$140,000
$160,000	$180,000	$83,580+68%	$160,000
$180,000	$200,000	$97,180+69%	$180,000
$200,000	....	$110,980+70%	$200,000

Fig. 10-1

(4) *Contributions.* Deductible are donations to any charitable, educational, or other philanthropic organization that has been qualified by the Treasury Department. Not only cash contributions are deductible but also amounts paid by the taxpayer (for gasoline, etc.) in order to carry out duties as a volunteer.

(5) *Casualty or theft losses.* If a taxpayer had personal property stolen or damaged, he is able to deduct the loss over the amount of any insurance received, less $100. This $100 limitation applies to each occurrence rather than to the total for the year.

(6) *Miscellaneous deductions.* Care of children can be deducted up to $400 a month per child. There are also many other types of miscellaneous expenses that would be listed in a tax guide.

EXAMPLE 5.

A taxpayer's adjusted gross income is $15,000 and his medical expenses are: medical insurance, $200; drugs and medicines, $260; other medical expenses (doctors' fees, medical equipment, and hospitalization), $580. The computation to arrive at the medical expense deduction would be:

Medical insurance premium (1/2 of $200)			$100
Medicines and drugs	$260		
Less: 1% of adjusted gross income	150		
Allowable deduction for medicines		$110	
Medical expenses (doctors' fees, equipment, etc.)		580	
Medical insurance premium (remaining balance)		100	
Total		$790	
Less: 3% of adjusted gross income		450	$340
Medical expense deduction			$440

STANDARD DEDUCTION

If the taxpayer has few expenses of the above six types, the standard deduction may allow him more than itemized deductions. This standard deduction is a fixed percentage, 15%, of adjusted gross income, but not to exceed $2,000.

EXAMPLE 6.

A taxpayer with adjusted gross income of $10,000 has itemized deductions of $1,200. The taxpayer is allowed to elect the standard deduction, $1,500 (15% of $10,000).

EXAMPLE 7.

A taxpayer with adjusted gross income of $20,000 has itemized deductions of $1,700. The taxpayer would be wise to elect the standard deduction at the maximum rate of $2,000. Note that he cannot take a standard deduction of $15\% \times \$20,000 = \$3,000$, as that would exceed the allowed maximum.

10.7 EXEMPTIONS

In addition to the allowable deductions from adjusted gross income, the taxpayer may claim an exemption of $750 for himself and $750 for his spouse. Being blind or being over 65 years of age (or both) qualifies husband or wife for an additional exemption of $750 (or $1,500). Further, an exemption of $750 may be claimed for each dependent. A *dependent* is a person who meets the following tests:

Relationship. He must bear a relationship to the family or must be a member of the household for the entire year.

Support. He must have been given more than half of his support during the taxable year by the taxpayer.

Gross income. The dependent must have had less than $750 of gross income for the year. This test is waived if the dependent is under 19 or is a full-time student.

Citizenship. The dependent must be a United States citizen or a resident of Canada, Mexico, the Canal Zone, or the Republic of Panama.

10.8 TAX CREDITS

The majority of taxpayers, those on salaries, have income taxes withheld from their wages, while professionals and businessmen pay an estimated tax on their earnings. Both of these *prepayments* are considered tax credits and are deducted from the tax liability. Other forms of tax credits are overpayment of FICA tax, retirement income credit, investment credit, and foreign tax credit.

10.9 OTHER TAX CONSIDERATIONS FOR INDIVIDUALS

CAPITAL GAINS AND LOSSES

The law defines as *capital assets* all items of property except "stock in trade" (that is, real estate, inventories, notes receivable, etc.). Special tax treatment is accorded to gains and losses resulting from sale or exchange of capital assets. The capital assets most frequently bought and sold by the individual are stocks and bonds.

A *short-term capital gain* is a gain on the sale of a capital asset that was held for six months or less. This gain is fully taxable. A *long-term capital gain* is a gain on the sale of a capital asset held for more than six months. If the net long-term capital gain exceeds the net short-term capital loss, a deduction of 50% of the excess is allowed. In other words, only half of net long-term gain need be included in gross income.

EXAMPLE 8.

Net long-term capital gain	$6,000	
Net short-term capital loss	2,000	
Net capital gain	$4,000	
Less: Long-term capital gain deduction	2,000	
Amount to be included in gross income		$2,000

EXAMPLE 9.

Net long-term capital gain	$2,000	
Net short-term capital gain	2,000	
Net capital gain	$4,000	
Less: Long-term capital gain deduction	1,000	
Amount to be included in gross income		$3,000

EXAMPLE 10.

Net long-term capital loss	$2,000	
Net short-term capital gain	6,000	
Net capital gain	$4,000	
Less: Long-term capital gain deduction	...	
Amount to be included in gross income		$4,000

INCOME AVERAGING

Because the income tax is a progressive tax (see Fig. 10-1), individuals whose incomes fluctuate greatly from year to year might be taxed more than those who receive the same total income in the same period of time.

EXAMPLE 11.

Gray and Brown each receive $40,000 in taxable income during a two-year period. Gray receives $10,000 the first year and $30,000 the second year, while Brown receives $20,000 each year. Because of the progressive tax structure, Gray would pay $9,700 for the two-year period, while Brown would pay only $8,760, a tax differential of $940.

To overcome this unfairness Congress added to the tax law a provision which allows a taxpayer to pay taxes on *average income* for the most recent five-year period.

Summary

(1)   The four types of taxes designed to produce revenue in the United States are _____, _____, _____, and _____ taxes.

(2)   The initials IRC stand for _____, and IRS stands for _____.

(3)   A _____ tax is a tax whose rate becomes smaller as the base increases, whereas the rate of a _____ tax becomes larger as the base increases.

(4)   The term "double taxation of corporate income" refers to income that is taxed first in in the hands of the _____ and then again in the hands of the _____.

(5)   The corporation's tax structure is based on two taxes, a _____ of 22% and a _____ of 26%.

(6)   _____ bonds are tax exempt.

(7)   If a taxpayer finds it disadvantageous to itemize his deductions, he may use the _____.

(8)   All items of property except stock in trade are considered _____ _____.

(9)   Individuals whose incomes fluctuate greatly from year to year are allowed to pay taxes on _____ for the most recent five-year period.

Answers: (1) income, sales, excise, property; (2) Internal Revenue Code, Internal Revenue Service; (3) regressive, progressive; (4) corporation, stockholders; (5) normal tax, surtax; (6) Municipal; (7) standard deduction; (8) capital assets; (9) average income

Solved Problems

10.1. A condensed income statement of the Schlossberg Corporation for the year ended December 31, 197–, appears below.

Net Sales	$240,000
Cost of Goods Sold	160,000
Gross Profit	80,000
Selling and General Expenses	56,000
Net Income Before Taxes	$ 24,000

Compute the tax of the Schlossberg Corporation as of December 31, 197–, (a) for the data as above; (b) assuming a net income before taxes of $64,000.

(a) _____

(b) _____

SOLUTION

(a) $24,000 × 22% = $ 5,280

(b) $25,000 × 22% = $ 5,500
                            $39,000 × 48% =   18,720
                  Total corporate tax $24,220

The corporate tax consists of a normal tax of 22% on all income and a surtax of 26% on income in excess of $25,000. An alternate method of computing the corporate tax would therefore be:

$$\$64,000 \times 22\% \;=\; \$14,080$$
$$(\$64,000 - \$25,000) \times 26\% \;=\; \underline{10,140}$$
$$\$24,220$$

10.2. The following condensed estimated income statement of the Sullivan Taxi Service is for the year ended December 31, 197–.

Taxi Income	$550,000
Less: Business Expenses	400,000
Net Income Before Taxes	$150,000

James Runabout, the owner, asks his accountant to compare the amounts of taxes he would have to pay as a sole proprietorship and as a corporation. Perform this comparison, if Runabout's personal itemized deductions and exemptions come to $36,000 and he withdrew $30,000 as his salary for the year. Assume that Runabout is married.

AS SOLE PROPRIETORSHIP

Business Taxation

Personal Taxation

AS CORPORATION

Business Taxation

Personal Taxation

SOLUTION

AS SOLE PROPRIETORSHIP

Business Taxation

Taxi income	$550,000
Less: Business expenses	400,000*
Net income before taxes	150,000
Taxes	....
Net income	$150,000

Personal Taxation

Net income	$150,000
Less: Itemized deductions and exemptions	36,000
Taxable income	$114,000
Tax liability (from tax table, Fig. 10-1)	$ 53,860

* Salary expense is not deductible as a business expense of a sole proprietorship

AS CORPORATION

Business Taxation

Taxi income	$550,000
Less: Business expenses	430,000**
Net income before taxes	120,000
Taxes	51,100
Net income	$ 68,900

Personal Taxation

Net income	$ 68,900
Salary from corporation	30,000
	$ 98,900
Less: Itemized deductions and exemptions	36,000
Taxable income	$ 62,900
Tax liability (from table, Fig. 10-1)	$ 23,837
Add: Corporate tax	51,100
Total tax liability	$ 74,937

** Salary expense is deductible from corporate income

The comparison shows that a sole proprietorship would produce tax savings in the amount of $74,937 − $53,860 = $21,077.

10.3. Rework Problem 10.2 on the assumption that Mr. Runabout decided to withdraw only half of the corporation's net income after taxes and to retain the balance in the firm.

AS SOLE PROPRIETORSHIP

Business Taxation

Personal Taxation

AS CORPORATION

Business Taxation

(continued next page)

Personal Taxation

SOLUTION

AS SOLE PROPRIETORSHIP

Business Taxation

Taxi income	$550,000
Less: Business expenses	400,000
Net income before taxes	$150,000
Taxes	....
Net income	$150,000

Personal Taxation

Net income	$150,000
Less: Itemized deductions and exemptions	36,000
Taxable income	$114,000
Tax liability (from tax table, Fig. 10-1)	$ 53,860

AS CORPORATION

Business Taxation

Taxi income	$550,000
Less: Business expenses	430,000
Net income before taxes	$120,000
Taxes	51,100
Net income	$ 68,900

Personal Taxation

	50%
Net income	$ 34,450
Salary from corporation	30,000
	64,450
Less: Itemized deductions and exemptions	36,000
Taxable income	$ 28,450
Tax liability (individual)	$ 7,275
Add: Corporate tax	51,100
Total tax liability	$ 58,375

The tax savings as a sole proprietorship now amount to only $58,375 − $53,860 = $4,515, because Runabout now takes a much smaller amount out of corporate income. Indeed, if he retained all of corporate income in the business, the corporation would yield a tax savings over the sole proprietorship.

10.4. Mr. and Mrs. Gary Fellows, whose adjusted gross income for the year was $18,000, have two dependent children. The following are amounts paid for medical expenses: medical insurance premium, $240; medicines and drugs, $245; doctors' fees, $520; hospital bills (portion not covered by insurance), $125. How much may they claim as a medical deduction?

_____
_____
_____
_____
_____
_____
_____
_____
_____
_____

SOLUTION

Medical insurance premium			$120
Medicine and drugs	$245		
Less: 1% exclusion	180	$ 65	
Doctors' fees		520	
Hospital bills		125	
Balance of medical insurance premium		120	
Total		830	
Less: 3% exclusion		540	290
Allowable medical expense deduction			$410

10.5. In Problem 10.4 a medical insurance premium of $600 instead of $240 would change the deduction considerably. Compute the new medical deduction.

_____
_____
_____
_____
_____
_____
_____
_____
_____

SOLUTION

Medical insurance premium			$150*
Medicine and drugs	$245		
Less: 1% exclusion	180	$ 65	
Doctors' fees		520	
Hospital bills		125	
Balance of medical insurance premium		450	
Total		1,160	
Less: 3% exclusion		540	620
Allowable medical expense deduction			$770

* Allowable deduction for medical insurance premium is one-half of premium up to $150. Balance to be combined with other medical expenses.

10.6. William Simpson, whose adjusted gross income for the year is $11,200, claims $480 in allowable medical deductions. His computations are:

Medical insurance premium	$180
Medicines and drugs	110
Doctors' fees	170
Medical equipment (eyeglasses)	20
Total	$480

Recompute his allowable medical deductions.

SOLUTION

Insurance premium			$90
Medicines and drugs	$110		
Less: 1% exclusion	112	$ 0	
Doctors' fees		170	
Medical equipment		20	
Balance of insurance premium		90	
Total		$280	
Less: 3% exclusion		336	0
Allowable medical deductions			$90

10.7. Compute the taxable income of Taxpayers A, B, and C.

	A	B	C
Adjusted gross income	$10,000	$12,000	$18,000
Itemized deductions	900	1,900	1,600
Exemption	750	750	750

	A	B	C

SOLUTION

	A		B		C	
Adjusted gross income		$10,000		$12,000		$18,000
Standard deduction*	$1,500				$2,000	
Itemized deductions			$1,900			
Exemption	750	2,250	750	2,650	750	2,750
Taxable income		$ 7,750		$ 9,350		$15,250

* The standard deduction may be used in place of itemized deductions. It is computed as 15% of adjusted gross income but not to exceed $2,000.

10.8. State the amount, if any, which Mr. and Mrs. John Smith may claim as an exemption for: (*a*) Mr. John Smith, age 68; (*b*) Mrs. John Smith, age 59; (*c*) John Smith Jr., age 22, earning $4,000 annually; (*d*) James Smith, age 20, earning $2,000 while a full-time student; (*e*) Mary Smith, age 16, earning $1,500; (*f*) Agnes Smith (mother of John), age 86, blind and relying solely on him for support.

(*a*) _____
(*b*) _____
(*c*) _____
(*d*) _____
(*e*) _____
(*f*) _____

SOLUTION

(*a*) $1,500 ($750 for himself, $750 because he is over 65)
(*b*) $750 (for herself)
(*c*) none (this son must file as an individual because he does not meet the gross income test)
(*d*) $750 (a full-time student's income is not included in gross income)
(*e*) $750 (under 19 years of age and does not have to meet the gross income test)
(*f*) $750 (fully supported by taxpayer; blindness and age allow extra exemptions only to husband and wife)

10.9. Determine the amount to be added to gross income in each of the following cases (losses are shown in parentheses):

	A	B	C
Net long-term capital gain (loss)	$4,000	$7,000	$(4,000)
Net short-term capital gain (loss)	7,000	(4,000)	7,000

	A	B	C

SOLUTION

	A	B	C
Net long-term capital gain (loss)	$ 4,000	$7,000	$(4,000)
Net short-term capital gain (loss)	7,000	(4,000)	7,000
Capital gain	$11,000	$3,000	$ 3,000
Less: Long-term gain deduction	2,000*	1,500*	. . .*
Amount to be added to gross income	$ 9,000	$1,500	$ 3,000

* Net long-term gain in excess of short-term loss is allowed a deduction of 50%:

	A	B	C
Long-term gain	4,000	7,000	. . .
Short-term loss	. . .	(4,000)	. . .
Excess	$4,000	3,000	. . .
Deduction (50% of excess)	$2,000	$1,500	. . .

10.10. Mitch Ziplow completed the following stock transactions during the taxable year:

Stock	Total Cost	Selling Price	Time Held
Acme Corporation	$ 6,000	$ 8,000	9 months
Belledy Company	7,000	5,500	4 months
Callor Corporation	12,000	18,000	2 years
Dundy Industries	5,200	7,200	5 months
Evans Company	2,400	100	4 years

Determine the amount to be added to his gross income.

SOLUTION

Long-term capital gain			
Acme Corporation	$2,000		
Callor Corporation	6,000	$8,000	
Less: Long-term capital loss, Evans Company		2,300	
Net long-term capital gain			$5,700
Short-term capital gain, Dundy Industries	2,000		
Less: Short-term capital loss, Belledy Company	1,500		
Net short-term capital gain			500
Total capital gain			6,200
Less: Long-term gain deduction (50% × $5,700)			2,850
Amount to be added to gross income			$3,350

10.11. C. Darro and W. Bryon both have $60,000 in taxable income for a three-year period. Darro has $15,000 for the first year, $20,000 for the second year, and $25,000 for the third year; Bryon has $20,000 for each of the three years. Both men are married and file according to the tax table, Fig. 10-1. Determine the total tax to be paid by each man.

	Darro	Bryon
1st year		
2nd year		
3rd year		
Total tax paid		

SOLUTION

	Darro	Bryon
1st year	$ 3,010	$ 4,380
2nd year	4,380	4,380
3rd year	6,020	4,380
Total tax paid	$13,410	$13,140

Because the tax is progressive, Darro's high third-year income overbalances his low first-year income.

10.12. Marc Bradley, 25 years old and married, furnished more than half of his widowed mother's support. His salary for the year was $12,400, of which $1,600 was withheld for federal income tax. Other income earned during the year was: interest on the bonds of Winesburg, Michigan, $70; interest on a savings account (not withdrawn), $120; tips earned as a part-time waiter, $450. He had paid during the taxable year: state income tax, $314; interest on auto loan, $275; interest on home mortgage, $1,240. Determine the amount of tax due or to be refunded.

SOLUTION

Income		
Salary	$12,400	
Savings account interest	120	
Tips	450	
Adjusted gross income		$12,970
Itemized deductions		
State income tax	314	
Interest on auto loan	275	
Interest on home mortgage	1,240	
Total itemized deductions		1,829
		$11,141
Less: Exemptions ($750 × 3)		2,250
Taxable income		$ 8,891
Tax liability		1,576
Less: Tax credit (federal income tax withheld)		1,600
Refund		$ 24

10.13. Below is a list of ten income items that are to be considered in preparing a tax return. For each determine the amount, if any, to be reported as income.

(a)	Cash withdrawn from sole proprietorship (net income $22,000)	$15,000
(b)	Earned bank interest (not withdrawn)	500
(c)	Rent income $1,800; rent expenses $1,200	600
(d)	Interest income from bonds of the city of Westchester	250
(e)	Long-term capital gain, $8,000; short-term capital gain, $6,000	14,000
(f)	Bank loan	2,000
(g)	Tips	350
(h)	Receipt of inheritance from uncle's death	3,000
(i)	State unemployment benefits	1,200
(j)	Christmas bonus	275

(a) _____

(b) _____

(c) _____

(d) _____

(e) _____

(f) _____

(g) _____

(h) _____

(i) _____

(j) _____

SOLUTION

(a) $22,000 (net income is the taxable amount)

(b) $500 (withdrawal is irrelevant: the interest was earned and is taxable)

(c) $600 (income less expenses)

(d) 0 (municipal bonds are tax-free)

(e)
Net capital gain	$14,000
Less: Long-term capital gain deduction	4,000
Amount to be included in gross income	$10,000

(f) 0

(g) $350

(h) 0

(i) 0

(j) $275 (a bonus is treated as income earned)

10.14. Opposite each item below place a check mark in the appropriate column. State the type of each deduction.

	Deductible from Gross Income	Deductible from Adjusted Gross Income	Not Deductible
Auto expense driving to job			
Standard deduction			
Gift to sick friend			
Interest on mortgage of home			
Interest on mortgage of income-producing property			
Child care			
State income tax			
Federal income tax			
Damage of $300 to personal auto not covered by insurance			
Depreciation of business machines			

SOLUTION

	Deductible from Gross Income	Deductible from Adjusted Gross Income	Not Deductible
Auto expense driving to job			✓ (only travel from 1st job to 2nd is deductible)
Standard deduction		✓ (15% of adjusted gross income, not to exceed $2,000)	
Gift to sick friend			✓
Interest on mortgage of home		✓ (interest deduction)	
Interest on mortgage of income-producing property	✓ (business deduction)		
Child care		✓ (miscellaneous deduction)	
State income tax		✓ (tax deduction)	
Federal income tax			✓
Damage of $300 to personal auto not covered by insurance		✓ (loss in excess of $100 can be claimed as a casualty loss)	
Depreciation of business machines	✓ (business deduction)		

10.15. Calculate the tax obligation of Paul and Carol Silvergold (spouses), whose receipts and disbursements for the past year are as follows:

Cash Receipts

Gross Salary (withheld for federal income taxes, $3,800; withheld for hospitalization policy, $320)		$23,750
Dividend on Corporation Stock		
Owned by Paul Silvergold	620	
Owned by Carol Silvergold	80	700
Capital Gains		
Long-term Capital Gains	200	
Short-term Capital Gains	100	300
Interest Earned		
Bonds of Triborough Bridge (municipal bonds)	250	
U. S. Government Bonds	100	
From Bank (not withdrawn)	50	400

Cash Disbursements

Interest on Mortgage Note		$ 1,000
Taxes		
Personal Property Tax	200	
Sales Tax	600	800
Charitable Contributions		1,500
Medical Expenses		
Drugs	450	
Doctors' Fees	800	1,250

SOLUTION

Salary			$23,750
Dividends			
Paul Silvergold	$ 620		
Carol Silvergold	80		
	$ 700		
	− 180		520
Long-term gain		200	
Short-term gain		100	
		300	
Capital gains deduction (50% × $200)		100	200
Bond and bank interest			150
Adjusted gross income			$24,620
Deductions (itemized)			
Charities	$1,500		
Interest	1,000		
Taxes	800		
Medical expenses			
Insurance premiums (limit $150)	150		
Drugs	450		
Less: 1% of adjusted gross income	246		
	204		
Doctor's fees	800		
Balance of insurance premiums	170		
	$1,174		
Less: 3% of adjusted gross income	739	435	
Exemptions		$1,500	
			$ 5,385
Taxable income			$19,235
Tax liability (from tax table, Fig. 10-1)			$ 4,166
Tax credit (tax withheld)			3,800
Tax due			$ 366

Examination III
Chapters 8-10

1. The Nell Corporation had the following financial position data:

	Year 2	Year 1
Cash	$105,000	$145,000
Accounts Receivable (net)	65,000	35,000
Inventories	90,000	35,000
Prepaid Expenses	40,000	10,000
Accounts Payable	100,000	150,000
Notes Payable	40,000	25,000

Compute (a) working capital, (b) current ratio, (c) acid-test ratio.

2. Borak Company had the following income and expense data:

	Year 2	Year 1
Net Sales	$420,000	$340,000
Cost of Goods Sold	280,000	240,000
Expenses	95,000	75,000

Prepare a comparative income statement for Year 2 and Year 1, showing each item in relation to sales.

3. The Sunshine Company's income statements show the following data:

	Year 2	Year 1
Sales	$1,400,000	$1,000,000
Inventories (beginning)	300,000	250,000
Purchases	750,000	700,000
Inventories (ending)	150,000	140,000

Compute for each year (a) the inventory turnover, (b) the number of days' sales in inventory.

4. The Caren Corporation had the following data for each December 31:

	Year 2	Year 1
Cash	$ 45,000	$ 41,200
Accounts Receivable (net)	36,200	35,000
Inventories	180,000	181,000
Prepaid Expenses	72,000	68,000
Equipment	94,000	80,000
Accumulated Depreciation, Equip.	12,000	7,000
Accounts Payable	47,000	45,400
Notes Payable	21,600	21,600
Dividends Payable	5,000	7,000
Common Stock	122,000	122,000
Retained Earnings	51,500	42,400

Prepare a schedule of changes in components of working capital.

5. Indicate the effect of the following transactions on working capital by placing a check-mark if there is no effect, or by indicating the amount of increase or decrease.

Transaction	No Effect	Increase	Decrease
(a) Bought merchandise, $3,000, on account			
(b) Sold $2,000 of merchandise for $2,800			
(c) Paid $4,200 for operating expenses			
(d) Purchased equipment, $6,900, on account			
(e) Paid $3,200 on notes payable			
(f) Received $1,000 on account from customers			
(g) Borrowed $1,500 on a 30-day note			
(h) Declared and paid a cash dividend of $2,500			

6. The Anita Company reported net income of $30,000, exclusive of extraordinary items, for the current year. Depreciation for the year was $8,000. Prepare the "cash provided by operations" section of the Statement of Change in Financial Position (cash form), using the following data:

	Current Year	Previous Year
Accounts Receivable	$25,000	$20,000
Inventories	55,000	51,000
Prepaid Expenses	6,000	5,000
Accounts Payable	21,000	17,000
Taxes Payable	9,000	10,000

7. A condensed income statement of the Gillespie Corporation for the year ended December 31, 1973, appears below.

Sales	$300,000
Cost of Goods Sold	210,000
Gross Profit	90,000
Selling and General Expenses	68,000
Net Income Before Taxes	$ 22,000

Compute the tax as of December 31, 1973, (a) for the data above; (b) assuming a net income before taxes of $60,000.

8. Mr. and Mrs. H. Halpern, whose adjusted gross income was $19,000, have three dependent children. The following amounts have been paid out for medical expenses:

Medical insurance premium	$280
Medicine and drugs	260
Doctors' fees	600
Hospital bills (not covered by insurance)	200

Determine the amount they may claim as a medical deduction.

9. Compute the taxable income of the following three individuals:

	A	B	C
Adjusted gross income	$11,000	$12,000	$17,000
Itemized deductions	900	1,850	2,100
Number of exemptions	1	2	2

Note: The standard deduction may be substituted for the itemized deductions.

10. State the amount, if any, which **Mr.** and **Mrs. Agin** may claim as an exemption for:

    (*a*)   Mr. Agin (husband), age 69

    (*b*)   Mrs. Agin (wife), age 61

    (*c*)   Son, age 24, earning $5,000 annually

    (*d*)   Daughter, age 20, full-time student earning $3,000 annually

    (*e*)   Mother-In-Law, age 84, relying on them for full support

11. Determine the amount to be added to gross income for each taxpayer below (losses are shown in parentheses).

	A	B	C
Net long-term capital gain (loss)	$ 5,000	$ 6,000	$16,000
Net short-term capital gain (loss)	6,000	5,000	(5,000)
Capital gain	$11,000	$11,000	$11,000

12. Evan Flora, 26 and married, furnished more than half support for his widowed mother. Evan's salary was $15,600, of which $2,200 was withheld for federal income tax. Other income earned during the year consisted of:

Interest on savings account (not withdrawn)	$200
Interest on municipal bond	80
Tips earned as bellhop (part-time)	560

Itemized deductions were:

State income tax	$ 460
Interest on loan	240
Interest on home mortgage	1,200
Charities	150

Determine the amount of his tax balance due or his refund. (Assume for simplicity a flat rate of 25%.)

Answers to Examination III

1.

		Year 2	Year 1
(*a*)	Current assets	$300,000	$225,000
	Less: Current liabilities	140,000	175,000
	Working capital	$160,000	$ 50,000

(*b*) Current assets ÷ Current liabilities

$$\frac{300,000}{140,000} = 2.1 \text{ to } 1$$

$$\frac{225,000}{175,000} = 1.3 \text{ to } 1$$

(*c*) Quick assets ÷ Current liabilities

$$\frac{170,000}{140,000} = 1.2 \text{ to } 1$$

$$\frac{180,000}{175,000} = 1.0 \text{ to } 1$$

2.

	Dollars		Percentages	
	Year 2	Year 1	Year 2	Year 1
Net Sales	$420,000	$340,000	100%	100%
Cost of Goods Sold	280,000	240,000	67%	71%
Gross Profit	140,000	100,000	33%	29%
Expenses	95,000	75,000	22%	22%
Net Income	$ 45,000	$ 25,000	11%	7%

3.

	Year 2	Year 1
(a)	$900,000 ÷ $225,000 = 4.0	$810,000 ÷ $195,000 = 4.2
(b)	$900,000 ÷ 365 = $2,466	$810,000 ÷ 365 = $2,219
	$150,000 ÷ $2,466 = 61 days	$140,000 ÷ $2,219 = 63 days

4.

Increase (Decrease) in Current Assets

Cash	$ 3,800	
Accounts Receivable (net)	1,200	
Inventories	(1,000)	
Prepaid Expenses	4,000	$8,000

Increase (Decrease) in Current Liabilities

Accounts Payable	$ 1,600	
Notes Payable	..	
Dividends Payable	(2,000)	(400)
Increase in Working Capital		$8,400

5.

	No Effect	Increase	Decrease
(a)	√		
(b)		$800	
(c)			$4,200
(d)			$6,900
(e)	√		
(f)	√		
(g)	√		
(h)			$2,500

6.

Net Income		$30,000
Add: Deductions		
Depreciation	$8,000	
Increase in Accounts Payable	4,000	12,000
		$42,000
Deduct: Applications		
Increase in Accounts Receivable	$5,000	
Increase in Inventories	4,000	
Increase in Prepaid Expenses	1,000	
Decrease in Taxes Payable	1,000	11,000
Total Cash Provided		$31,000

7. (a) $22,000 × 22% = $ 4,840

(b) $25,000 × 22% = $ 5,500
$35,000 × 48% = 16,800
$22,300

An alternate method applies 22% to all income and a surtax of 26% to income in excess of $25,000:

$$\$60,000 \times 22\% \qquad = \$13,200$$
$$(\$60,000 - \$25,000) \times 26\% = \underline{9,100}$$
$$\underline{\underline{\$22,300}}$$

8.

Medical insurance premium			$140
Medicine and drugs	$260		
Less: 1% exclusion	190	$ 70	
Doctors' fees		600	
Hospital bills		200	
Balance of medical insurance premium		140	
Total		$1,010	
Less: 3% exclusion		570	440
Allowable medical expense deduction			$580

9.

	A		B		C	
Adjusted gross income		$11,000		$12,000		$17,000
Itemized deductions	$1,650*		$1,850		$2,100	
Exemption	750	2,400	1,500	3,350	1,500	3,600
Taxable income		$ 8,600		$ 8,650		$13,400

* standard deduction used

10.   (a) $1,500, (b) $750, (c) none, (d) $750, (e) $750

11.

	A	B	C
Net long-term capital gain (loss)	$ 5,000	$ 6,000	$16,000
Net short-term capital gain (loss)	6,000	5,000	(5,000)
Capital gain	$11,000	$11,000	$11,000
Less: Long-term gain deduction	2,500	3,000	5,500
Amount to be added to gross income	$ 8,500	$ 8,000	$ 5,500

12.

Income		
Salary		$15,600
Interest on savings account		200
Tips		560
Adjusted gross income		$16,360
Itemized deductions		
State income tax	$ 460	
Interest on loan	240	
Interest on home mortgage	1,200	
Charities	150	2,050
		$14,310
Exemptions (3 × $750)		2,250
Taxable income		$12,060
Tax liability (assumed 25%)		$ 3,015
Less: Tax credit		2,200
Tax due		$ 815

INDEX

Accounts receivable
  and average daily sales, 193
  ratios for, 193
  turnover of, 193
Accrued interest, 75-76
Amount and percentage changes, 189-190
Appropriation of earnings, 51-52
Assets
  noncurrent, increases and decreases in, 211
  partners admitted by contribution of, 2-3
  plant, ratio of, to long-term liabilities, 195
  ratio of net sales to, 195-196
  revaluation of, 3
  total, rate earned on, 196

Balance sheet budgets, 153
Balance sheets, 212-213
  budgeted, 158-160
Boards of directors, 24
  and preferred stock, 26
Bond sinking funds, 78-79
Bond transactions, authorized, recording of, 73
Bonded indebtedness, appropriations for, 51-52
Bonds
  accrued interest on, 75-76
  callable, 72, 77
  characteristics of, 71
  collateral trust, 71
  convertible, 72, 77
  coupon, 72
  face value of, 73-74
  funding by, versus funding by stock, 72-73
  interest rate on, 74
  maturity date for, 71
  options for conversion or recall of, 72
  premium and discount on, 73-75
  redemption of, 77
  registered, 72
  serial, 71
  sinking fund, 71
  unsecured, 71
Book value of stock, 29-30
Budget report, 161
Budgeted balance sheet, 158-160
Budgeted income statement, 153-158
Budgeting, 153
Budgets, 153-184
  balance sheet, 153
  capital expenditures, 159-160
  cash, 159
  cost of goods sold, 155-157
  direct labor, 156-157
  factory overhead, 157
  flexible, 160-161
  income and expense, 153

Budgets (cont.)
  master, 153
  materials purchased, 155-156
  moving or continuous, 154
  operating expenses, 157-158
  production, 155
  sales, 154
By-products, 103-104

Callable bonds, 72
  redemption of, 77
Capital, paid-in, 25
Capital assets, defined, 235
Capital expenditure budget, 159-160
Capital from Forfeited Subscriptions, 48
Capital gains and losses, 235
Capital stock, 25
Capital Stock Subscribed, 47
Cash, 210
Cash budget, 159
Cash dividends, 53
Cash form, 214
Casualty losses, as tax deduction, 234
Charters, corporation, 24, 28, 73
Chattel mortgages, 71
Collateral trust bonds, 71
Common stock, 26
  earnings per share on, 196-197
Component percentages, 190-192
Contingencies, appropriation for, 51-52
Contract rate, 74
Contributions, as tax deduction, 234
Control accounts, agreement of subsidiary
    accounts with, 124
Controllable variance, 163
Convertible bonds, 72
  redemption of, 77
Corporations, 23-92
  advantages of, 23
  bonds and, 71-92
  characteristics of, 23
  charters for, 24, 28, 73
  disadvantages of, 23-24
  equity accounting for, 25-26
  retained earnings of, 25, 51-52, 54-55
  stock subscriptions and, 47-48
  taxation of, 23-24, 230, 232
  terminology used in, 24
  treasury stock of, 24, 48-51
Cost of goods manufactured, 101-102
Cost of goods sold budget, 155-157
Cost systems, 120-152
  job order, 120-124
  process, 124, 131
Costing, direct (variable), 124-125

Costs
  average unit, 120
  fixed and variable, 160-161
  flow of, 126-127, 131
  of goods sold, 131
  manufacturing or production, 99
  price and, 120
  process, comprehensive illustration of, 127-131
  research and development, 99
  semivariable, 160
  standard, 124, 161
  variances in, 161-163
Coupon bonds, 72
Current ratio, 192

Debt and equity funding, 73
Direct (variable) costing, 124-125
Direct labor budget, 156-157
Direct labor cost, 100
Direct labor variances, 162-163
Direct materials variances, 162
Discount on bonds, 73-75
Dividends
  cash, 53
  defined, 52
  earnings and, 196-197
  effect on retained earnings, 54-55
  restriction of, 78-79
  stock, 53-54, 196
  taxes on, 24
Donated Capital, 49

Earnings
  retained, 25, 51-52
  per share, on common stock, 196-197
Equity
  ratio of, to liabilities, 195
  stockholders', decreases in, 211
Equity accounting, 25-26
Equity and debt financing, review of, 79-80
Equivalent units, 125-126
Excise taxes, 230
Expansion, appropriation for, 51-52

Factory overhead, 100
Factory overhead budget, 157
Factory overhead variances, 163
FIFO (first-in-first-out), 101, 126-127, 130-131
Financial budgets, 153
Financial position
  changes in, 210-229
  statement of change in, 212-215
Financial statement analysis, 189-209
  horizontal, 189-190
  by ratios, 192-197
  vertical, 190-192
Financial statements, worksheet and, 101
Fixed assets, 99
Flexible budget, 160-161
Flow of costs, 126
Flow of goods, 125-126
Franchise tax, 24

Funding, by stock versus funding by bonds, 72-73
Funds
  defined, 210
  sources and applications of, 210-211

General expenses budget, 158
Goods, flow of, 125-126
Goods sold, cost of, 131
  budget for, 155-157
Goodwill, 3-4
Gross income
  adjusted, deductions from, 233-234
  deductions from, 233
  defined, 232-233
  tax exemptions and, 235

Horizontal analysis of financial statements, 189-190

Income, gross, 232-235
Income averaging, 235-236
Income and expense budgets, 153
Income statement, 103
  budgeted, 153-158
Income tax formula, for individuals, 232
Income taxes, 23, 230-249
Individuals
  income tax formula for, 232
  other tax considerations for, 235-236
  tax credits for, 235
  tax deductions for, 233-234
  tax exemptions for, 234-235
Interest
  accrued, 75-76
  payment of, 71-72
  as tax deduction, 230
Interest rate, on bonds, 74
Internal Revenue Code (IRC), 230
Internal Revenue Service (IRS), 230
Inventories, 99-101
  number of days' sales in, 194
  ratios for, 194
  turnover of, 194
  unit cost and, 100
Issue of stock
  at par, 28
  at premium or discount, 28-29

Job order cost systems, 120-124
Joint products, 103-104

Ledger accounts, 122-124
Liabilities
  long-term, ratio of plant assets to, 195
  ratio of equity to, 195
Liability
  in corporations, 23
  in partnerships, 1
LIFO (last-in-first-out), 101, 126-127
Long-term capital gain, 235

Losses
  division of, in partnerships, 4-6
  participation in, 1

Manufacturing accounting, 99-119
Manufacturing cost
  analysis of, 99-100
  total, 101
Market value of stock, 24
Master budget, 153
Materials purchases budget, 155-156
Maturity date of bonds, 71
Medical and dental expenses, as tax deduction, 233
Monthly transactions, cost systems and, 121-122
Mortgages
  chattel, 71
  real estate, 71
Moving or continuous budget, 154

Net sales, ratio of, to assets, 195-196

Opening balances, 121
Operating budgets, 153
Operating expenses budget, 157-158
Options, for conversion or recall of bonds, 72
Organization costs, corporate, 24

Par value of stock, 24
Partners
  new, admission of, 2-4
  unlimited liability of, 1
Partnerships, 1-22
  characteristics of, 1
  defined, 1
  dissolving of, 1
  division of net income or loss in, 4-6
  formation of, 1-2
  goodwill in, 3-4
  liquidation of, 6-8
  new partners admitted to, 2-4
  taxation of, 230-231
Performance reports, 161
Periodic inventory method, 100-101
Perpetual inventory method, 100-101
Plant assets, ratio of, to long-term
      liabilities, 195
Plant and equipment, 99
Preferred stock, 26-28
  cumulative, 27-28
  earnings per share on, 196-197
  participating and nonparticipating, 26-27
Premium on bonds, 73-75
Price, cost and, 120
Process cost system, 124
Process costs, comprehensive illustration of,
      127-131
Production budget, 155
Profits
  net, division of, 4-6
  participation in, 1

Progressive taxes, 230
Property, co-ownership of, 1
Property taxes, 230
Proportional taxes, 230

Quick or acid-test ratio, 192

Ratios
  for accounts receivable, 193
  of equity to liabilities, 195
  financial statement analysis by, 192-197
  for inventory, 194
  of net income to average total assets, 196
  of net sales to assets, 195-196
  of plant assets to long-term liabilities, 195
  quick or acid-test, 192
  for working capital, 192
Raw materials, cost of, 99-100
Real estate mortgages, 71
Redemption of bonds, 77
Registered bonds, 72
Regressive taxes, 230
Research and development costs, 99
Retained earnings, 25, 51-52
  effect of dividends on, 54-55
  statement of, 55

Sales budget, 154
Sales taxes, 230
Security, bonds and, 71
Selling expenses budget, 157-158
Shares of stock, 24
Short-term capital gain, 235
Sinking fund bonds, 71
Sinking funds, 78-79
Sole proprietorship
  accounting for, 25-26
  taxation and, 230-231
Standard costs, 124, 161
Standard deduction, 234
Stock
  book value of, 29-30
  common, 26
  funding by, versus funding by bonds, 72-73
  issue of, 28-29
  preferred, 26-28
  treasury, 48-51
Stock dividends, 53-54
Stock subscriptions, 47-48
  default on, 48
Stock Subscriptions Receivable, 47
Stockholders, 24
  and preferred stock, 26
Subsidiary accounts, agreement of control
      accounts and, 124

Tax credits, 235
Tax deductions
  itemized, 233-234
  standard, 234
Tax exemptions, 234-235

Taxation
   of businesses, 230-232
   of corporations, 23-24
Taxes
   deduction for, 233
   on dividends, 24
   excise, 230
   franchise, 24
   income, 23, 230-249
   property, 230
   proportional, 230
   regressive, 230
   sales, 230
Theft losses, as tax deduction, 234
Treasury stock, 24, 48-51
   appropriation for, 51
   donation of, 49-50
   purchase of, 50-51
Trust indentures, 71

Turnover
   of accounts receivable, 193
   of inventory, 194

Uniform Partnership Act, 2

Variances in cost, analysis of, 161-163
Vertical analysis of financial statements, 190-192
Volume variance, 163

Weighted Average, 126-127
Working capital, 210
   applications of, 211
   changes in, 210-212
   joint sources and applications of, 212
   sources of, 211
Working capital form, 213-214
Working capital schedule, 210-211
Worksheet, 101

Catalog

If you are interested in a list of SCHAUM'S
OUTLINE SERIES in Science, Mathematics,
Engineering and other subjects, send your name
and address, requesting your free catalog, to:

SCHAUM'S OUTLINE SERIES, Dept. C
McGRAW-HILL BOOK COMPANY
1221 Avenue of Americas
New York, N.Y. 10020